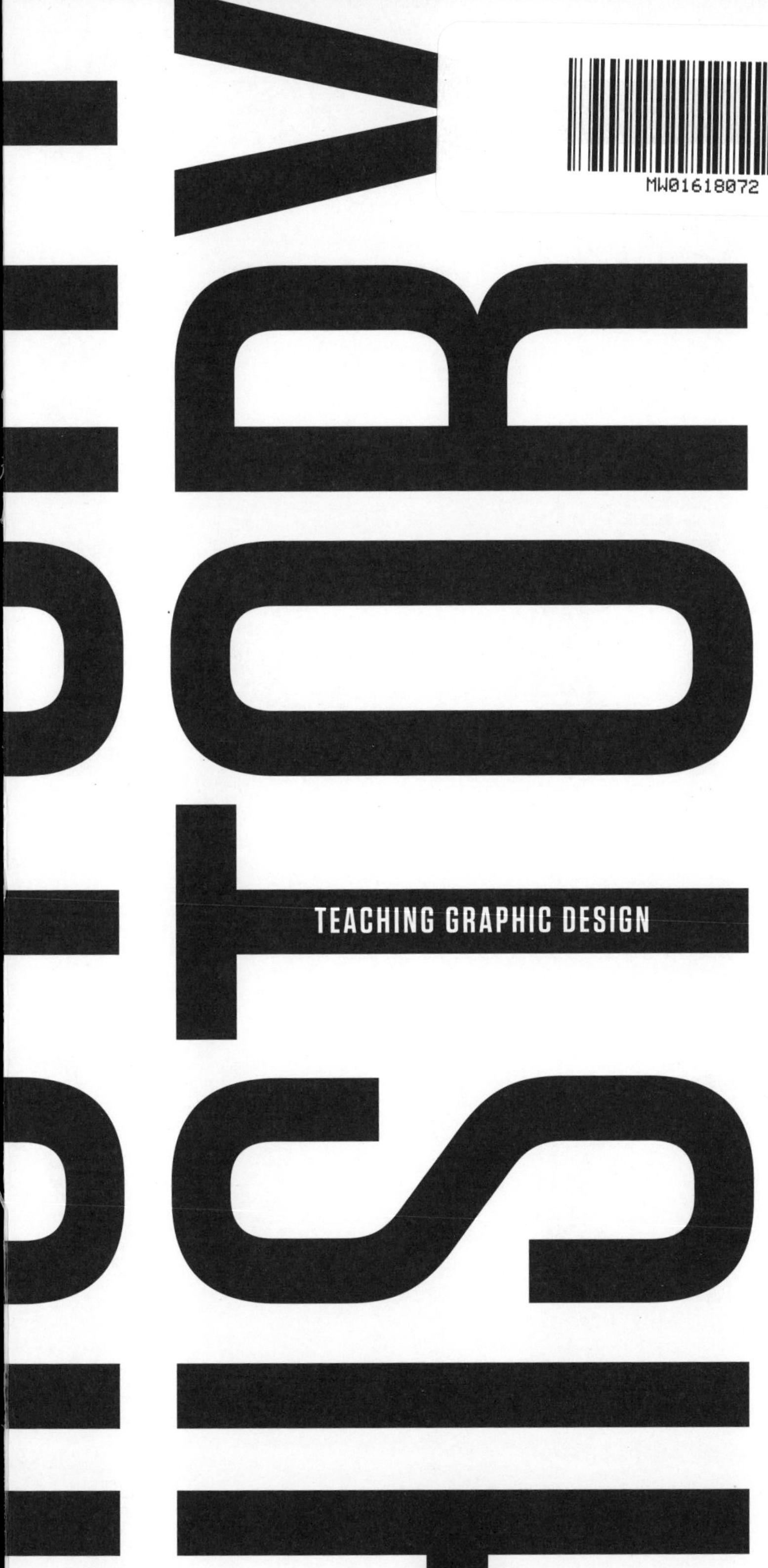

TEACHING GRAPHIC DESIGN

EDITED BY
STEVEN HELLER

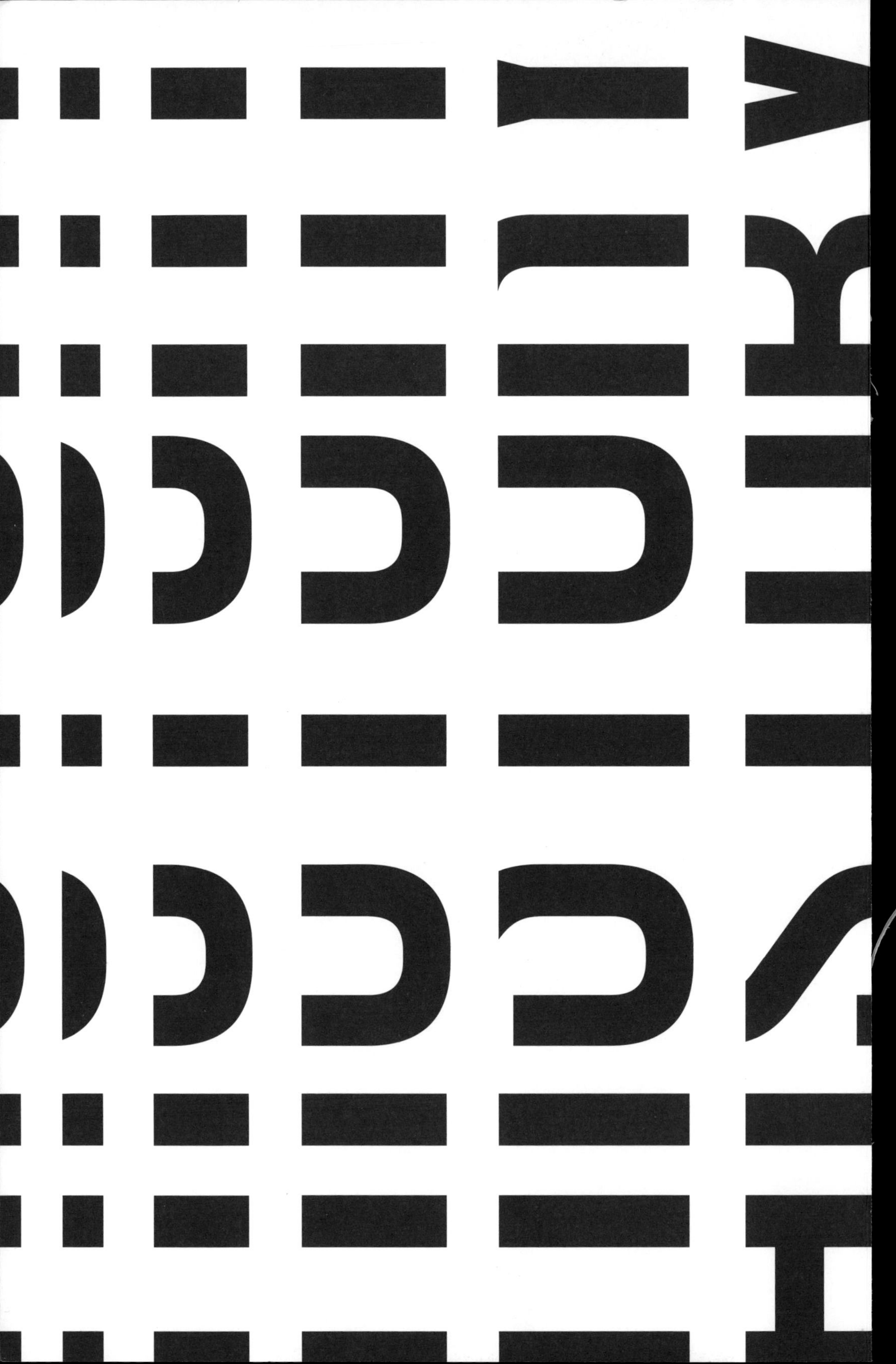

HISTORY

TEACHING GRAPHIC DESIGN

EDITED BY
STEVEN HELLER

ALLWORTH PRESS
NEW YORK

Allworth Press books may be purchased in bulk at special discounts for sales promotion, corporate gifts, fund-raising, or educational purposes. Special editions can also be created to specifications. For details, contact the Special Sales Department, Allworth Press, 307 West 36th Street, 11th Floor, New York, NY 10018 or info@skyhorsepublishing.com.

23 22 21 20 19   5 4 3 2 1

Published by Allworth Press, an imprint of Skyhorse Publishing, Inc. 307 West 36th Street, 11th Floor, New York, NY 10018. Allworth Press® is a registered trademark of Skyhorse Publishing, Inc.®, a Delaware corporation.

www.allworth.com

Copublished with the School of Visual Arts
Cover and interior design by Rick Landers

Library of Congress Cataloging-in-Publication Data

Names: Heller, Steven, author.
Title: Teaching graphic design history / Steven Heller.
Description: New York, New York : Allworth Press, an imprint of Skyhorse Publishing, [2019]
Identifiers: LCCN 2018056698 (print) | LCCN 2018057010 (ebook) | ISBN 9781621536857 (eBook) | ISBN 9781621536840 (paperback)
Subjects: LCSH: Graphic arts--History--Study and teaching (Higher) | Graphic design (Typography)--History--Study and teaching (Higher) | BISAC: DESIGN / History & Criticism. | DESIGN / General. | DESIGN / Graphic Arts / General. | EDUCATION / Teaching Methods & Materials / Arts & Humanities.
Classification: LCC NC998 (ebook) | LCC NC998 .H457 2019 (print) | DDC 741.6071/1--dc23
LC record available at https://lccn.loc.gov/2018056698

Print ISBN: 978-1-62153-684-0
eBook ISBN: 978-1-62153-685-7

Printed in China

READY?

BEGIN

George Santayana, the philosopher and novelist who famously coined the phrase "Those who cannot remember the past are condemned to repeat it," also said, "History is always written wrong, and so always needs to be rewritten." While these aphorisms may be in conflict, for the purposes of this book they are spot-on. Both describe the difficulty of teaching (and studying) the history of *graphic design*. Designers cannot afford to be ignorant of what came before, yet a lot of misinformation gets passed on, resulting in a discipline rife with major and minor inaccuracies, and murky understanding of its origins.

Graphic design history as an academic discipline is arguably still in its adolescence, because graphic design—a.k.a. commercial art, visual communications (or viz com)—has only just reached middle age. Since in the nineteenth century this ersatz field was a loss leader within the printing and typesetting industries, its backstory was subsumed under a broader graphic arts narrative. So, when commercial art—posters, books, magazines, packages, logos, signs, and more—as surveyed seriously during the 1970s (even before Philip B. Meggs published his landmark *A History of Graphic Design* in 1983), there were many gaps and missing attributions that are now being rectified (although new ones, notably many gender and racial omissions, are likely to emerge).

The role of the historian today is concerned with approving what is worthy of study and what can *legitimately* be ignored. So many reams of graphic design have been produced over the past century and a half that historical research includes determining where and about whom teaching graphic design history should focus: On form-givers? Form-users? Form-receivers? Form and content drivers? One thing is certain: A massive amount remains to be uncovered, analyzed, and codified in this ever-expanding graphic design universe—and it all must be digested by students, who must find its relevance to their work as designers.

It should go without saying that learning graphic design history is indeed relevant as a model for present and future design practice. The past is hardwired into everything designers do, whether it is so-called "retro" or contemporary work. In recent years, more inclusive graphic design narratives have been produced that attempt to make amends for underrepresented people, groups, and genres.

Graphic design history has ostensibly developed on two tracks—objective record and subjective interpretation. The "interpretation" part is important, since graphic design history is as much an act of storytelling as it is data collection. While facts are the foundation of credible historical records, graphic design is not simply defined by dates or confined to places, people, and things. Graphic design history is a crisscrossing timeline of collective accomplishments, individual expressions, and hybrid practices—in short, it is mass communication transmitted through multiple visual languages and graphic styles.

Graphic design narratives chronicle how the customs of particular cultures are viewed through signs, symbols, and all those many artifacts designed for displays in the public spaces and isolated niches. Graphic design history explains what was popular or not in business and society. Design history, unlike art history, examines phenomena where design is a means to an end—a consequence, not a goal.

There could be no graphic design if not for the industries and institutions that employ designers to make ephemeral visual communication. Conversely, graphic design would be narrowly limited if not for an array of progressive experiments conducted regardless of the patronage of a client. This mass of designed "stuff" would be landfill-in-the-making were it not pieced together into a contextual narrative. The historian's role is to help explain the contexts in which graphic design artifacts make an impact.

Nonetheless, the history is by and large taught by self-professed graphic design experts, who use personal and eclectic methods to scrutinize, categorize, criticize, and even proselytize. While the number of scholars who formally practice graphic design history is actually few when compared to legions of historians in other areas of culture, politics, commerce, and technology, the field has been increasing in various positive ways on its own terms.

Teaching graphic design history has evolved over the decades from informal lectures by veteran practitioners (like folklore handed down by wise and knowledgeable elders) into structured classes and symposia by scholars and hands-on practitioners. Some use textbooks that codify the history as well as examples drawn from their own research. A critical mass of firsthand knowledge and canonical history can be an enlightening teaching method.

Yet, truth be told, teaching graphic design history is not the highest priority for most design schools and departments, which have little time to prepare students to enter a job market that cares less about historical literacy than the virtues of conceptual talent, aesthetic skills, and technological know-how. For most design programs, learning about legacy is viewed as extracurricular.

Some schools do not even offer design history courses, while others append them to studio classes because there is no space in tightly packed curricula. Sometimes, they are offered through art history or humanities departments, often because there is a fundamental relationship between art and design. A common teaching method is incidental inclusion—based on a kind of osmosis achieved through including historical research covertly into solving otherwise design-centric assignments.

Over the past decade, there have been a large assortment of text-and-picture books, videos, and museum exhibitions devoted entirely or in part to graphic design history, including "eye-candy" compilations, so basic historical information is now more accessible than ever before. Add to this the dozens of self-generated research explorations (much of this found online), and it is more possible than ever before to teach

"The historian's role is to help explain the contexts in which graphic design artifacts make an impact."

oneself certain aspects of graphic design history. By virtue of thorough research, one can even become a bone fide expert in specialties and subdisciplines that may never had been explored before.

It is, however, still perplexing that in recent years, with so many resources available (including this very book), that there is such a paucity of dedicated (and competent) historian-scholar-teachers. Maybe it is because graphic design history is still a hybrid practice—somewhere between art, psychology, and sociology. There are so few capable teachers that I am frequently asked by colleagues to recommend people to teach history classes whether or not they have necessary academic degrees. The actual numbers of "trained" instructors is surprisingly low—or, to the contrary, it is not surprising, since making a living as a design history scholar is not easy, even with a résumé full of degrees. And, honestly, having read a few books or even doing a bit of original research on particular periods or designers does not make one a full-fledged graphic design historian—but it's a start.

Building a foundation of historical expertise can be accomplished by various means. There are many experts in various design and typography disciplines who deliberately have invested time and money in learning their craft and heritage. Take type design, for example. The proliferation of annual international type conferences is evidence of a sizeable number of design "geeks" who will converse, instruct, and otherwise preach at length about the finer points of type, typography, and the typographic legacy. Most are practitioners, but scholars are in the mix, too. This is one of the most populated areas, but poster, illustration, and package design mavens also abound. Many of these deep-seated interests have produced valuable papers, books, and exhibits. With type, the need for history is self-evident; since so many typefaces are modeled on the past, not to acknowledge and study the history would be as ridiculous as not knowing the names Bodoni, Jenson, or Goudy. Yet, in truth, there is not the same necessity to know about graphic design's legacies, just as (don't shoot me for saying it) it is not necessary for the plumber, butcher, or policeman to know their histories (though some are eloquent on their subjects).

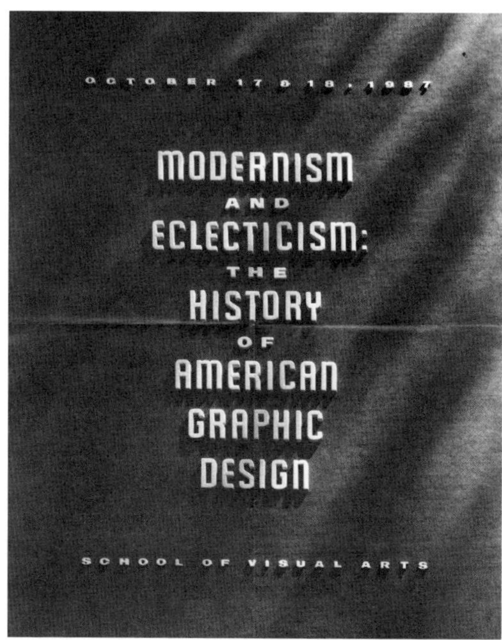

SVA Modernism and Eclecticism Poster, designed by David Connolly, 1987.

So, rather than ask the foremost question underpinning this book about "how" to teach this subject, we will begin by asking "why"—why teach students about graphic design history?

First, history is not a musty cloud stifling innovative practice. History may be a cloud, but only in the current argot of being a storage facility where the inventions and reinventions, legacy and heritage of the art, craft, and profession are stored. Some of these are neatly arranged in easily accessible buckets; some are messily disarrayed awaiting future excavation and orderly categorization. History is not a lockbox of ancient rules and taboos, but a key that opens founts of understanding —exploring the past illuminates the present and influences to the future, which makes the question, *Why teach graphic design history?* more essential than ever.

Every nation, region, or city has a design story of its own, and while individual work should be celebrated, the universality of graphic design and typography is necessary to appreciate its value in the world. Despite the dominance of Latin letters, increasingly more non-Western design is appearing throughout the world. Everyplace graphic design is practiced has a story waiting to be told and legacy needing to be discovered. The *why* is, therefore, pretty simple: design is powerful and knowledge is power. Designers work in a powerful medium and should be as knowledgeable as possible.

Now comes the *how*. This prompts more difficult questions like: Should there be standardized curricula? What amount of class time should be devoted? Can history be taught so that it parallels studio requirements? Can history be efficiently taught in a survey, or must more granular courses be mandated? How can personal preference and bias be accommodated in presenting history? Does criticism have a role in this study? How far back must history go, and where does it end? What about cross disciplinary history, incorporating other art forms and diverse media? Must there be a canon, or should history be expansive and unlimited? What does an effective graphic design history syllabus look like?

The why and how lead to the *who*. Who would benefit from the study of graphic design history? The students, for reasons already addressed; the professionals, for the same reasons, plus knowing the origins and interconnections of the field would add to contemporary professionals' design literacy; and the nondesigners, including media critics, popular culture enthusiasts, art aficionados, and others involved in visual arts. Top on my list, however, are high school–age students, who are currently exposed to and entrenched in a media-persuasive-saturated world. They should understand that every interaction, anything they watch and touch and imagine, has a story. Of course, it is easy to list potential candidates, but let's go back in time (and history) to see how exposure to the practice of graphic design and its legacy inspired some today's historic exemplars. One of the first "modern" graphic design textbooks to shed light on history was Leon Friend and Joseph Hefter's *Graphic Design: A Library of Old and New Masters in Graphic Arts* (1936). As a high school textbook, it was at once instructive and inspiring for a Depression Era generation that wanted creative alternatives to boring jobs, and doing commercial work expanded their artistic options. That is the goal of graphic design history—to instruct in ways of working while informing the reader that there are reasons behind and consequences for graphic design.

This book, *Teaching Graphic Design History*, will offer recommendations on how to teach graphic design history. The field is changing quickly as are those entering its ranks. This is a resource for future development in an age of digital tools and platforms. What makes history fascinating is not just the stories and legends and lore, but the fact that so much of today's practice was indeed done before, maybe in more primitive ways, but for similar outcomes.

CH1

TEACHING METHODS

Author and critic Tom Wolfe, in his keynote speech at the first AIGA Conference in Boston, famously warned that designers were habitually plundering "The Big Closet," a repository of passé styles and historical forms. It was 1984, the height of graphic design's precomputer "retro" period, when designers calling themselves postmodernists rejected modernist minimalism, replacing it with a kind of ersatz historicism and passé veneer. Yet their appropriations also produced certain positive unintended consequences, like providing history tutorials that gave enlightenment to an unknowing and inexperienced younger generation through exposure to a slew of forgotten or lost tropes and mannerisms. The sampling of historic artifacts was not always the most effective way to teach designers history, but it certainly made some of them anxious to learn more—at least that is what I saw happening.

Borrowing from the past was not new. In the late 1950s and 1960s, Push Pin Studios became known as exemplars of the creative reinvention of various passé styles. In their hands, these were not elegiac pastiches, but rather a unique Push Pin '60s style, which is today celebrated as being timely then and iconic now. Graphic design from the mid-'80s until 2000 was defined, in part, by the reappreciation and reapplication of ignored art-historical eras, mostly of European avant-garde design, including Russian Constructivism, the Bauhaus, Dada, and Futurism. Indeed, thirty years from now, this period of appropriation might very well be proclaimed as a defining moment in graphic design history. It all depends on how the history is spun and who does the spinning.

Graphic design history is written (and taught) by people with predilections for certain approaches above others. How the stories are framed determines how the histories are codified and which stick. There is room for interpretation, and graphic design scholarship should never be a rote recitation of bygone events, but an ongoing investigation. For teachers and students, there are various ways to ingest, digest, and debate formal and philosophical issues through design history courses. Here are a few possible survey approaches (there may be others):

Chronological

The most elementary approach to teaching graphic design history is to follow the accepted time line laid down in current history books. Some begin at the dawn of visual representation (cave painting), the introduction of moveable type and printing (Gutenberg), or the beginning of the industrial, commercial, or mechanical ages (with the advent of advertising, which gave birth to graphic design). All are

“Graphic design history is somewhere between science and superstition (or fact and anecdote).”

legitimate entry points, depending on how far back you want to go. The problem is that while chronology is necessary to establish context, it can also become too rote—it is not enough to remember dates. Although there is nothing wrong with learning how one event or object leads to another, it does, however, suggest that following an accepted time line must be supplemented by more information—sidebars or tangents—that shed light on particularly important or peculiar intersections—let’s say, between design and its function in industry or how politics or technologies have impacted the field or how comics influenced typography.

Canonical

Usually, the chronological approach takes into account a consensus about which individuals, events, innovations, objects, or styles should be studied as paradigms. Every student needs to know the unquestionable facts. This is known as a canon. It is the historical foundation on which the field sits. A canon is indeed essential to any historical pursuit, but it also has its speed bumps, as design historian Martha Scotford wrote in “Is There a Canon of Graphic Design History?” (*AIGA Journal* Vol. 9 No. 2, November 2, 1991): “The concept of *canon* is under debate right now in literary/educational circles, as its existence is alleged to produce a culturally narrow and elitist university curriculum, among other cultural problems.” Using five graphic design history books as examples, Scotford set out to show that “Given what I believe is its unintentional nature, it may be that there are ‘mistakes’: this could be *a* canon, but not *the* canon of graphic design. It could very well be that some designers and their work do not belong here or that others have been overlooked.” Since she wrote her findings in 1991, further discovery of significant designers that had been ignored are being inducted into the canon. This is an ongoing process, which continues through research and teaching.

Form-Givers

Another way of building a canon is through categorizing history according to pioneering accomplishments. Of course, only a few designers are worthy of close scrutiny, but the ones who have uniquely contributed to graphic design languages, styles, and forms by making marks that have helped define the field should be held up as models. For instance, the Czech designer Ladislav Sutnar was a pioneer of information design; American Alex Steinweiss introduced the first record album cover art; Cipe Pineles was the doyen of cinematic magazine pacing. The list of form-givers goes on. Looking at their individual work as building blocks of popular culture gives more breadth to history as it adds the human element to graphic design.

Thematic

A historical overview of themes including politics, entertainment, food, travel, industry, and culture routinely intersects with genres like type, typography, posters, packages, displays, advertisements. Paul Rand rightly declared "design is everywhere," in every nook and cranny of life. Although thematic genres are sometimes general umbrella topics, drilling into specific areas, including the histories of data visualization, music packaging, comic art, propaganda, and book and magazine publishing, these can be surveyed through a wide range of perspectives, like time, place, style, and more. The history of corporate identification or branding, for instance, is a huge field that opens onto many cross-cultural concerns, like feminism and racism, that have long been ignored in design history.

Geographical

Graphic design is a global field—now more than ever. Prior to the Internet design styles, schools and movements signified particular times and places throughout the industrial world. Type designs, for example, that were once unique to certain countries or regions are now made universally accessible through online foundries and streaming services. Once, different nationalities and languages were known for uniquely designed typefaces. When type fonts were made from heavy metal, the distribution costs were prohibitive, so America had its faces and Europe its own. Now the borders are fluid. Everyone has access to everything. So, using demographics as signpost for historical pathways can be a valuable way of examining a wide range of communication cultures.

Vernacular

Technically speaking, all graphic design is vernacular. It is the textual/visual language or dialect in common usage by the people of particular countries or regions. Vernacular is also, however, a bona fide graphic style comprised of design tropes that echo certain stereotypes or clichés. In terms of style, these days, it is a self-conscious application of primitive or untutored type and typography used to achieve certain aesthetics. The study of real commercial art and stylized vernacular design reveals the evolution of the art.

TEACHING TOOLS

You have entered a realm of scholarship, to paraphrase Rod Serling's introduction to *The Twilight Zone,* "as vast as space and as timeless as infinity. It is the middle ground between light and shadow, between science and superstition, and it lies between the pit of man's fears, and the summit of his knowledge."

This is an area which we call graphic design history.

Perhaps this is stretching the quotation to the outer limits, but it has a nice ring. Graphic design history is somewhere between science and superstition (or fact and anecdote). To *teach* graphic design history demands a critical knowledge "as vast as space"—design space and the universe for whom graphic design is made. And it must be imparted it in a way that is insightful and entertaining. To teach graphic design history means communicating knowledge that brings the past to life in the present. This suggests that reaching the summit of our knowledge requires using a variety of tools and resources. So before digging deeper into the points of view in this book, it is time to discuss the various themes and numerous ways that history is taught and review which tools and resources (obvious and not) are most useful.

Books

The most reliable repositories of shared information, criticism, theory, and discovery past and present are design and art books: omnibus histories, monographs, and surveys. They are knowledge warehouses. Over the past few decades, the market has swelled for design history text-and-picture books covering all manner of design heritage and legacy (see Further Reading for selected titles).

Decks

Once called slideshows (and actually shown on a projector with slides in a Kodak carousel), the contemporary equivalent—PowerPoint, Keynote, and PDF presentations—are referred to as "decks." They include a slew of available special visual and sound effects and technical capabilities unheard of in the era of the carousel projector. Illustrated lectures continue to be one of the most effective ways to reach students.

Decks come in many formats: there are chronologies, biographies, and surveys. Some are thematic—and, depending on the respective teacher's interests and insights, the deck can drill as deeply as a documentary film. Current audio/visual technology, combining still, motion/animation, and sound, makes the deck a classroom essential as a supplement to live lectures. It can also be referenced online and be useful with and without narration.

Symposia

History comes alive when it is shared with others. Classroom lectures are no doubt incredibly important; symposia and conferences bring people together with common interests to learn, discover, and debate. I recall the first graphic design history conference I attended at Rochester Institute of Technology, organized by Professor R. Roger Remington (see page 90); it was a blast of fresh air and new ideas. Meeting others with specialized research goals was as invigorating as it was informative. Whether largely attended or intimate, a symposium provides a platform to exchange research and resources.

For ten years, I coorganized the School of Visual Arts' "Modernism & Eclecticism: A History of American Graphic Design" with Richard Wilde. In addition to lectures by scholars presenting their original research (often on subjects that were unknown to the audiences), the pioneers of graphic design, Paul Rand, Henry Wolf, Muriel Cooper, Leo Lionni, and others were invited to speak about their careers. The concept was to introduce attendees (students, scholars, and professionals) to a range of themes and movements, ideologies and methodologies, prompting more expanded interest in the obvious and obscure aspects of the design legacy.

Original Objects

Books and decks do not offer students contact with original material—and nothing can be better than touching and feeling an original document. Although the vast majority of graphic design objects are printed multiples, the older they are, the rarer they are. The more ephemeral they are, the more fragile. Through secondary reproduction in publications, students can see the image, but tactile qualities of the printed material, whether a poster or package, provides additional appreciation of the material being studied. Borrowing from libraries and archives (which is often impossible) or buying original graphic design is definitely worth the expense and effort, if only to examine the ways that some of design's greatest icons existed in their original contexts. But originals are hard to come by . . . so the next best thing is . . .

Facsimiles

Paging through vintage Dada journals, El Lissitzky's *For the Voice*, or Depero's bolted book should provide more than vicarious design thrills. Hands-on contact with important graphic design artifacts such as these can influence how a design scholar views a body of work or inspire a graphic designer regarding how to practice his craft. The photographic reproductions of rare design pieces that appear in history books and magazines provide a glimmer of insight, but to truly savor historic design objects, one must understand nuances of form and structure. This derives from scrutiny. Yet, as noted above, such relics are not so easy to scrutinize, since many of them from the late nineteenth and early twentieth century are so fragile that turning their pages can be risky. Librarians and curators are justifiably reluctant to let even the most serious scholar finger through these valuables lest they get damaged or destroyed.

There is an alternative. Near-perfect duplications of originals are more practical research tools for historians and students. In fact, many limited edition facsimiles (and most of them are published in limited quantities) are often as valuable as those precious originals. The best of them are produced by master printers who capture the nuanced details of the original, from the coverage of ink to the texture of paper. A photographic reproduction records a particular version of the document—imperfections and all—but a facsimile preserves the essence of the original. Facsimiles are not the poor man's design artifacts—far from it. Like restrikes of Rembrandt or Goya etchings, the best design facsimiles are so faithful to the original that they have their own artistic integrity.

Videos and Films

The number of highly produced video documentaries has greatly increased, and with streaming, they are more accessible than ever. There are plenty of DIY amateur YouTube documentaries, but a higher level of production has increased the viewability of films on graphic design and related arts and crafts. In recent years, docs on individuals, including Milton Glaser, Herbert Matter, Max Bill, Massimo and Lela Vignelli (and many others), have added to our collective knowledge. Moreover, docs on Linotype, wood type, letterpress, predigital tools, as well as the typeface Helvetica, have not just increased knowledge, but have also put a human face and voice to the process of producing design. Developing a library of films and videos for class or individual viewing is an excellent supplement to the deck or slideshow.

Websites

Between scholars and fans, the exclusive design history websites have contributed greatly to the knowledge base and consequent accessibility of significant information. Time lines, articles, factoids all contribute to a wealth of design history data. Some websites devoted to individual designers are the result of intense scholarship by experts; others are the result of student interest. Creating a multileveled site that includes bibliographic, biographic, videographic, and other documentary material is useful for the information it provides and to serve as a platform for the addition of more or updated material.

Periodicals

Despite the increasing decline in design magazines, these are still the raw (and cooked) ingredients of historical research. Over the course of the late nineteenth, and throughout the twentieth, century, design periodicals have been chronicles of styles, forms, and practices. Access to magazines, past and present, is often the primary resource for design history scholars and teachers.

Archives

When graphic design was commercial art, preservation of ephemeral documents—from notes to sketches to comps to finished work—was considered unimportant. Today, maintaining access to the building blocks of packages, posters, books, magazines, etc., is just as useful for the student and scholar as the final work. Archives in libraries, schools, design organizations, etc., are not just warehouses for ephemerality, but staging areas for research.

LEARNING METHODS

It is always useful to integrate history studies into actual practice. Like copying the great master painters of old, students today can learn a lot by copying or reinterpreting the great master designers. Do a poster in the manner of . . . Solve a problem using the style of . . . For one of my classes, I have students read about the life of Czech designer Ladislav Sutnar, then develop a display and/or text alphabet based on the influence of his work. The results by students from a few classes have contributed to how the typefaces have performed and their relevance today.

Sutnar Arabic and Farsi Alphabet, Influenced by Ladislav Sutnar, by Mahya Soltani and Tala Safie

Sutnar Alphabets

Ladislav Sutnar was known in the United States as much for his unique shapes and geometric manipulations as for his compositional order and signature color palette. The typefaces he used were more or less limited to a group of sans, including Futura, and a few serifs for body copy. In fall 2016, after the republication of *Ladislav Sutnar: Visual Design in Action* (Lars Muller), which I helped revive thanks to a crowdsourcing campaign in the United States, I asked my students—most of whom had come to New York's School of Visual Arts MFA Design / Designer as Author and Entrepreneur from around the world—to reinterpret Sutnar's work as alphabets or fonts. The range of materials was incredibly diverse. Mahya Soltani from Iran and Tala Safie from Lebanon collaborated on a Farsi and Arabic modular alphabet based on Sutnar's interest in geometric shapes and primary colors. Melissa Rojanapongpun from Thailand was inspired by Sutnar's Venus paintings. Other students did their fonts with geometric precision, while others were more abstractly basing the letters on his fundamental sense of precisionist order. In the end, the influence Sutnar had on the students—many of whom had never known Sutnar's work before—was both exciting and innovative. The work shows that visionaries like Ladislav Sutnar work in their own times and have influence in future times.

Sutnar influenced font by Beatrice Sala

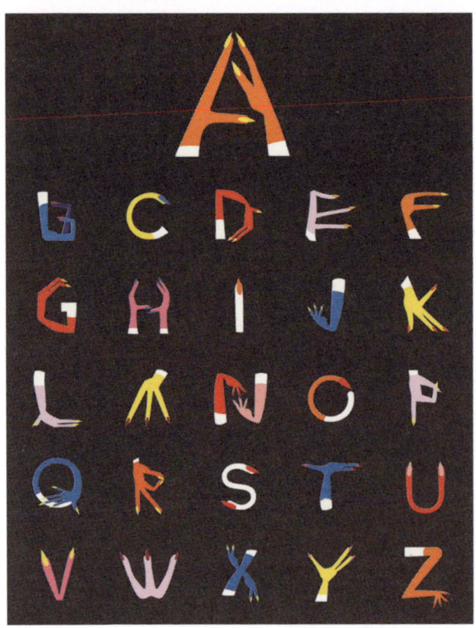

ABCDE
FGHIJ
KLNMO
PQRST
UVWXY
Z

Sutnar influenced fonts by (Top) KrongpornThongongarj, (Bottom left) Julia Marsh, (Bottom right) Yuxin Luo

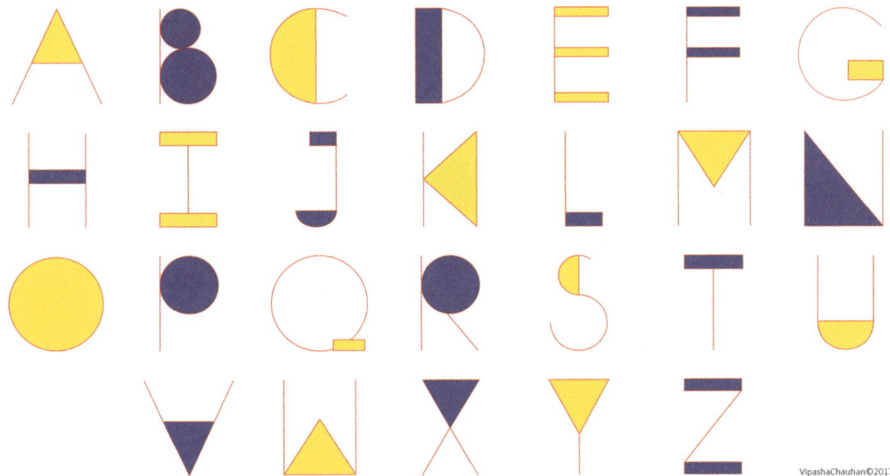

72 pt glorious states of america

60 pt opal is the second best apple

48 pt still no room for cheesemongering

36 pt the importance of following rules

24 pt hempseeds live in argentina and are healthy substitutes for oatmeal candy

Sutnar influenced fonts by (Top) Vipasha Chauhan, (Bottom) Shira Chung

"Type Class" assignment by Weronika Racz

PRACTICAL HISTORY

One of the best ways to learn practice, pragmatics, and history is to assign students to create a new idea based on vintage principals. Learning about type and typography is essentially the lingua franca of design, so assignments that allow the student to draw from history to construct a contemporary project are both engaging and illuminating. The following project exemplifies the fusion of old and new.

Type Class
In her type design and practice class, Weronika Racz, a graduate student at the Polish-Japanese Institute of Information Technology, was assigned to create a typographic game that examines the structure of different type families and styles. It was her responsibility to include the practical aspects and aesthetics as well as delve into the history of the typefaces she worked with. The entire project included many interactive analog parts and was an efficient, creative way to learn legacy and functional details.

CH2

PIONEERING GRAPHIC DESIGN HISTORY

Keith Godard

It started about 1970 after I was invited to come to the California Institute of the Arts to costart a course in graphic design within the newly formed Design Department. I discovered whilst I was teaching a studio course in typography that most of the young Californians and adventurous students from other locations believed that Helvetica was the be-all and end-all of modern design and that sans serif was invented yesterday.

Thus, I embarked on investigating how to start a history of graphic design lecture series. I did not have much to go on, except in my youth at the London College of Printing, Harry Beck (the inventor of the London Underground map) came to our classroom one afternoon a week to tell stories in a most engaging way. The hearsay and gossip of the cutting of the fonts, along with the nuances of the lives of Nicholas Jenson, Bodoni, and the notorious Eric Gill—the last made some of my classmates giggle, further making his lectures memorable.

I had had no academic history training. I recalled the architectural lectures by Vincent Scully that I had attended at Yale were so flamboyant, opinionated, and occasionally enhanced by hitting the screen with his pointer to stress details; this was very effective. As he did all this without notes was remarkable, an experience that changed my thinking that academicians were dry, boring, and even induced sleep.

I realized that if I were to invent this lecture series, it had to be personal, intriguing, and somewhat theatrical. On remembering my arrival in Los Angeles in the late 1960s, and meeting Louis Danziger, one of the important influential designers of the '50s and '60s, I recalled that he had a large library with a green pool table in the middle of the room along with a copy stand in a small closet in his studio. His house was airy and open, being one of the first designed by Frank Gehry, and was a good environment as a starting point for research.

Abandoning the attempt to teach studio design, I embarked on formulating sixteen weeks of one-and-a-half-hour lectures, expanding from the Industrial Revolution to the Modern International Style of the 1970s. Each week, I copied examples of design, making 35mm slides from Lou's books, and read ideologies about various movements—cultural, social, political implications and those that were artistically influential. I recorded, in my voice onto cassette tapes with appropriate foreign accents, the thoughts on design and manifestos of El Lissitky, Walter Gropius, and F. T. Marinetti and others from their various writings. I played these to the students as if authentic, enthralling and motivating them to remember important philosophical aspects of history.

At the end of the lecture, I revealed the impersonator. They seemed to look forward to what would be coming in the following weeks.

My belief is that the best way to explain to students the somewhat nebulous discipline of this practice of graphic design, which emerged out of commercial art and over the past hundred years has been coined graphic design, is done by practicing designers, knowledgeable of their heritage, rather than by art historians. Why? Because the practitioner brings a biased way of working and seeing the world as a designer of practical function and social responsibility, taught as a helping hand coinciding with students' studio coursework.

Recently, in one of my lecture courses, Graphic Design Studies and History, I gave an assignment to students to choose one particular designer's work or a movement from one of the past decades that I had shown as a sample that we had discussed. It had to be either a work that they admired or with which they had an affinity. They were asked to use the actual text and visual subject matter of that design of the past and to redesign it for today's audience in contemporary typography and updated imagery.

To conclude, here are some points related as to why studying the history of graphic design is important:

1. To help students find role models that relate to their work.
2. To realize visual solutions are often repeated over generations of time, especially with the advancing of production technology.
3. To search for appropriateness in creating solutions.
4. To understand which designs are based on literal concept ideas to communicate their message and which by abstraction imagery to evoke an emotional response.
5. To be able to tell the difference between eclectic, minimal, derivative design, *et a la mode en chaque* epoch.
6. To do good work.

Keith Godard attended the London College of Printing and Graphic Art, studying under Tom Eckersley. After eighteen months' service in the Royal Army Medical Corps, he became assistant to George Him (AGI). In 1960, he became a graphic designer. Following employment as an assistant at Town *magazine working under Dennis Bailey, he met Robert Brownjohn, Bob Gill, and Alan Fletcher, through whose encouragement he was awarded a full scholarship to attend the MFA program at Yale School of Art and Architecture. He studied with Paul Rand, Herbert Matter, and Bradbury Thompson. He has developed a personalized history of graphic design lecturing for over thirty years, which has become a creative fabric of influence for his own design practice and teaching.*

TEACHING DESIGN HISTORY: PRACTICE, PROCESS, AND CONTEXT

Franc Nunoo-Quarcoo

The evolution of graphic design in this moment is such that it is now widely identified as visual communications design because of the scope of the practice, tools, intent, and audience of the field at large. Therefore, teaching that history would encompass practices, processes, and contexts; hence, a diverse and inclusive global account of practitioners, their work, processes, and context. Perhaps Victor Margolin's multivolume *World History of Design* is the fount for revisioning the history of graphic design for what Steven Heller notes as "unique for its inclusivity, which reaches far beyond Western design research's usual orbit."

The evolution of design practice and the evolution of its history have opened the door to the formulation of disciplinary threads such as participatory design, codesign, and human-centered design that influence designers' creative and intellectual decisions and how design concepts for addressing "wicked problems" for social good take final form. It is important to note that pioneering visual communications designer Otl Aicher initiated the aforementioned threads in his practice in postwar Germany and hence influenced how design practice and its histories are inextricably interconnected and interwoven.

With the rapid ignition of post-World War II concepts of design as a professional practice, fueled by political, social, economic, technological, and digital innovations, graphic/visual communications design was in dire need of global understanding of what it is and of its value to society. This notion is ever more amplified now, especially in this first quarter of the twenty-first century, a century that is messaged and irrefrangibly linked with design through its very practices and activities. Visual communications design has assumed the mantle of lingua franca for twenty-first century multiple media communication.

Teaching graphic design history enables students to study various practices, thus providing a range of syntax for the students to begin to develop their own visual language and processes for identifying and formulating approaches for developing specific and particular skill sets to specific design problems at particular points in time. At the University of Michigan Penny W. Stamps School of Art & Design, where I teach visual communications design, the majority of courses are structured to address both practice and context across the art and design curriculum. One such course I taught for multiple years was ARTDES 150–*Art and Design Perspectives I: The Creators* (ADP I). It was a highly successful course formulated as a core gateway course for all

"Instructors must continue to create diverse, inclusive, contextual, and constructive learning environments that provide meaningful learning experiences leading to activities aimed at achieving multimodal values to positively affect the problems and possibilities in teaching design history."

first-year art and design students. Surprisingly, the course was sought after by students in the humanities, architecture, business, and engineering.

ADP I was the first in a trilogy of core gateway courses. In succession, students enrolled in ADP II: Society and ADP III: Technology and the Environment. Because the faculty who taught these courses acknowledged that it was impossible to explore any of these in a vacuum, all three courses included slight overlaps and redundancy so that the aggregate of ADP I, II, and III engaged students with the broadest range of creators, visual expressions, ideas, technology, and global issues. All of this was to demonstrate to students how art and design could be inspiring and productive forces in the world they inhabit.

The objective of the course was to introduce students to what it is to be a creator—an artist or designer. The course was organized to introduce students to contemporary art and design practice and relative histories of the disciplines so they could contemplate their place within it. Films, lectures, practicing artists' and designers' presentations, a combination of both historical and contemporary readings, and instructor-led discussions helped foreground how students might develop their own practice(s) during their time at the school and beyond. Which methods work well to accomplish this, and which examples of teaching have proved successful? The overall pedagogical goal of ADP I was to foster in students a deep interest in the acquisition, understanding, and comprehension of the history of contemporary art and design, thinking, practice, and related contexts—all in relation to other histories including architecture, the performing arts, humanities, science, and technology. With this goal in mind, a contextual and inclusive teaching philosophy is aligned with the belief that students must be critical and active participants who must consider design practice inseparable from design history in relation to all it engages.

Paramount in this enterprise was to facilitate and mentor students in learning environments to practice design holistically. In this "ideal" environment, students were assigned a bibliography with audio and visual materials that helped them understand the histories of designers, their processes, and relevant ancillary histories. An equally important aspect of the enterprise was to alert students to specific elective courses (across the campus in other schools and departments) that put in context design history as it relates to allied fields in art, architecture, product, industrial, and advertising design.

In the Stamps School of Art & Design curriculum, there is a required and active participation in the Penny Stamps Speaker Series (free, open, and avidly attended by the university community and general public), a highly successful and popular weekly multidisciplinary speaker/lecture/ presentation series featuring practitioners, theorists, futurists, historians, and documentarians from the spectrum of art and design. In concert with the school's curriculum and range of course syllabi, this speaker series provides a continuum that helps students establish a vivid and much-needed contextual thread of a discipline in its ever-evolving history. Collectively, all this helps to map and record the histories of design and related disciplines in context.

This model for teaching design history, then, is well served when the past and the present are held together to privilege emphasis on process, practice, and history in context. Over time, these methods of teaching the history of design to students have proved successful. Instructors must continue to create diverse, inclusive, contextual, and constructive learning environments that provide meaningful learning experiences leading to activities aimed at achieving multimodal values to positively affect the problems and possibilities in teaching design history.

Franc Nunoo-Quarcoo is professor of design at Penny Stamps School of Art & Design, University of Michigan

THE VISUAL CONTEXT OF GRAPHIC DESIGN HISTORY

Patrick Argent

> *"Publicity has in fact understood the tradition of the oil painting more thoroughly than most art historians. It has grasped the implications of the relationship between the work of art and its spectator-owner and with these it tries to persuade and flatter the spectator-buyer."*
> —JOHN BERGER, *WAYS OF SEEING*

Graphic design, in the hands of a master and at its most accomplished, is an image that can be presented and subsequently perceived as a de facto work of art, a consequential function far beyond that of its primary purpose.

John Berger made an emphatic correlation between the way publicity (in broader terms *graphic design*) and fine art can be viewed in *Ways of Seeing*, his analysis of the interpretation of the language of images. Despite its traditionally perceived lesser role in the hierarchy of the visual arts, it has nonetheless held a significant place in the evolution of artistic movements of the past two centuries.

What bearing might this relationship between the two disciplines have on the importance of teaching graphic design history to students training to become practitioners, as opposed to academics?

Visual perception.

Training to be a future professional demands fundamentally that a student be fully conversant in visual expression. Seeing, evaluating, and developing an astute perspective rather than just simply looking is an essential part of any designer's armory of specialist skills.

Fine art students are continuously immersed in the history and historiography of their own creative discipline. This approach is part of the integration of theory and practice emphasizing the development of a critical awareness and of independent judgment. In practical terms, this is seen as a reflective method to enhance and develop a higher level of critical thinking, analysis, and interpretive skills. The understanding of semiotics, design, and systemized visual language helps enable students to advance and cultivate their own individual work.

Similarly, graphics students, by the critical study of the work of a predecessor, substantially enhance their capacity for visual thinking and consciousness, further developing their own approach to design. Keenness of perception, a capacity for analysis, a refinement in aesthetic discernment, combined with a meaningful engagement with the work of others, create visual vocabulary that promotes greater understanding of the art, rationale, and methods of design practice.

In addition to the recognition of past influences on modern design thinking and culture, knowledge of contemporary issues and developments within the profession is a crucial element to any aspiring designer wishing to practice on the conclusion of their training.

A heightened sense of visual literacy is also vital in a designer's ability to *communicate* about *communications* authoritatively, an essential prerequisite for establishing one's professional standing in the eyes of any prospective client.

Reflecting the interdisciplinary fine art approach, the extension of historical and contextual studies toward studio tasks, provides an abundant scope for a range of assignments that widen and enrich other areas of applied study.

A brief outlining the production of individual magazine articles relating to a specific designer, period, movement, or historical theme involves visual and academic research and writing skills, in addition to a range of practical design techniques.

Contextual studies can also introduce a fertile source of separate yet directly related design projects into the general program. Graphics for an exhibition space devoted to an individual topic or a poster series for a museum are particularly applicable examples.

Often the results of these integrated collaborative projects subsequently constitute important components in the students' final-year exhibitions and portfolios.

This fluid and expansive approach to the subject can also be further broadened—for instance, with students creating short documentary films or presenting illustrated talks to their faculty peers based on their research.

A fundamental requirement for any student designer is to possess an open and ever-enquiring mind. Cognizance of the visual history of one's own profession, apart from its obvious relevance, also offers the opportunity to learn by example and be inspired by the best of the past.

In his unyielding essay "Confusion and Chaos—The Seduction of Contemporary Graphic Design," excerpted from his 1993 book *Design, Form and Chaos,* Paul Rand alluded to this in stating:

> *But for the familiarity with a few obvious names and facts about the history of painting and design, history is a subject not taken too seriously. This does not imply that just because some work is a product of the past it is privileged to join the ranks of the immortals. The historical process is (or should be) a process of distillation and not accumulation. In a certain sense it is related to natural selection—survival of the fittest. Furthermore to shun history is to re-invent the wheel—with the probability of repeating what has already been done.*

In a wider educational sense, the study of historical graphic design also encompasses the investigation of the social, cultural, economic, political, aesthetic, and technological contexts from which it emerged.

Exploring those contexts leads importantly to the appraisal of and subsequent discussion about the essential visual communication of ideas: the what, when, where, why, how, by whom and for whom those ideas were created and the subsequent inherent meaning, messages, and information they convey.

In *How Designers Think*, author Bryan Lawson emphasizes the significance of students requiring a wealth of visual experience to draw upon in order for them to develop and hone their creative skills.

> *Thus for Laxton (1969) creativity in design is promoted by initially concentrating on filling the reservoir with a supply of ideas. This is very much in step with psychologists writing on creativity. Kneller (1965) goes so far to say: 'One of the paradoxes of creativity is that, in order to think originally, we must familiarize ourselves with the ideas of others. . . . These ideas can then form a springboard from which the creator's ideas can be launched.*

The uninitiated student who has little or no experience of investigating design of the past is summarily consigned to a ghetto of visual impoverishment.

Conclusively, the evolution of graphic form from antiquity to the present day is one of the most potent and integral aspects of the development of civilization itself. A substantively informed critical overview of that development, graphic design's extraordinarily rich and kaleidoscopic history, has never been nor ever will be extraneous to becoming a designer.

Bibliography

John Berger, *Ways of Seeing* (London: BBC/Penguin Books, 1972), 2008 edition, 135.

Bryan Lawson, *How Designers Think* (London: Butterworth Architecture, 1988), 118, 119.

Paul Rand, "Confusion and Chaos—The Seduction of Contemporary Graphic Design" (London: *Design Review* Issue 5, Volume 2, 1992), 45.

Patrick Argent is a graphic designer, writer, and lecturer. In design education, he has taught in both further and higher education sectors, including a period in the University of Lincoln BA (Hons) Graphic Design program. Additionally, he has acted as an academic adviser to the University of Hull. His contributions to numerous periodicals and newspapers in the UK include articles for The Independent, Design Week, Creative Review, *and* Baseline, *in addition to* Frame *(the Amsterdam-based interior design journal). He is also a former editor of the Chartered Society of Designers' magazine* CSD.

WHAT WE TALK ABOUT WHEN WE TALK ABOUT GRAPHIC DESIGN

Scott-Martin Kosofsky

Ever since the fifteenth century, people of a mathematical turn of mind have posited theories about the underlying geometric principles of the Classical Latin capital letters. It was thought that these perfect forms, which reached an apogee in Imperial Rome, must have been the product of some divine truth, like those put forward by Pythagoras as the "music of the spheres." Luca Pacioli, a collaborator of Leonardo da Vinci's, published such a set of geometrically composed letters in a 1509 book about mathematical and artistic proportions. Fra Luca was a supremely organized man—he is considered the father of modern accounting—but to graphic designers of my generation he is best remembered for his drawing of the letter M that, for thirty-five years, was the logo of the Metropolitan Museum of Art.

One might ask if any of these theories ever influenced professional letterers or type designers. They did not—not in their own day and not later—because each one fell flat somewhere, creating distortions that the professional letterers, able to see subtleties more clearly than the theorists, would not tolerate. The work of the best hands and eyes always rise above formulas. The old Met logo was likely the highest use ever made of Fra Luca's drawings, chiefly because it is visually interesting and alluring, but also because it is a symbol of inquiry and careful observation, like Leonardo's Vitruvian Man.

In graphic design, being interesting and alluring—and clear—is always the higher truth. It's what we're after. But it is also a field that, like architecture and fashion design, makes use of its past in a remarkably full way, often for entirely different purposes. While Fra Luca's theory of letterforms failed to pass muster for one group of designers, it succeeded famously for another. This is an example of how history provides our "stuff," the things that are embedded into our consciousness, the material through which we draw ideas and develop our taste and critical judgment. It's what we talk about when we talk about graphic design. What makes it so compelling is the way it can spring to life at any moment, such as when letters that were carved in stone two thousand years ago can suddenly become the hot new thing. Who could have predicted in 1988 that a digital font released the next year, based almost slavishly on the letters carved onto the base of Trajan's Column, in 114 CE, would become the most popular typeface ever for movie posters? And that it would also become ubiquitous in packaging, advertising, and signage of all kinds? To realize that it was precisely the same style of lettering that Fra Luca and Albrecht Dürer

Questa lettera .M. se caua del tondo e del suo quadro le gambe suttili uogliáo esser per mezo de le grosse comme la senistra del. A. le extreme gambe uogliano esser al quanto dentro al quadro le medie fra quelle e le intersecationi de li diametri lor grosseze . grosse e sutili serefereſcano a quel le del. A. cõme di sopra in figura aperto poi comprendere.

(Top left) M, logo of the Metropolitan Museum of Art, 1971–2016 (Top right) M from Fra Luca de Pacioli, De divine proportione, Venice, 1509.

(yes, *that* Dürer) had dissected five hundred years earlier says quite a lot about how the waves of history resonate in graphic design, and not only in our letterforms. The codex, the bound book, had overtaken the scroll early in the Christian era, yet the scroll, a form long left for dead, made a comeback—shocking when you think about it—as the underlying form of the World Wide Web and most other things we read on screens. We are, as designers, constantly reviving and adapting, sometimes directly, though most often in ways that suit our current sense of style, and, more important, the needs of the content we are designing.

Why, then, do graphic design students say, as I am told they do, that history is irrelevant to them, that the courses often fail to reach them? Is it the way the subject has become segregated into a textbook-driven course without much, or any, connection to the problem-solving exercises in studio classes? I believe it may be. I also believe that the textbooks themselves reinforce the disconnection, in no small part because of their similarity to the stiff and leaden social studies textbooks that students yawn through in high school. What the books present is, by and large, a long cavalcade of instances arranged chronologically—too much to absorb, yet with too little effort invested in showing how the subjects and problems addressed by graphic design are common across the eras, and how their solutions may migrate or transform over time and into our day. It is by weaving these connecting threads that we make history usable for students and for ourselves, whether it's old letterforms that appear as new again, art nouveau posters as the inspiration for psychedelic art in the 1960s (lately showing signs of revival), or how the organization of sixteenth-century science books can become the useful models for "big data" today.

My friend Lance Hidy, who was a friend of Philip Meggs's, told me that central among Meggs's purposes in writing *A History of Graphic Design*, the most popular textbook in the field, was to establish graphic design as a discipline distinct from, and equal to, painting, sculpture, and architecture, and equally worthy of scholarly inquiry. Indeed, its organization is similar to that of the ubiquitous *Janson's History of Art*.

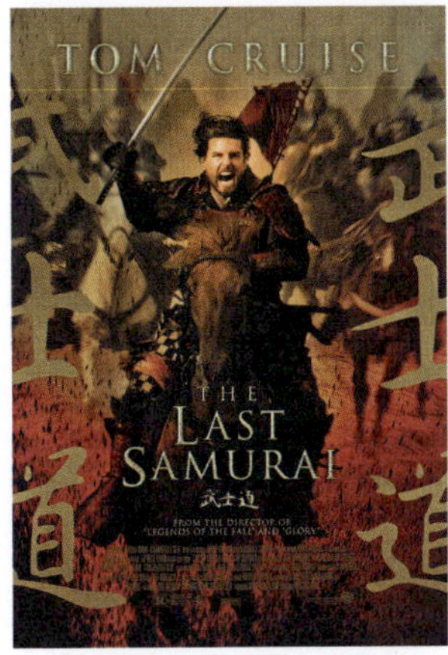

The inscription on the base of Trajan's Column, Rome, 114 ce. Photograph by Richard Kindersley and Movie posters featuring Adobe Trajan

If Meggs gives the impression of equality, it fails the "distinct from" test, and that's unfortunate for graphic design students. First, the audiences for the two books are quite different from each other and have different needs. Janson's primary users are liberal arts students on the grand tour of culture (art students are a small minority), whereas Meggs's users are largely students in graphic design programs. Second, graphic design, which is a métier and not an art, has far more diverse applications. Students who find employment as graphic designers will work in a far greater variety of fields than will art students: the design of texts in books and journalism, information and data design, type design,

This is an example of what can be seen through the use of modern digital imaging techniques. Image courtesy of E. M. Ginger, 42-Line, Oakland, CA.

Baths of Diocletian, Rome, engraving by Roland Freart, The Whole Body of Antient and Modern Architecture. London: C. Wilkinson, etc., 1680.

High-quality reproductions make a big difference. Clockwise from top left: detail from Filippo Marinetti, *Les Mots en Liberté Futuristes, Edizionii Futuriste di Poesia*, Milan, 1919; detail from Kazimir Malevich, *Pervyi Tsikl Lektsii* by Nikolai Punin, St. Petersburg, 1920; detail from Piet Zwart, commercial brochure, 1931; detail from a manuscript leaf on vellum showing the late Carolingian minuscule, Northern Italy, ca. 1120; detail from a flong (stereotype matrix) used as the cover of *PM* magazine, New York, 1935; detail from Giovanni Antonio Tagliente, *Lo Presente Libro*, Venice, 1544; detail from Harrild and Sons, wood type specimen, circa 1895; detail from Nicolas Jenson's *Euclid*, Venice, 1474. Images courtesy of The Letterform Archive, San Francisco, CA.

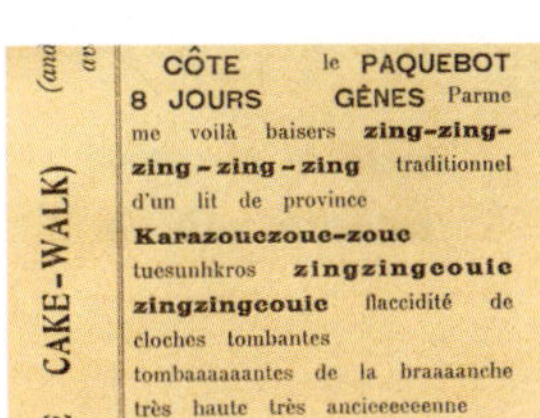

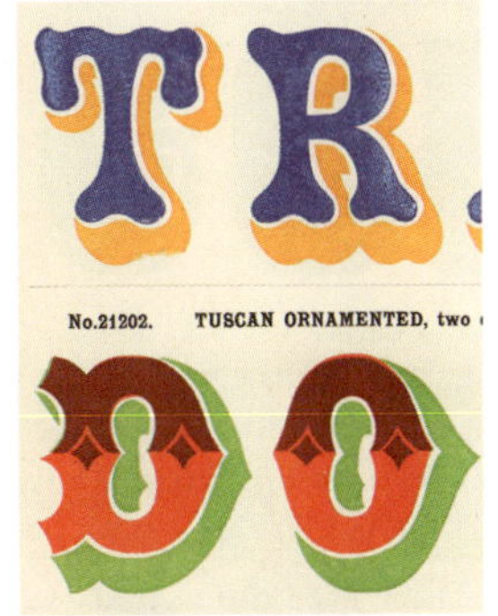

advertising and marketing, packaging, logos and signage, public and broadcast communications, printed ephemera—and the Web and multimedia implementation of all of them. Graphic design history should be organized accordingly, by content and application, keeping in mind that among them all there is common ground: typography, the use of images, the use of space, and, most important, getting a message across clearly.

"If graphic design education were to become more content-centered, an approach in which style is the response, not the driver, then we might see a revival in students' interest in history, and in literacy, too, as they begin to search more widely for models and inspiration."

Architecture is a better model than art for a history of graphic design, because it, too, has diverse applications. In the professional practice and education of architects, a distinction is made between building architecture and interior architecture. There were, and are, architects who excel at both (think Frank Lloyd Wright) and others who seldom, if ever, cross the line. There are schools and course paths that emphasize design and others that emphasize engineering. While there are all-inclusive histories of architecture that are organized chronologically, the ones used by students on a professional path are arranged by typology (and sometimes by geography): dwellings, government buildings, industrial buildings, commercial spaces, houses of worship, museums, and so on.

A graphic design textbook organized by applications will not appear overnight, and one has to wonder whether a textbook is what's needed at all, considering the vast number of area studies that are now in print. Yet, something must be done, as students need exposure to the best examples drawn from all of graphic design history. Real examples. Ask any prominent designer about their formative experiences, and they will tell you about the connections they made with certain works that excited their interests. While it is only in the rarest institutions that students might have access to original books and documents, it is conceivable that a number of schools could band together to create an organized online repository of expertly photographed images that could be printed on-demand by high-end inkjet at full or near full size by each teacher. The examples could be brought into the classroom and discussed critically, passed around or viewed after class—and made available for the students to download themselves. The images could form the basis for a wiki, in which students and teachers could participate in expanding the knowledge base and share opinions. Each department and each instructor could use these images to make their own curricula, according to the needs of their students and the subjects at hand.

The digital images will be a help, but not an end. I believe strongly that opportunities to view great work of the past are an urgent need of graphic design students, just as they are for art students. This will mean visits to library special collections, museums (who often own more graphic art than they exhibit), and rare book dealers and shows. I know from my own experience that one can understand next to nothing about the work of, say, Bodoni or William Morris without seeing it in person, up close. The scale, the ink color and intensity, the paper, and the presswork are symphonic, working together in a way that that renders even the best reproductions inadequate. Experiencing such works, both as design and as high craft, will be transformative for students.

If graphic design education were to become more content-centered, an approach in which style is the response, not the driver, then we might see a revival in students' interest in history, and in literacy, too, as they begin to search more widely for models and inspiration. This approach would emphasize the why, as well as the how, design is integrated throughout a work, deep inside, not only as a veneer that sits on the surface. Moreover, a visual portal to the many kinds of work involving graphic design can point to career paths that students, whose exposure to design might still be limited to just a few things, might not have considered but may someday wish to follow.

Scott-Martin Kosofsky develops, produces, designs, edits, composes, and makes types for books in Rhinebeck, New York, where he is a partner in the Philidor Company. He is also an award-winning writer. His work falls largely into two categories: image-rich books on a wide range of subjects—from forgotten architecture to letterforms to the Apollo Lunar Program—and Judaic books in liturgy, Bible, and history.

TYPOGRAPHIC HISTORY

Jerry Kelly

Type is a tool: a tool for communication, and it can also be a tool to an aesthetic end (ideally concurrent with its use as a tool for communication). Like all tools, there are methods for its use to be learned, and better and worse ways to use it. We serve our mission as teachers of typography best by instructing beginners how to use this tool called type. We should also keep in mind that type is a very technical and complex item, so there is a lot to learn.

From what I have seen over many decades as a teacher, and also as a designer and producer of printed materials, most often only the aesthetic side of typography is covered in colleges, with little if any regard for its technical component. Therefore, students come out of school with little if any knowledge of how to use type, though they may have many examples of typographic design in their portfolios. If they are not taught the fundamentals of type, those portfolio examples will betray an ignorance of the subject, though they often show design talent. Having often been responsible for hiring designers myself, I have seen this again and again: good design sense, but poor knowledge of type and typography. This is really a shame, since if students learn about type in class, they will be much better able to realize their design goals, and to achieve finer results.

So, if we truly want to teach type and typography, we have to impart a great deal of technical information to students. Important factors such as leading, body size (and how it relates to point size), letter fit and kerning, typeface classification, parts of letters, the evolution of type design, and much else should be learned in order to use this tool most effectively. This is not what students expect in art school; they would like to deal solely with aesthetics, but they cannot realize their aesthetic potential if they do not know how to use the basic building block of typographic design: type. Students do not expect textbook-like information, memorization, and tests in typography class; they expect something more akin to a studio art class. Unfortunately, at most schools, teachers and administrators abdicate their responsibilities, and the students usually get what they want: a chance to play around with typographic design without learning the basic technical information needed to properly use type.

And there is a lot to learn. This could be taught in a most didactic manner, with a teacher presenting the information and expecting the students to memorize and apply it. In a way, there would not be anything wrong with that, if it worked; at least students would learn how to

"... students come out of school with little if any knowledge of how to use type, though they may have many examples of typographic design in their portfolios."

use type to achieve their goals. However, in order to truly understand the principles of type and its use, and for to students better remember what they are taught, a historical approach is best. Let me provide just a couple of examples: it would be simple enough to explain that leading is space between lines, and if a student is taught that and can remember it, that is good. But if the teacher were to explain that when type was set in metal, thin strips of an alloy consisting mostly of lead were inserted between lines if the typographer wanted more space between ascenders and descenders, then students will understand where the term "leading" comes from, and that understanding will greatly help them to remember the term and its meaning. Similarly, an instructor can simply state that kerning is adjusting the space between a pair of letters, but if students were to understand that in metal type, kerning meant undercutting the letterform on top of a piece of metal so it could overhang the adjoining letter, they would better understand the principle, and they would also then clearly know why the term "kern" is used both to explain this adjustment of letter fit AND the part of a letterform that overhangs its neighbor, such as the top of an "f." If the teacher goes on to explain how this term evolved with the use of phototype and digital type to mean not just cutting in, or removing, space between letters, but also adding space, they could then delve into the meaning of terms such as letterspacing and letter fit.

These are just a couple of examples; there are many, many more. To stay with the effects of kerning in typography: once the history of how this was used in metal is imparted, then the principle of how the Linotype machine could not accommodate individual kerned letters, then therefore we see distorted forms such as the Linotype Janson italic *f* or Optima roman "f" with its "hook" design. And with that, students will start to learn how to discern between better and worse versions of Janson and other fonts available today.

I sympathize with art school students' dread of history and technical information; I do not believe anyone went to art school with such study in mind. However, if when we teach historical and technical information we can throw in along the way how such information applies to computer typography today, they will appreciate its importance. The greatest appreciation will come, however, after the student leaves these beginning classes and either goes on to advanced type classes or working in the "real world"; then their greater knowledge of type and typography will serve them well.

One of my most profound moments as a teacher was running into a couple of my Type I and II students on campus the year after they took my beginning typography classes. I asked them how type III and IV were going. They replied, referring the other students in the class, "Man, those kids don't know anything about type!" Of course, that will be the end result if they are not taught anything about this highly technical subject with a rich history.

Jerry Kelly is a calligrapher, book designer, and type designer and has served as chairman of the American Printing History Association, president of the Typophiles, and an active member of several committees at the Grolier Club. He has written many articles as well as several books on calligraphy and typography, including The Noblest Roman: The Centaur Types *(coauthored with Misha Beletsky, winner of the 2016 Bibliographical Society of America Prize). Before starting his own business in 1998, Kelly was vice president of the Stinehour Press, preceded by a decade as designer at A. Colish. He has taught at various institutions and has lectured widely.*

RECONSIDERING: PHILIP MEGGS AND RICHARD HOLLIS

Johanna Drucker

Note: This piece was written just as Emily McVarish and I had finished our Graphic Design History: A Critical Guide *(2008) and was meant to position our project in relation to the two most popular texts in the field. Our debt to both was and is apparent, but our approach was driven by critical, theoretical principles rather than a narrative approach to the history of individual accomplishments. While Philip Meggs's book remains a major reference work, and Richard Hollis's convenient and succinct overview a useful introduction to social history in the field of graphic design, neither combined the historical scope and critical frameworks of social forces that we brought to our project. The analysis offered here was a justification for introducing a new text but was meant as a respectful homage. It was also intended to offer students and scholars in the field a way to think about history metacritically and to make explicit the ways models shape understanding about form and design. (JD, November 2017)*

Originally published in Design and Culture*, volume 1, issue 1, pp. 51–78.*

Establishing a New Field

Philip Meggs made a bold move when he first published *A History of Graphic Design*, rather than of visual communication, in 1983. In choosing his title, Meggs knew his readers understood that the field had emerged fully from commercial art, the printing trades, public relations, and fine arts.[1] This distinct identity had emerged with the establishment of professional organizations, publications, and curricula in the early twentieth century. By the 1970s and early 1980s, graphic design had taken its place among the professions in the United States, Japan, and Europe.[2] As an area of study with a claim to its own history, graphic design was still relatively undeveloped. Meggs's publication not only created an outline of graphic design history, but also defined the discipline.

Any intellectual discourse constitutes its objects according to various models, and Meggs's book is of course shaped by many such models. These include concepts of history, graphic design, the designer, and even the purpose and form of a book meant for pedagogy. While Meggs conscientiously updated his own research and reading in subsequent editions (the expanded bibliographies are testimony to his diligence), he never rethought his conceptual premises.[3] The works published by the Allworth Press, *Eye,* the volume *Graphic Design in America,* the writings of Ellen Lupton and J. Abbott Miller, Steven Heller, Jessica Helfand, and many others who absorbed lessons of theory into a method, all provided models for radically transformed criticism in the field. Though sometimes referenced in his later bibliographies, they were not absorbed into his approach.

The scope of Meggs's contribution is best understood when weighed against that of Richard Hollis's *Graphic Design: A Concise History*, the next historian to study the field in depth. Their combined legacy challenges us to formulate a clear argument of historical study and a method suitable to our times. In reconsidering Meggs, we must describe the fundamental assumptions that shape his ideas of graphic design history and understand that many go unnoticed or are still followed unreflectively. By the time he published his book in 1994, Hollis could draw on a much richer spectrum of critical writings. The sharp distinctions between these two show that they were conceived at different moments in intellectual history. But each also embodies conceptual distinctions that are ideological as much as generational. Meggs's positivist and celebratory approach reflects a progressive teleology in which technological improvements mark gains and benefits, while Hollis's analyses are rooted in a left-oriented critique of signs and language as ideological formations. The implications of these differences are profound. Equally important, each defines history and historical methods and exposes basic critical assumptions about how *knowledge* is understood.

Meggs's Intellectual Formation

Meggs brought his background as a practitioner and teacher to his study, and his book came out of the lectures and syllabi developed for teaching. After he received his MFA from Virginia Commonwealth University, he worked as a graphic designer for Reynolds Aluminum and art director for A. H. Robins Pharmaceuticals. He returned to his alma mater in 1968 to teach. When Meggs began teaching the history of visual communication in 1974, this contribution was still rare in design curricula. To prepare, Meggs surveyed the field; using a grant from the National Endowment for the Arts in the late 1970s, he traveled to other institutions teaching the subject more widely. Highly informed and seriously literate, he made use of every resource that he thought might be relevant to inform the set task. But he had only a handful of precedents with which to conceptualize the history of the field as we now know it.

Meggs drew on two then-distinct intellectual traditions in conceiving his project. One was the history of what are known as *graphic arts*:

printing, books, signage, and posters (including various technological innovations and their development). Its methodology is an inventory of artifacts or a chronology of technical processes. The other was what we now think of as the history of *visual communication*, with its roots in formal principles. Together, these provided Meggs with a wide range of primary and secondary materials to inform his study. Both are conspicuously visible in the titles that populate the bibliography of the 1983 edition.

Weaving together the history of graphic arts, Meggs consulted works from the history of fine art and printing, book arts, posters, typographic design. Many still-essential texts, such as Douglas McMurtrie's *The Book: The Story of Printing* (1943), Daniel Berkeley Updike's *Printing Types: Their History and Use* (1937), or John Lewis's *Anatomy of Printing* (1970), provided basic information about printing, type, designers, or technologies. Their chronological narratives bear the stamp of each author's own training and formation. Though all of the authors listed in the bibliography are humanists who clearly value the artistry of the works they study, some, like Max Gallo, have stronger roots in Marxist theories of social history. Others, like Stanley Morison (well known for his work as a practitioner), used their knowledge of archival resources to develop sophisticated critical discussions of historical material.

The depth of Meggs's scholarship is impressive and still provides a useful starting point for work in this field. His bibliography lists many studies only available in a research library, such as the papers of the Arts and Crafts Society, published in 1893, and a 1901 work by Charles Ashbee on John Ruskin and William Morris. Classics and contemporary titles from art history and criticism, many of them still in print are featured in his list: *Futurist Manifestos* (Apollinio 1973), a monograph on Theo van Doesburg (Baljeu 1974), another on Mondrian and de Stijl (Jaffe 1979), Edmund Fry's *Cubism* (1978), and Stephen Bann's *The Tradition of Constructivism* (1974). When appropriate, he consulted specialized publications focused on the early periods, such as the work of the major early Egyptologist E. Wallis Budge (1909), for studies of *The Book of the Dead* and the Rosetta stone. Though some of these have been superseded by archaeological discoveries or recent research, these are landmark publications in their own fields.

Technically focused texts dealing with mechanical processes and equipment sit alongside primary sources such as the eighteenth-century printing manuals of Pierre Fournier (1764, 1768). Most of the imprints (and reprints) are issued from commercial publishers: Dover, Watson-Guptill, Viking, Thames and Hudson, and Reinhold. Aside from the art historical titles, almost none of the works Meggs cited for reference

"A good place to begin comparing Meggs and Hollis is with differences in their decisions about historical scope and periodization. Each begins and ends their histories in different places, subdivided according to different criteria."

were from academic or scholarly presses, another sign of the marginal status of graphic design history at the time. Scattered among the studies of woodblocks, mechanical typesetting methods, and posters are occasional titles with the word "design" in them. Remarkably, however, the phrase "graphic design" does not appear in any title in that original bibliography—and never in conjunction with the word "history."

In gathering materials to track the second contributing strain of intellectual thought, he tracked the roots of visual communication through texts with a theoretical commitment to the formal language of graphics. Several works embodied this sensibility: Karl Gerstner's 1959 publication *Die Neue Graphik* (1959 a, b) was "the first comprehensive survey of the history and rationale of the Modern Movement." Gerstner's modern focus was complemented by Josef Muller-Brockmann's *History of Visual Communication* (1967), another work in which historical issues are subservient to arguments about the principles of form. These shared more with each other than they did with books on the history of printing because their approach to design was grounded in formal principles that are the hallmark of mid-twentieth-century paradigms. These authors saw design as structured like a language. This attitude was a direct outgrowth of Constructivist principles—the work of Wassily Kandinsky (1926), Lazar El Lissitzky, Sergei Eisenstein, and others—that prevail through the Bauhaus, even though the tendencies go further back, into the work of Walter Crane, John Ruskin, and the aestheticist writers of the late nineteenth century. In the mid-twentieth century, this attitude was expressed in the works of Georgy Kepes (1951) and Laszlo Moholy-Nagy (1947a), whose quintessentially modernist writings reinforced the "language of design" paradigm. Their goal was to elaborate universal principles and attitudes toward form. They viewed history as a catalog of examples, but their larger project was to outline fundamental features of visual "language" without questioning the fundamental difference between linguistic and visual modes of expression. This tradition is heavily stamped by a formal assumption in which language terms like syntax, semantics, or semiotic categories of icon, index, and symbol are invoked as metaphors but also as organizing categories of analysis and practice. In the mid-to-late-twentieth century, the textbook industry for graphic design practice built on this paradigm, with a proliferation of publications with "language of" in their titles—including one by Meggs (1992b) published in 1992: *Type and Image: The Language of Graphic Design*.

Scope and Periodization

A good place to begin comparing Meggs and Hollis is with differences in their decisions about historical scope and periodization. Each begins and ends their histories in different places, subdivided according to different criteria. A look at each table of contents provides a useful overview of these frameworks (Meggs 1983: n.p.; Hollis 1994, 5). Meggs starts in prehistory and extends to the Information Age. For him, the term *graphic design* is not constrained by a historical definition (it was not in existence and common use until the early twentieth century). Meggs's perspective includes cave paintings, the artifacts of preliterate and traditional cultures, and embraces many forms of visual expression. He considers graphic design interchangeable with "visual communication." As a consequence, he sees this large historical sweep within a single continuum, albeit one demarcated by major technological and cultural shifts.

In Meggs's approach, graphic design is not defined as a profession, but a set of skills and objects that include the work of symbol makers, scribblers, scribes, and individuals in the craft and trade of print, signage, or web design. His five major subdivisions consist of twenty-five chapters, with a fairly even distribution of four to six per section, though a larger proportion of attention is given to the modern and contemporary periods.[4] His chapter titles like "The German Illustrated Book" or "Photography, the New Communications Tool" emphasize his attention to formal properties or technological developments.

Hollis is more orthodox in his allegiance to the historical specificity of the term graphic design. He begins his study in the modern period, with the late nineteenth century, when industrialism is well advanced and the separation of graphic design from print production has become established practice. His seven thematically defined sections (containing nineteen chronological chapters) are each associated with geographical locations ("Italy," etc.). The implication is that graphic design can be understood within the framework of specific local cultures and social networks. From the outset, clear differences are

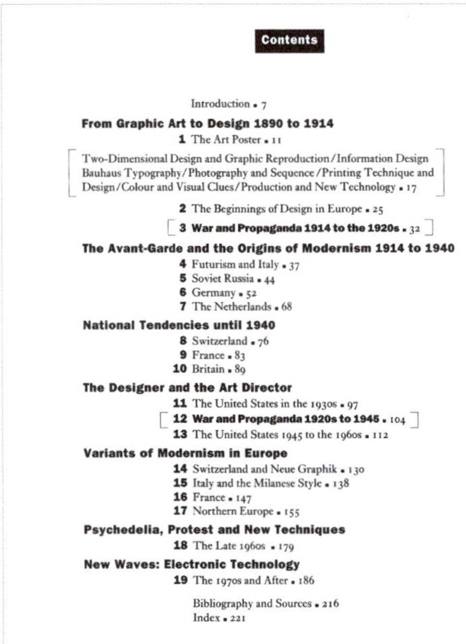

Contents

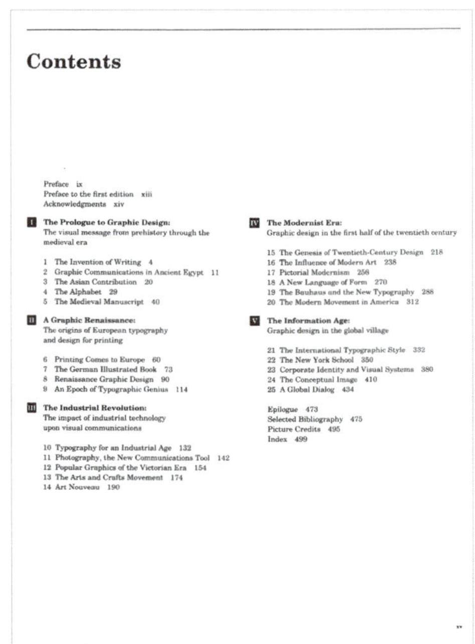

Contents

(Left) Richard Hollis, *Graphic Design: A Concise History* contents page. (Right) Phillip Meggs, *A History of Graphic Design* contents page.

apparent. Meggs leads with artifacts. The archive and collection are primary in his conception, even if discussion of designers becomes a way to create a connecting narrative among the individual objects. Meggs takes artifacts as self-evident. For him, they comprise a discrete record outside of the conditions of their production and reception, as formal, aesthetic expressions. Hollis begins with a social world and its history, within which designed artifacts arise, shaped by the situation and circumstances of their execution. For Hollis, objects are never self-evident but are instruments and means of mediating relations of power and influence, ideology and meaning production. These differences of scope and periodization reflect contrasting attitudes toward technology and notions of historical progress.

Technology as Progress

The first three historical periods of Meggs's book are demarcated by changes in production methods. Within this conceptual frame, the break after Section I, "The Prologue to Graphic Design: The visual message from prehistory through the medieval era," has a logical endpoint in the invention of printing and moveable type in the 1450s. Section II, "A Graphic Renaissance: The origins of European typography and design for printing," spans 350 years of stylistic and formal development that ends in the late eighteenth century with the arrival of industrialization. Throughout these three centuries, many radical cultural and social changes occurred, such as changes in media formats and functions, colonial expansion, revolutions, new democratic forms of government, and capitalist entrepreneurship. But Meggs relies on technology as a periodizing device for the graphic arts.[5] Section III, "The Industrial Revolution: The impact of industrial technology upon visual communications," starts in the late eighteenth century and traces the automation of print production. Using industrialization as a technological milestone makes good sense, but the impacts of steam, factory-style labor, and changes in the social organization of Europe and the United States resonate with social implications in which printed matter is an active participant. Meggs treats cultural changes as a backdrop against which graphic works stand out with clear and discrete autonomy.

Meggs uses the start of the twentieth century as a default milestone for Section IV, "The Modernist Era: Graphic design in the first half of the twentieth century." Rather than pointing to the striking changes in media and the innovations brought by radio and electricity, he shifts away from the logic of his own technologically based argument. In the early twentieth century, the self-identified field of graphic design comes into being, along with new institutions, professional roles and identities, technologies, and practices. The division between the industrialization of the nineteenth century and the twentieth century is awkward. The cultural transformations within which modernism arises are intimately bound to the nineteenth century, including radical changes in the political sphere, artistic activity, and mass communication. In the 1890s and 1900s, impulses that derived in large part from the longer development of the Arts and Crafts movement were transformed as they came under pressure from radically altered economic and political circumstances. The transformation of attitudes toward the role of graphic designers in industrial production doesn't map onto decades in this period. The early-twentieth-century avant-garde extended the programs of social radicals and progressives and other strains of politically informed aesthetics with roots in the work of Henri de Saint-Simon and other progressive thinkers. These impulses were transformed under pressure of changed political and economic circumstances. Likewise, the relation of these activities to technological change is as nuanced as their connections to innovations in Russian Constructivism or International Dada.

Meggs wrote in advance of the full integration of digital technologies into design practice, since he finished his first edition in 1983. But his final section, Section V, "The Information Age: Graphic design in the global village," traces the systematization of graphic design within corporate environments and networks of information. Following World

War II, popular and corporate culture were permeated with the notion of the information age; such talk evoked the rhetoric of progress that Meggs engaged enthusiastically. Published in 1998, the third edition adds chapters on "Postmodern Design" and "The Digital Revolution."[6]

Meggs's divisions make sense if one accepts his larger conceit: the chronology of Western media and communication maps onto the history of its technology. As mentioned above, sometimes this produces problems, particularly when Meggs introduces a hard division between the nineteenth and early twentieth centuries. Placing the 1902 establishment of the Weimar Arts and Crafts Academy in Section II but the 1900 founding of the Darmstadt Colony within the modernist movement creates an uncomfortably forced distinction between closely related activities. Many changes in social conditions helped shape the thinking and action of key players like Peter Behrens, Henry van de Velde, the Grande Duke of Saxe Weimar, and powerful industrialists who backed these experiments.[7] Nationalistic impulses combined ideological and financial agendas. Artists working with the formal legacy of the Arts and Crafts, but a different set of cultural beliefs, applied their talents to the very industries that had been so seriously criticized by William Morris several decades earlier.[8]

Meggs does not provide a platform to examine these contradictions. Instead, his chronological scaffolding rises above social complexity, explaining these developments simply as changes in the role of the designer and the form of the objects produced. The chronological structure actually works against analysis of ideological forces, since it naturalizes sequence as a self-evident fact. These are surface details, and analysis of the deeper conceptual model reveals more interesting issues.

Meggs's method creates a continuous narrative that describes artifacts in sequence, in keeping with traditional art historical conventions. This narrative approach inevitably requires selection; fraught decisions of inclusion and exclusion are smoothed over by the unified appearance of the text. Rhetorically, Meggs creates a "story" of graphic design, its forward momentum shaped largely by technological progress.[9] He chronicles inventions that are conceived empirically as self-evident and straightforward. As per his title, Meggs wants to provide *a history*, a linear account of forms of graphic expression.[10] It is worth noting, in regard to Meggs's approach, that several titles by Marshall McLuhan are listed in his extensive bibliography, including the highly influential *Understanding Media* and *Gutenberg Galaxy*, published in 1964 and 1962, respectively (Meggs 1983: 500). Though Meggs draws lightly on the media studies and theory that McLuhan brought into the popular and scholarly spotlight, his emphasis on the historical progression of technological developments suggests echoes of the Canadian author's thinking. A title that is conspicuously absent from Meggs's bibliography is Elizabeth Eisenstein's *The Printing Press as an Agent of Change*, published in 1979. The controversial volume must have come to Meggs's attention, and the notion of agency suggested in its title would have resonated with some of his own perspectives.

Events provide a "context" for print culture, which is therefore understood as a quasi-autonomous, discrete zone of activity "within" this "context." For instance, the section titled "A Graphic Renaissance" describes Johann Gutenberg's innovations and financial difficulties and the dissemination of print technology through specific individuals. Combined with his ability to call attention to the graphical qualities of type and design in the illustrations, this argument works well. Meggs connects the control of printing and migration of printers from Germany and France into Switzerland and the Low Countries with the religious wars in Europe, situating the development of the Dutch printing industry within a narrative linked to political events. But even as political eventspunctuate an otherwise unbroken continuum, they appear to stand outside of graphic design.

Meggs conforms to a mainstream art historical approach in which "context" was (and still often is) described as if it were a stable "setting" for the autonomous gems of art history or graphic design.[11] This concept of context as a static setting is uninflected by dialectical thinking. Meggs's attitude toward history is not solely the result of the historical moment of his writing. Social art history and cultural studies were already well-established approaches to the analysis of visual and graphic form by the late 1970s and early 1980s, and Marxist theory had been well-integrated into historical explanations for over a century. From a dialectical perspective, graphic expressions in fine or commercial arts can be conceived as codependent with circumstances of production and use. They arise in a dynamic relation to ideological and cultural forces. But for Meggs, context remains a set of circumstances, a preexisting frame in which to place an autonomous work or object functions. This mechanistic notion of history pervades his work.

The Force of Narrative

Meggs's "story of" approach is so strong that we quickly forget it is rhetorical. Discussing each era's celebrities and major accomplishments, he never extracts principles from his observations on style or form. For instance, he describes the invention of typography as "one of the most important advances in civilization after the invention of writing," because it "allowed the economical and multiple production of alphabet communication" (Meggs 1983: 71; 1998: 58). He provides information about the process of punch-cutting, matrix stamping, and casting and the need for an alloy with specific properties. But he never suggests that the standardization and modularization that are part of letterpress technology imposes rationality on human production in a way that broke with the holistic guild approach and provided a model for attitudes toward knowledge production as well as labor. The fragmentation of processes into distinct parts that had to fit—literally in the case of letterpress—is part of larger changes. The development of the printing press exemplifies the organizing principles for discourse formation in the larger social order. The rationalization of sight according to perspectival principles and the introduction of mapping system to organize space according to a mathematical representation register related and equally striking shifts aligned with these principles.

At times, Meggs's parade of persons and works can be highly entertaining. Meggs's tale of the German Friedrich Koenig, who in 1814 introduced two double-cylindered steam-powered printing presses to print the London *Times*, reads like an extended gag joke. Fearing sabotage, the *Times*' editor told workers to assemble for "news" from the Continent. At six a.m., he entered the pressroom where newspaper staff gathered, anticipating an announcement about Napoleonic campaigns. Instead he walked in and announced, "The *Times* is printed—by steam" (Meggs 1983: 164; 1998: 132). Meggs's breezy and incident-filled approach comes under visible strain as it reaches the modern period. Facts overwhelm argument; information, rather than ideas or insights, populates the pages. The twentieth century takes up half the book. Moreover, when dealing with recent events, the details of the foreground often obscure a longer view. Meggs's knowledge of practitioners and important graphic campaigns explodes into a plethora of profiles, one after another, without a sense of an argument.

Such narrative histories are usually criticized for their inclusions and exclusions. In the 1980s, for instance, H. W. Janson was attacked for his Western-centric approach and his failure to cite females and artists of color.[12] But the real limitation of narrative history is not only in its selections. The intellectual problem is that narrative approaches assume that a totality exists, a priori, outside of the narrator's activity. The failure of a unified narrative is not that it is incomplete, but that it is based on an assumption that somewhere there is a whole, preexisting history to which it could be responsible. This model of history presumes completeness as an ideal in which an account would mirror or mimic a preexisting "real" that is self-identical and replete. This carries the methodological implication that the unified whole can be objectified in its completeness by an observer standing outside of its events—an empirical historian. This distinction of subject and object as an underlying construct and worldview drives descriptive narration. It assumes that we stand outside a history that could, had we but world enough and time, be fully rendered in a descriptive text. But this attitude is premised on a mechanistic cause-and-effect sequence of discrete events, a model of knowledge that comports readily with the technological positivism underpinning *A History of Graphic Design*. The enterprise conjures an image of history as a vast virtual museum waiting to be explored, a concept that has very little currency in contemporary critical thought.

Underpinning such positivist approaches is another unquestioned construct; Meggs believes that a discrete free-willed subject can observe an a priori world. Moreover, he believes that this world is equally self-defined, bounded, limited, and available for description. This view is part of the scientific method in the seventeenth and eighteenth centuries and expressed in Newtonian physics, Linnean classifications systems, or, closer to graphic forms, the perspectival systems that rationalize visual representation. These are challenged by dialectical approaches such as historical materialism in Marx's analysis of historical forces, the decentering of the rational subject in Freud's psychoanalytic approach, ideas of relativity and quantum mechanics, and other probabilistic and codependent formulations of knowledge that conceive of knowledge as an emergent process of elements in a dynamic system of relations. Not surprisingly, this earlier, self-sufficient model of subject serves as the basis of Meggs's figure of the designer.

The Designer as Free Agent

Meggs's artifact-based model of graphic design history posits an equally autonomous designer. Some of these individuals are known by name; their characters and sensibilities are pertinent to our understanding. According to Meggs, graphic designers make free-willed choices about style and form in keeping with the needs and spirit of an age. Meggs's designer is an autonomous producer, not a produced subject.

For instance, Meggs explains Will Bradley's style by his Americanness. Bradley knows his audience is not ready for the unconstrained eroticism of his inspiration, Aubrey Beardsley. The power of such explanations is that they appear to show cause and effect, as if the designer were operating as a fully self-aware and autonomous agent. But Bradley's business acumen and aesthetic missionary opportunism can be construed as a case of codependent formation, not individual character traits. Down to the way he uses a clean, descriptive line, his wholesomeness

"... he insists that graphic design serves a client's needs and is driven by that relationship, while fine art is subject to a very different set of regimes for creation and success."

is endemic. Even his nudes are chaste, lacking any hint of the perverse eroticism in the Beardsley lines. Bradley had internalized the values of his culture; he does not hold himself back from making decadent aesthetic statements. They are outside of his range of expression. They fall into the domain described by Michel Foucault as forms that cannot be expressed because they cannot be imagined. The designer is a produced subject, not a free agent who produces.

Because Meggs's designers are always active agents, they create new styles for clear and logical reasons, as if their taste and judgment were not part of larger trends but merely a response to technological opportunities. Meggs characterizes the nineteenth-century French poster artist Jules Chéret, for instance, as making a conscious decision to create campaigns for advertisers to demonstrate the beauty in lithography (Meggs 1983: 223, 1998: 194). This is not untrue. But it does not explain the sources for these images and their role in changing attitudes toward the commodification of women and sexuality in the burgeoning consumer culture. This approach contrasts with writers like Adrian Forty, a Meggs contemporary, who published *Objects of Desire* in 1986 and erased the designer from design history entirely.

Though it may seem counterintuitive, this assumption echoes Meggs's implication that designers produce their work independently, simply choosing styles appropriate to the times. Designers are not conceived as historically produced subjects or as an effect of the ideological conditions in which these "reasons" cause them to act. Designers not only master form and style, but also their own destiny. The only exceptions are those caught in the web of large-scale events (Meggs recounts that Etienne Dolet is burned at the stake, Tschichold threatened, and Alvin Lustig dies young). But even then, designers are acted on by, not complicit in, these events, and Meggs's reading of these incidents is fatalistic rather than analytical. Lustig's early death intensifies the aura of his (certainly remarkable) work, as do Tschichold's persecution and Dolet's torment, but these ideas are not analyzed for their effect on our concepts of heroism or radical aesthetics, or the discursive formations within which these figures, and their fates, were manipulated for symbolic purposes—or for the ways Dolet's and Tschichold's decisions to position themselves strategically in relation to power formations allowed them to be used as symbolic figures.

The Hollis Contribution

Richard Hollis shares some of Meggs's methodological assumptions, but he analyzes activities rather than objects or people. Building on Meggs's foundation, Hollis brings additional critical perspective to the field. He is not a radical deconstructionist, taking apart metanarratives of truth or logocentrism. His leftist orientation draws on British cultural studies rather than a poststructuralist critique of discourse. The strategic decisions that distinguish his work expose a different model of graphic design, its history, and the designer. He begins his book in medias res, at the moment he identifies as the shift "From Graphic Art to Design 1890 to 1914." In so doing, Hollis frames his project as necessarily incomplete. This starting point contrasts with Meggs's totalizing scope, but even more, with his presumption that there exists an already complete, preexisting history to be narrated. Bracketing his focus and beginning with the modern period, Hollis points to historical and cultural realms outside of graphic design. In his introduction, he justifies this decision, discussing the specific activities that distinguish graphic design from fine art. Most specifically, he insists that graphic design serves a client's needs and is driven by that relationship, while fine art is subject to a very different set of regimes for creation and success. Hollis's telescopic prose risks being cursory, and the foundations on which he establishes modernism lack the depth of Meggs's longer view.

Hollis is a working designer, keenly aware of the tensions brought into play by the various identities of fine art, commercial work, and client interests in a profession that has "existed only since the middle of the twentieth century" (Hollis 1994: 8). Hollis's own credentials come from his professional track record, rather than academic training. His formal design education was sporadic, and coupled with National Service and stints working as a printer. Like Meggs, Hollis has had a career as an educator and designer, and his activist stance is evident (Wilson 2006: 26). Hollis worked with many clients, including the CND, *New Society*, and *New Middle East*, as well as cultural and arts organizations. He cofounded the School of Design at West of England College of Art and has sometimes been credited with seeing design as "social service" (Wilson 2006: 28). The very "conciseness" of Hollis's book extends his model of partial knowledge yet provides sharp conceptual insights within its limits. He constantly situates design works into the play of social forces or conceptual shifts. In a statement that suggests a rapidly shifting field, he describes László Moholy-Nagy at the Bauhaus as gradually transforming from "improvising craftsman" to an "industrial designer" (Hollis 1994: 63). In another paragraph, he calls attention to the use of German nationalist colors in John Heartfield's cover design for Kurt Tucholsky's *Deutschland über alles* (Hollis 1994: 62). Though brief, and often confined to qualifying clauses, these statements constantly link graphic works and cultural realms. Even his introductory remarks identify three roles for graphic design: 1) identification, 2) information and instruction, and 3) presentation and promotion. He introduces a metalanguage of function into his model right at the outset. Instead of starting with the archive, he grounds his study in the idea of design as a set of activities a designer enacts within a system of social relations of production and reception.

Though necessarily brief (in sheer surface area, Hollis's entire book is one third the area Meggs allots to this period), Hollis has a critical edge. He organizes his historical chronology thematically. The chapter titles make clear his critical disposition. "National Tendencies until 1940" or "Psychedelia, Protest, and New Techniques" suggest an integration of cultural conditions and graphic expressions. Hollis pays special attention to the two major World Wars of the twentieth century, in part because they offer an opportunity to assess propaganda campaigns across a range of media and national situations (studying British recruitment policies, for instance, vs. the American draft). But they also establish rhetorical continuities that are sometimes a counterpoint to other strains of graphic design activity. So though Chapter 12, "War and Propaganda 1920s to 1945," takes up where Chapter 3, "War and Propaganda 1914 to the 1920s," leaves off, it is placed squarely with the section on "The Designer and the Art Director." Chronology does not overdetermine the reading of works, nor are they fixed in a single chronological scaffold. Artifacts are read back into an understanding of circumstances, and motivations for formal choices become vivid aspects of aesthetic expression within a field of possibilities. Noting that Lucien Bernhard's poster style was unsuccessful in New York, Hollis describes the gap between American notions of idea and image; a purely visual concept was likely to fail, while a graphic expressing "human interest" could succeed (Hollis 1994: 67). Hollis's categories offer a vocabulary for analysis, not just description. Style choices are neither inevitable nor predetermined. As the Bernhard example shows, graphic design is constrained by conditions of reception as well as production means.

Instead of portraying designers as autonomous agents, Hollis presupposes that social connections among people are a fundamental part of style formations and changes. Tracing the development of Neue Graphik in Switzerland after the Second World War, for instance, Hollis exposes tensions in the way Emil Ruder puzzled over—and Jan Tschichold pushed—the perception that principles developed at the Bauhaus were becoming obsolete. Conversations and a professional community exert pressures. Decisions about style are formulated within that web. In another example, Hollis stresses that the connections that linked Max Bill, Siegfried Odermatt, and Rosmarie Tissi relate to the rise of international typographic style (Hollis 1994: 199). (By contrast, Meggs identifies its roots in the new typography of de Stijl and other formalist movements of the 1920s and 1930s, characterizing it as a style, not a value-laden expression of beliefs.)

Hollis's analyses are never far from the social sphere. A designer whose own career was shaped by his work for political and social causes, Hollis questions whose interests are served by advertising campaigns of the political propaganda to which designers lend their talents. Describing Dutch design of the 1920s and 1930s, he emphasizes "the enlightened tradition of imaginative design in the public services inherited by the students of Zwart, Schuitema, and Kiljan" (Hollis 1994: 75). In Hollis's model, graphic design depends on social circumstances and cultural functions. Artifacts may remain, but only by recovering their purpose and effect, Hollis suggests, can we fully interpret their graphic qualities. In the best of all possible scenarios, designers would work for a more equitable world in which the goals of progressive politics could be realized. Though their explicit beliefs fall in slightly different areas of the ideological spectrum, Meggs and Hollis share a moralistic commitment to design and to education in the service of progressive values.

Nevertheless, their ideological contrast is everywhere apparent. Hollis describes how Russian Constructivists "rejected the idea of the unique work of art as belonging to old bourgeois society" (Hollis 1994: 46). The statement contains a record of their attitude (stressing that it was key to the definition of their goals) and its radical push to restructure their world according to a new cultural order. While Meggs discusses at considerable length the Russians' innovation, the turbulence of World War I, and the role of artists in the Revolution, his characterization lacks Hollis's critical edge. Tellingly, Meggs puts the term "leftist" in scare quotes and says these artists "had been opposed to the old order and its conservative visual art." A world of difference opens between the analysis inherent in Hollis's brief statement and Meggs's description.

The Status of Design History

What is the use of the study of the history of graphic design? Should we assume that designers *ought* to know anything about the production of letterforms in the Roman period? Or the way the forms of manuscript hands migrate into the variants of early type design? The marked contrasts between Meggs and Hollis raise fundamental questions about the function of history in the education of a young designer, or as a contribution to the field.

Design history's place in pedagogy and long climb to status is reflected in the books' material qualities. Meggs's original 1983 publication had low production values. With images reproduced in mixed-quality black-and-white reproductions, its margins cramped to reduce costs, its design is serviceable at best. Van Nostrand saw this publication as a gamble. No excess capital was invested. Subsequent editions suggest that Meggs had proved the market for his text existed. By the 1992 edition, a section of color plates had been introduced and the layout had been reorganized. Radically overhauled, the 1998 third edition offers a coffee-table-book experience, with lots of color, coated stock, but an even smaller font size. The 2005 fourth edition, supplemented by Meggs's one-time student and contemporary, Alston Purvis, demonstrated the ongoing value of this book as a reference text while appealing to a wider audience. Likewise, Hollis's book has become a standard in the field. Reissued and kept in print with a second edition reissued in 2001, it maintains its small format and postage-stamp-sized images.

Meggs's text-heavy continuous narrative contains a mild moral imperative. Students of graphic design *should* know its history; their interest in the field is taken as a given. Written twenty-five years ago, Meggs's book assumes patterns of reading and concentration that may be changing. Meggs derives from humanist legacies to an Enlightenment period; education forges connections between the natural sprit of human intelligence and the social contract. We inherit that attitude through the influence of the nineteenth-century figure Matthew Arnold. Exposure to the best of what has been writ, made, or wrought, Arnold tells us, enlightens the spirit and uplifts the soul. Meggs requires students to submit themselves to a whole program, from beginning to end. Being exposed to the best designs, they know the origin of forms used daily.

Hollis, on the other hand, considers the tools of political analysis valuable to a designer's practice. He wants designers to assess the implications of their own activities in ways that are not possible with Meggs's more descriptive narrative. Whose interests do graphic communications serve? How can style choices carry ideological meaning?

Hollis's answers seem like survival skills—not just for the individual designers, but for the culture as a whole. Hollis explores the complicity between design and monoculture, the spread of American-style consumerism and its fantasmatic desires. While these themes may not be shared by all designers and critics, an activist sensibility has broad support within the design community and among its educators. On the side of cultural legacy and its preservation, design historians have the opportunity to pass an appreciation of the work of earlier generations into a broader recognition as accomplishments that shape the material world. I frequently note the surprise and interest of laypersons when introduced to the history of type, book design, posters, or other elements of a graphic world that seems natural because of its familiarity. They love finding out the history of Times New Roman and Gill Sans or knowing that the Declaration of Independence is printed in Caslon or that the letters have a longer history of use than any other communication technology.

The scholarly opportunity is what brings me back to Meggs and Hollis directly. Meggs's text was modeled so strongly on art historical precedents that it did not offer new methodological insight into the way visual forms work historically and culturally, nor the ways knowledge is formed with a partial, particular perspective. Graphic design historians, and here I mention Max Gallo's *The Poster in History* (1973, 1975) again as a striking example, can read visual forms as the expression of cultural forces through the work of an individual, rather than seeing individuals as the force that shapes the graphic world. A subtle distinction, perhaps, but an important one.

That distinction reorients our understanding, humbling us with a wake-up call to our own thought processes. Values and beliefs produce us as subjects of history and culture. The ideological blindness that enables us to imagine ourselves as autonomous subjects is reinforced by the positivist approach to historical knowledge that imagines it as a field to be described from outside, rather than from within. The recognition that that *knowledge* is always partial, rooted in particular circumstances of individual perception, radically alters our understanding of the role artifacts play in shaping our models of the world. Graphic design history can shift its methods from claims of knowledge (positivist, objective, empirical) of static representations toward knowing (probabilistic, intersubjective, interpretative) as a dynamic process of thinking and analyzing. In that model, incompleteness becomes a stimulant, driving the reader to inquiry and research. I value Meggs for his erudition and accuracy. My equally deep respect for Hollis stems from his shift toward critical principles, ways of thinking about design history as an unfinished, indeed, unfinishable process. Next-generation histories should synthesize lessons from both, while absorbing new models of scholarly activity, as well.

Ahead lie the opportunities for production of an ongoing interpretative history. As networked (and print) resources grow, the artifacts available for study of the history of graphic design expand. Physical and virtual archives and collections in the future will take account of the assumptions that shape past approaches, knowingly or not. As models of pedagogy, research, and critical insight change, they will shape the future of graphic design history to embody the diversity of thought and viewpoint that currently enriches debates within the profession. As the available inventory of materials expands, this history will not be limited to an inventory of artifacts to be thought about, but will also include lively discourse about the ways of thinking.

References

Apollinio, Umbro (Ed.). 1973. *Futurist Manifestos*. New York: Viking Press.

Arts and Crafts Exhibition Society. 1893. *Arts and Crafts Essays*. London: Longmans Green and Co.

Ashbee, Charles R. 1901. *An Endeavor towards the Teaching of John Ruskin and William Morris*. London: Edward Arnold.

Bann, Stephen (Ed.). 1974. *The Tradition of Constructivism*. New York: Viking Press.

Beirut, Michael. 1994. *Looking Closer: Critical Writings on Graphic Design*. New York: Allworth Press.

Bojko, Szymon. 1972. *New Graphic Design in Revolutionary Russia*. London: Lund Humphries.

Brady, Elizabeth. 1974. *Eric Gill: Twentieth Century Book Designer*. Metuchen, NJ: The Scarecrow Press.

Broude, Norma and Mary D. Garrard. 1982. *Feminism and Art History: Questioning the Litany*. Boulder, CO: Westview Press.

Budge, Sir E. A. Wallis. 1909. *The Book of the Dead*. London: British Museum.

Crane, Walter. 1898. *The Bases of Design*. London: George Bell and Sons.

Durant, Stuart. 1972. *Victorian Ornamental Design*. London: Academy Editions; New York: St. Martin's Press.

Eisenstein, Elizabeth. 1979. *The Printing Press as an Agent of Change*. Cambridge: Cambridge University Press.

Ferebee, Ann. 1970. *A History of Graphic Design from the Victorian Era to the Present*. New York: Van Nostrand Reinhold.

Forty, Adrian. 1986. *Objects of Desire*. London: Thames & Hudson.

Foucault, Michel. 1972. *The Archaeology of Knowledge*. New York: Pantheon.

Fournier, Pierre Simon. 1764, 1768. *Manuel Typographique*, Vols I & II. Paris.

Friedman, Mildred S. 1989. *Graphic Design in America*. Minneapolis, MN: Walker Art Center.

Friedman, Mildred S. and Joseph Giovannini. 1989. *Graphic Design in America: A Visual History*. Minneapolis, MN: Walker Art Center; New York: H. N. Abrams.

Fry, Edward F. 1978. *Cubism*. London: Thames & Hudson, 1966; New York: Oxford University Press.

Gallo, Max. 1973. *The Poster in History*. New York: American Heritage Pub. Co.

Gallo, Max. 1975. *The Poster in History*, Concise edn. Milan: Arnoldo Mondadori Editore.

Gerstner, Karl. 1959a. *Die Neue Graphik*. Teufen: Arthur Niggli.

Gerstner, Karl. 1959b. *The New Graphic Art: Its Origins, Its Evolutions, Its Peculiarities, Its Tasks, Its Problems, Its Manifestations and Its Future Prospects; die neue Graphik, etc.; le nouvel art graphique, etc*. New York: Hastings House Publishers.

Gerstner, Karl. 1968. *Designing Programmes*. Teufen: Verlag Arthur Niggli AG.

Gillon, Edmund V. Jr. 1969. *Art Nouveau: An Anthology of Design and Illustration from the Studio*. New York: Dover.

Glaser, Milton. 1973. *Milton Glaser: Graphic Design*. Woodstock, NY: The Overlook Press.

Gluck, Felix. 1969. *World Graphic Design: Fifty Years of Advertising Art*. New York: Watson-Guptill.

Gorb, Peter (Ed.) 1978. *Living by Design: Pentagram*. London: Lund Humphries; New York: Whitney Library of Design.

Gowan, Al. 1984. "[Review] A History of Graphic Design by Philip Meggs and A History of Graphic Design and Visual Communications by Clive Ashwin." *Design Issues*, 1(1): 87.

Greer, Germaine. 1979. *The Obstacle Race*. New York: Farrar, Straus, and Giroux.

Hanks, David A. 1979. *The Decorative Designs of Frank Lloyd Wright*. New York: E. P. Dutton.

Hauser, Arnold. 1951, 1952, 1957, 1958. *Social History of Art*, Vols 1–4. New York: Knopf (1951 and 1952); New York: Random House (1951); New York: Vintage Books (1951, 1957, 1958).

Helfand, Jessica. 1996. *Six Essays on Design and New Media*. New York: W. Drenttel.

Heller, Steven. 1988. *Graphic Style: From Victorian to Post-modern*. New York: H. N. Abrams.

Heller, Steven and Julie Lasky. 1993. *Borrowed Design: Use and Abuse of Historical Form*. New York: Van Nostrand Reinhold.

Heller, Steven and Marie Finamore. 1997. *Design Culture: An Anthology of Writing from the AIGA Journal of Graphic Design*. New York: Allworth Press, American Institute of Graphic Arts.

Heller, Steven. 2002. "Philip B. Meggs, 60, Educator and Historian of Graphic Design." *New York Times*, December 1.

Hobart, Michael and Zachary Schiffman. 1998. *Information Ages*. Baltimore: Johns Hopkins University Press.

Holland, D. K. and Abbott J. Miller. 1994. *Signs and Space*. Rockport, MA: Rockport/Allworth Editions.

Holland, D. K. and Michael Bierut. 1993. *Graphic Design: America*. Rockport, MA: Rockport/Allworth Editions; Cincinnati, OH: Distributed by North Light Books.

Holland, D. K., Jessica Helfand, and others. 1997. *Graphic Design: America Two.* Rockport, MA: Rockport/Allworth Editions.

Hollis, Richard. 1994. *Graphic Design: A Concise History.* London: Thames & Hudson.

Hollis, Richard. 2002. *Graphic Design: A Concise History.* London: Thames & Hudson.

Hollis, Richard. 2005. *Graphic Design: A Concise History.* London: Thames & Hudson.

Hurlburt, Allan. 1977. *Layout: The Design of the Printed Page.* New York: Watson-Guptill.

Itten, Johannes. 1964. *Design and Form: The Basic Course at the Bauhaus.* New York: Reinhold.

Jaffe, Hans L. C. 1971. *De Stijl.* New York: H. N. Abrams.

Jaffe, Hans L. C. 1979. *Mondrian und De Stijl.* Obenmarspforten: Galerie Gmurzynska.

Kallir, Jane. 1986. *Viennese Design and the Weiner Werkstätte.* New York: George Braziller and the Galerie St. Etienne.

Kandinsky, Wassily. 1926. *Punkt und Linie zu Fläche: Beitrag zur Analyse der malerischen Elemente.* München: Albert Langen.

Kaplan, Wendy. 2004. *The Arts and Crafts Movement in Europe and America: Design for the Modern World.* New York and London: Thames & Hudson with the Los Angeles County Museum of Art.

Kepes, Gyorgy. 1951. *Language of Vision*, with introductory essays by S. Giedion and S. I. Hayakawa. Chicago: Paul Theobald.

Lewis, John Noel Claude. 1970. *Anatomy of Printing: The Influences of Art and History on Its Design.* London: Faber.

Lonberg-Holm, K. 1950. *Catalog Design Progress.* New York: Sweet's Catalog Service.

Lonberg-Holm, K. and Ladislav Sutnar. 1944. *Catalog Design.* New York: Sweet's Catalog Service.

Lupton, Ellen. 1996a. *Mechanical Brides.* New York: Copper-Hewitt, National Museum of Design, Smithsonian.

Lupton, Ellen. 1996b. *Mixing Messages: Contemporary Graphic Design in America.* London: Cooper-Hewitt, National Design Museum, Smithsonian Institution, and Thames & Hudson.

Lupton, Ellen and J. Abbott Miller. 1996. *Design, Writing, Research.* New York: Kiosk.

Marinetti, Filippo T. 1971. *Marinetti: Selected Writings*, R. W. Flint (Ed.). New York: Farrar, Straus, and Giroux.

Martin, Marianne W. 1968. *Futurist Art and Theory 1909–1915.* Oxford: Clarendon Press.

McLuhan, Marshall. 1962. *The Gutenberg Galaxy.* Toronto: University of Toronto Press.

McMurtrie, Douglas C. 1943. *The Book: The Story of Printing and Bookmaking.* New York: Oxford University Press.

Meggs, Philip. 1964. *Understanding Media: The Extensions of Man.* New York: McGraw-Hill.

Meggs, Philip. 1983. *A History of Graphic Design.* New York: Van Nostrand Reinhold.

Meggs, Philip. 1992a. *A History of Graphic Design.* New York: Van Nostrand Reinhold.

Meggs, Philip. 1992b. *Type and Image: The Language of Graphic Design.* New York: Wiley and Sons.

Meggs, Philip. 1998. *A History of Graphic Design.* New York: Wiley and Sons.

Moholy-Nagy, László. 1947a. *The New Vision and Abstract of an Artist 1928*. New York: Wittenborn.

Moholy-Nagy, László. 1947b. *Vision in Motion*. Chicago: Paul Theobald.

Morison, Stanley and Kenneth Day. 1963. *The Typographic Book 1450–1935*. London: Ernest Benn Limited; Chicago: University of Chicago Press.

Morison, Stanley. 1972. *The Politics and Script*, edited and completed by Nicholas Barker. Oxford: Oxford University Press.

Müller-Brockmann, Josef. 1971. *A History of Visual Communication: From the Dawn of Barter in the Ancient World to the Visualized Conception of Today*. Teufen: Arthur Niggli.

Nye, David. 1994. *American Technological Sublime*. Cambridge, MA: MIT Press.

Steinberg, S. H. 1955. *500 Years of Printing*. London: Pelican.

Updike, Daniel Berkley. 1937. *Printing Types: Their History, Forms and Use*. Cambridge, MA: Harvard University Press.

van Doesburg, Theo (Ed.) 1968. *De Stijl, Vol. I—VII 1917–1931*, Reprint. Amsterdam: Athenaeum.

Wilson, Christopher. 2006. "Rational and Responsive, the Work of Richard Hollis Exemplifies a Very British Kind of Modernism." *Eye Magazine*, no. 59, March: 26.

Windsor, Alan. 1981. *Peter Behrens, Architect and Designer*. New York: Whitney Library of Design.

Endnotes

1. As Al Gowan's 1984 review of Meggs's first edition notes, the field had only recently been acknowledged by the US IRS and undergone multiple name changes. Designers, he asserts, "didn't know whether they were commercial artists, layout artists, communication designers, art directors, or what" (Gowan 1984: 7).
2. Al Gowan mentions that though W. A. Dwiggins had coined the term "graphic designer" in the 1920s, the profession was barely recognized by "architecture, medicine, law or"—here is the crucial entity (!)—"the U.S. Internal Revenue Service until recent years" (Gowan 1984: 88).
3. John Wiley acquired Van Nostrand Reinhold in 1997, hence the apparent change in publisher (Meggs 1991, 1998, 2005).
4. The standard assumption is that modern and contemporary design are more interesting for current practice, but this seems like a notion worth examining.
5. See, for example, the analyses of Steinberg (1955).
6. The 1983 edition had only four sections. The first three are the same as those of subsequent editions, but the fourth section was originally simply "The Twentieth Century" and ended with "The Global Dialog" in the early 1980s. The five-part distinction, breaking out "The Information Age" as a separate section, first appears in the second, 1993, edition. This structure remains in the 1998 edition, though it includes the two extra chapters. The only other change is the addition of a chapter at the beginning of Section IV in both the second and third editions that focuses on "The Genesis of Twentieth-Century Design."
7. Such developments are enumerated, for example, by Alan Windsor (1981) in *Peter Behrens, Architect and Designer* and Jane Kallir (1986) in *Viennese Design and the Weiner Werkstätte*.
8. For more background on this issue, see Kaplan (2004).
9. Meggs's attitude embodies the American sense of awe at technological progress described by David Nye (1994) in his work *American Technological Sublime*. Though Nye's work comes after Meggs's first edition, he is commenting on precisely the kind of triumphalist celebratory attitude Meggs exhibits.

10. By contrast, Hobart and Schiffman (1998), *Information Ages*, describes the development of cuneiform writing systems into information systems. Their model depends on distinctions grounded in reocentricism (words describe things, *res*, and language tries to conform to a supposedly a priori world) and logocentrism (words, *logos*, constitute meaning and things conform to their concepts). In Hobart and Schiffman's approach, the development of writing starts with literal accounting, develops into a classification system through list making, and is further advanced through the coming of a fully abstract notation system for concepts and ideas that displaces the early thing-based approach. This conceptual apparatus would not have been available to Meggs in 1983, but even had it been, it is somewhat outside the basic parameters of his more literal description (Hobart and Schiffman, 1998).

11. A remarkable exception to this norm is French Marxist historian Max Gallo's striking 1973 book *The Poster in History*. Gallo has a dialectical disposition that is characteristic of continental traditions and Marxist training. Likewise, Arnold Hauser's 1950s publication of his four-volume *Social History of Art* reflected the late 1930s Vienna world, which had been its intellectual crucible. For Hauser, as for generations of social art historians who have followed, sociological conditions and artistic expression are inextricably bound to each other in form, style, production, reception, value, and use (Hauser 1951, 1952, 1957, 1958).

12. Critiques of Janson and other surveys were instigated within the purview of feminist art history. Norma Broude and Mary D. Garrard's *Feminism and Art History: Questioning the Litany* (1982) and Germaine Greer's *The Obstacle Race* (1979) were premised on such critiques. In the 1980s, the field of art history was influenced by postmodern and poststructuralist theory, prompting systematic and sustained critique of master narratives, original talent, and the tradition of the white male artist. Diversity issues, the influence of British cultural studies, the rise of identity politics, the so-called "culture wars," and other major intellectual development contributed to a shift in methodology as well as changes in the approach to canon formation. Scholars from within art history, such as Michael Holly and Keith Moxey; critics Lucy Lippard, Lowrie Sims, Brian Wallis, and Abigail Solomon-Godeau; and many figures writing from literary or critical perspectives, like Normal Bryson and Adrian Piper, all changed the field dramatically.

Johanna Drucker is the Breslauer Professor of Bibliographical Studies in the Department of Information Studies at UCLA. She is internationally known for her work in artists' books, the history of graphic design, typography, experimental poetry, fine art, and digital humanities. Recent titles include: Graphesis: Visual Forms of Knowledge Production *(Harvard University Press, 2014),* The General Theory of Social Relativity *(The Elephants, 2018),* Downdrift: An Eco-fiction *(Three Rooms Press, 2018), and* Visualization: Modelling Interpretation *(forthcoming). In 2014, she was elected to the American Academy of Arts and Sciences and awarded an honorary Doctorate of Fine Arts by the Maryland Institute College of Art in 2017.*

GRAPHIC DESIGN HISTORY FOR WEB DESIGNERS

Patricia Belen

Educators who teach web design are in a precarious situation. Alongside the ongoing debate of whether coding should be included in a design curriculum, there's the fact that many websites are now created using WYSIWYG editors and predesigned templates. Despite these obstacles, I believe learning HTML/CSS, the backbone of web design, in conjunction with the basic principles of design and user experience is beneficial for students starting out in design, whether in a design school or a liberal arts program.

Technology moves so fast that I can't predict what web design on the Internet will look like by the time my students graduate, much less what it will look like in ten or twenty years, or even whether websites will continue to exist or be replaced by AI, VR, or some other immersive technology.

Nevertheless, being able to tell stories and create experiences using code teaches students to think analytically, critically, and logically (sometimes even using mathematics). These are skills and characteristics of any good designer.

Certainly, my class spends a lot of time looking at websites to understand their design techniques and dissect how they were developed. However, website examples shown in the classroom today to demonstrate a design principle or coding technique may look completely different tomorrow. A website may even look different later on in the same day. As a counterpart to the ever-changing nature of the Internet, I often turn to historic examples of design in the form of books, posters, and other printed materials. These iconic artifacts do not only belong in traditional graphic design and typography classes. In fact, graphic design history has the potential to teach students so much about web and digital design. These are two examples (although many more exist):

Responsive Web Design / Karl Gerstner

Responsive web design goes beyond creating a secondary, mobile version of a website. Ideally, a website should only have one version that is always mobile—flexible enough to fit in your pocket (on a smartphone), in your bag (on a tablet or laptop), or on your desk (desktop computer). Devices are simultaneously becoming smaller (watches) and larger (oversize smartphones and computers morphing into televisions), so the idea of a flexible website in which the design can work anywhere is more important than ever.

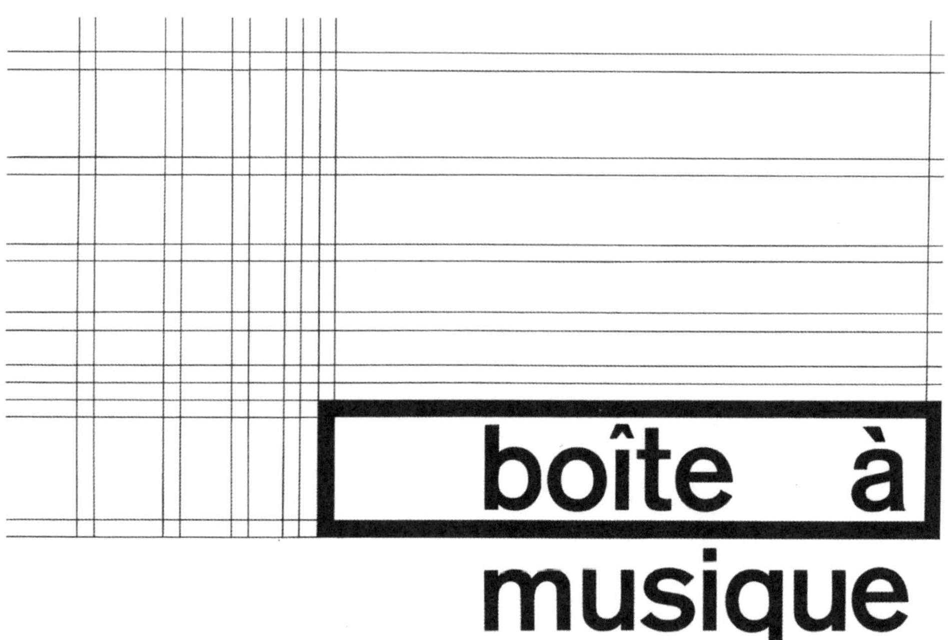

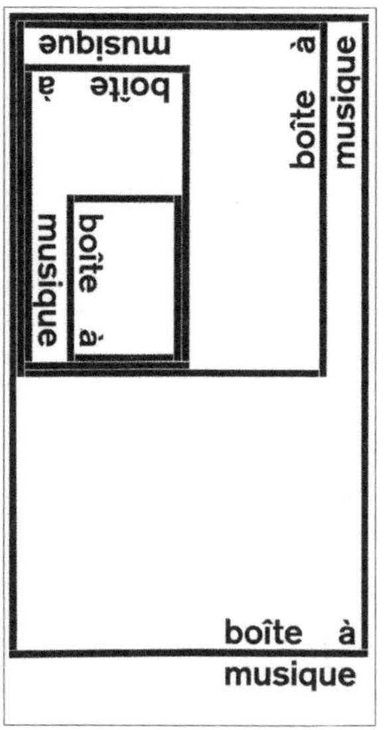

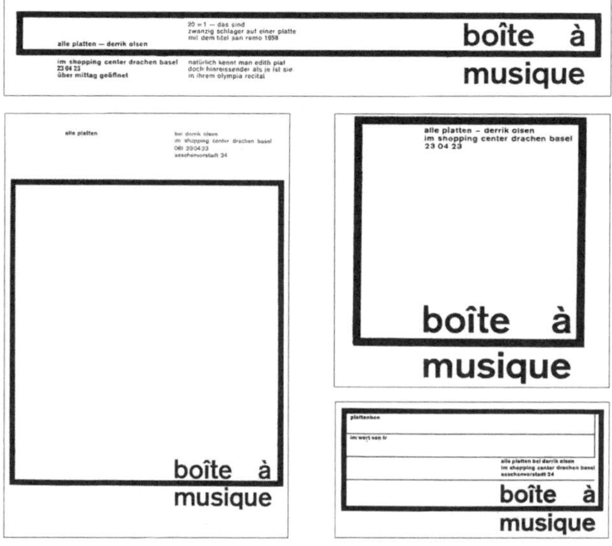

Identity structure and printed collateral, Boîte à musique, 1957–58.

"The concept of a flexible identity system is now widespread. However, in the 1950s, Gerstner designed logos and corporate identities that are not just flexible identity systems, they are also a precursor to responsive website design."

A pioneer of modern graphic design in Switzerland, Karl Gerstner developed ideas of flexible grids, systematic design, and integral typography—ideas adopted by web design. His books *Design Programs* (1964) and *Compendium for Literates—A System of Writing* (1974) detail these theories using examples of graphic design, typography, and art, including Gerstner's own work as a designer and partner at his advertising firm GGK (Gerstner, Gredinger and Kutter).

The concept of a flexible identity system is now widespread. However, in the 1950s, Gerstner designed logos and corporate identities that are not just flexible identity systems, they are also a precursor to responsive website design. Boîte à musique [Music Box], a record store in Basel, incorporates an actual "box" (rectangular frame) as part of its logo. The words "boîte à" are always in this frame, with "musique" directly underneath. The rectangular frame can be adjusted both vertically (upward) and horizontally (to the left) to accommodate any number of applications or proportions without modifying the original structure. The elements in and around the frame can differ, but the recognizable part of this identity remains the same.

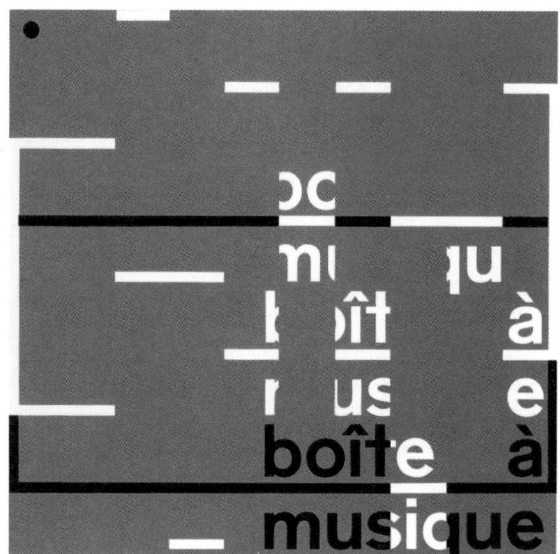

(Above) Bag and poster, Boîte à musique, 1957–58. (Opposite) Diagram, *Catalog Design*, 1944.

Gerstner writes "There is no case which is pre-eminent for its proportions. There are only variants of equal value; and the variant is pre-eminent when it is best adapted to the particular problem awaiting solution." Decades ahead of his time, Gerstner could have easily been describing websites. A website on a desktop is no longer the dominant view. The design on all devices must be considered equally.

The way Boîte à musique changes its proportions is similar to a website adjusting in a web browser. Certain elements remain the same, such as colors, typefaces, images, and copy; but within a responsive design, there are other variables that could be adjusted (the size and placement of the typefaces, images, and copy), depending on the size of the device where the website is being viewed.

Furthermore, with a responsive website design, there is room for experimentation. As Gerstner shows through Boîte à musique's bag and poster, dynamic color and clever cropping give these printed materials a sense of kineticism.

So what happens when a website responds in an unexpected manner? Should a website be predictable? What parts of a website can be animated without affecting usability? Can code be used to offer competing experiences of the same website based on device? Although Gerstner designed for print, his advanced design thinking can also be applied to web design.

User Experience Design / Ladislav Sutnar

Ladislav Sutnar is often referred to as a "pioneer of information design." As art director for Sweet's Catalog Service 1941–1960, Sutnar worked with researchers, writers, and designers to develop a wide range of visual print solutions for American industrial products. His publications *Catalog Design: New Patterns in Product Information* (1944) and *Catalog Design Progress: Advancing Standards in Visual Communication* (1950) are seminal texts in which Sutnar addresses his ideas and techniques for the advancement of catalog design standards.

Prior to Sutnar, the sight of a 1940s Sweet's Catalog File was quite daunting. They were huge and unwieldy, containing hundreds of dull, cluttered, and forgettable product catalogs for asphalt tile, unit heaters, condenser tubes, miniature precision bearings, cork products, and more. Sutnar's much-improved catalog designs are identifiable, functional, and visually dynamic. He organized information through coordinated visual systems of geometric shapes, navigational signals, and Constructivist colors.

At the heart of Sutnar's design theories is the user. Nowadays, "user" is thought of in terms of product or web design. In Sutnar's day, a "user" could be any person or customer who used a Sweet's catalog. Through various design techniques, Sutnar helped the user navigate complicated information quickly and easily, in a manner that provided a positive "user experience"—the same goal today's product and web designers strive to achieve.

As the first point of contact, a catalog cover is extremely important. Sutnar said, "the front cover should provide for quick suggestion of the catalog's content, by use of illustration, manufacturer's name, product name, trademark, color, shape, index, or other means." A website homepage has the exact same function. Web designers can take this even further by using video, animation, blocks of text, and other visual effects to quickly communicate the product, blog, service, or information being offered. While the homepage is not necessarily the first point of contact anymore, web designers still consider it crucial as an overview of what's "inside" the website.

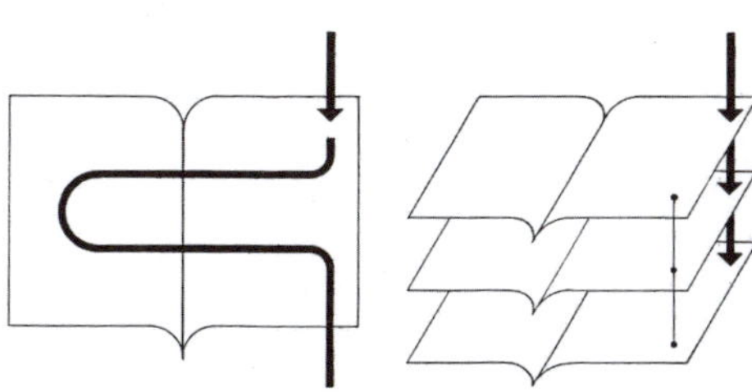

In a catalog, Sutnar thought of the upper right-hand corner of the right hand page as a natural focal point for the eye: "This space can be used to advantage for primary information . . . to lead the eye on the desired path for more efficient reading and to integrate the whole work into a cohesive design." This concept is not unlike website navigation. Whether in the form of a simple menu (denoted by parallel horizontal lines ☰) or cascading menu (expandable), website navigation is often located on the upper right or left corners of a web page. On an app, a bottom navigation bar may also be used. Primary placement of the navigation is essential to direct users through a website.

Sutnar was a proponent of controlling the visual flow of information by using design symbols to guide the user's eye so they can read quickly and efficiently: "These design symbols are visual *traffic signs*. Circles, triangles, etc. mark paragraph beginnings; hands and arrows point out important items in the body of the text." In web design, the same design symbols are still used to attract the user's eye and create visual hierarchy. Transitions, animations, and other gestural components aided by JavaScript enhance this experience. Arrows, graphics, text, hyperlinks, and buttons can blink, fade, change color, move, or have extra effects added to them. Hovering over an area of a website can reveal text to summarize what's behind a link. These visual cues tell the user where to look, what to read, and what to click (or tap)—they are not only functional, they also create a pleasurable user experience.

There is a misconception that print design has no place in a web design classroom; print is too limiting for the digital world; designers must move beyond the printed page to work with new technologies.

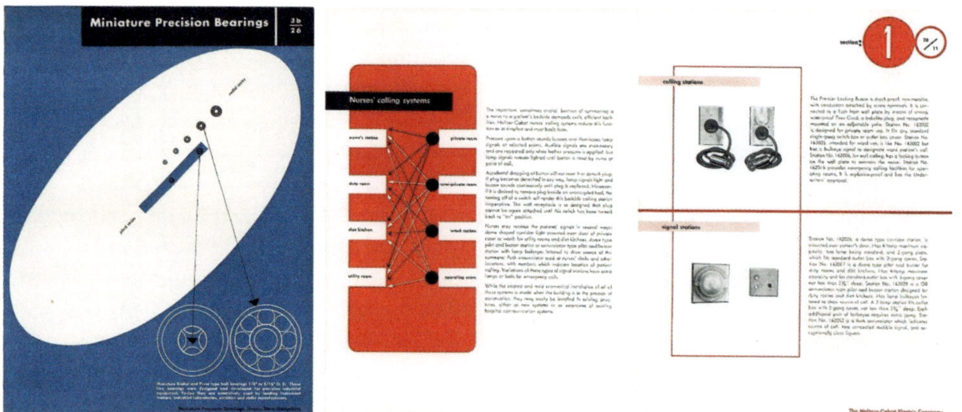

Cover, *Cuno Continously Cleanable Filters for Product Designers*, 1944. Interior, *Holtzer-Cabot Communication Systems*, 1944.

Diagram, *Controlled Visual Flow*, Design and Paper, No. 13, 1943.

However, how can I expect my web design students to move beyond the printed page if they don't even understand the principles behind the printed page? How can learning how to code open up possibilities for new ways of thinking in web design without first appreciating the thinking of graphic design pioneers like Gerstner and Sutnar? What about all the other examples: How using grids (or breaking them) creates unique website layouts? How typographers have been using variable type long before the idea of a singular file format? My hope is that the rich history of graphic design's past be used to inform the interactive, digital experiences of tomorrow.

Bibliography

Gerstner, Karl. *Designing Programmes*. Arthur Niggli Ltd., 1964.

Gerstner, Karl. *Karl Gerstner: Visual Language*. Hatje Cantz, 2001.

Heller, Steven. "Ladislav Sutnar, Web Design before the Internet." *Typotheque*, 29 Nov. 2004, www.typotheque.com/articles/ladislav_sutnar_web_design_before_the_internet.

Hewitt, Jon. "Speak Up Archive: Flexible Consistency, Consistent Flexibility." *A Former Division of UnderConsideration*, 13 Feb. 2008, www.underconsideration.com/speakup/archives/004431.html.

Lönberg-Holm, Knud, and Ladislav Sutnar. *Catalog Design*. Sweet's Catalog Service, 1944.

Sutnar, Ladislav. *Controlled Visual Flow, Design and Paper, No. 13*. Marquardt Company Incorporated, 1943.

Patricia Belen is a designer, educator, and cofounder of Kind Company (kindcompany.com) and Display, Graphic Design Collection (thisisdisplay.org). She teaches courses in graphic design and web design at Fordham University in New York City.

TEACHING GRAPHIC DESIGN HISTORY: A PERSONAL PERSPECTIVE

Susan Merritt

"Your students have no knowledge of the people and events that are the cornerstone of our profession. They don't even know who Milton Glaser is!" That jarring criticism by a professional in the community was the testimony I needed to support my proposal for a course in graphic design history at San Diego State University in 2000. Up until then, history had been informally covered in our studio classes. Obviously, that approach wasn't making the grade.

The only catch was that I'd have to teach the class myself. In addition to teaching, I was a practicing graphic designer with an acquired affection for design history but no academic credentials. I had, however, studied at the Basel School of Design from 1971 to 1976 with notable designers, like Armin Hofmann and Wolfgang Weingart, who were included in Philip Meggs's *A History of Graphic Design*—at that point in its third edition. I figured that experience gave me a leg to stand on.

I first explored teaching History of Graphic Design as an elective seminar, which allowed me to keep the group small while I got up to speed. I put study guides together and posted them on a website. This caught the attention of Wiley, the publishing company, and they enlisted me to develop an instructor's manual with study guides as a companion to Meggs's book. Although a long and arduous task, the manual proved useful to me as well as other professors who were developing similar courses. Wiley continues to update the manual with each new edition.

After four years, the course became a required lecture class at the 200-level, and two years later the faculty decided to move it to the 300-level, since the prerequisites were two lower-division art history classes. I taught History of Graphic Design from 2001 to 2018. As head of the program, I knew the curriculum intimately and often referenced studio assignments during lectures to help students understand the synergistic relationship between history and practice. And vice versa. In studio classes, I referred back to history lectures or introduced an assignment with a short review.

A lecture class can be challenging for design students who tend to be kinesthetic learners and learn best through active participation. It's a good idea to include some form of physical engagement during class, such as a handwritten activity or use of an electronic response device that allows the instructor to make a point and follow it up with a question or image to be identified. (I often think how fun and effective a graphic design history *Jeopardy!* game would be!) Discussion is also valuable although difficult when the time period is limited to an hour and fifteen minutes and the class is large, on average fifty to seventy students per semester in our program.

While teaching graphic design history, I was so inspired by what I was learning that soon pictures weren't enough. I wanted to hold the actual artifacts in my hands, study them, and feel that connection to the past or experience the human scale of things large and small. So, during summer breaks, I headed to archives, libraries, and museums in North America, Europe, and Asia, like Grolier Club Library and Butler Library at Columbia University in New York; Gutenberg Museum in Mainz, Germany; Printing Museum in Lyons, France; Plantin-Moretus Museum in Antwerp, Belgium; and Printing Museum, Tokyo, among them. I documented my trips and shot a lot of pictures that made their way into my lectures. I collected examples, brought them to class, and passed them around so students could compare the weight of a lead sort to a piece of wood type, run their fingers over an embossed or letterpress printed sample, and closely examine the subtle gradation of a nineteenth-century chromolithographic trade card.

I reached out to SDSU's Special Collections and was amazed by how many relevant objects they have: incunabula books, Euclid's *Geometriae elementa*, tomes by Aldus Manutius's Aldine Press, Diderot's *Encyclopédie*, William Morris's Kelmscott books, and my favorite, Henry van de Velde's *Also Sprach Zarathustra*. The librarians are very appreciative of our interest and bend over backward to accommodate large groups of students. These field trips proved so successful that I scheduled two during each fifteen-week semester. The first visit focused on materials up to the nineteenth century, and the second covered the Industrial Revolution and twentieth century. The librarians prepared presentations about each piece (with my occasional commentary to fill in), followed by a hands-on activity during which the students examined the artifacts and completed a worksheet. By incorporating the fieldwork into the course, Special Collections was encouraged to expand their holdings and began purchasing additional primary source materials to enhance the student experience and support learning outcomes, with a focus on much-needed twentieth-century acquisitions.

Exhibitions and visiting artists are also valuable aids for teaching graphic design history if resources are available. I helped organize a couple of poster shows at the University Art Gallery over the years, including *The Graphic Imperative*, an eye-opening traveling exhibition. This year, I curated *Give-and-Take: Poster Design by Nancy Skolos and Thomas Wedell* at the SDSU Downtown Gallery. We were fortunate to be able to bring Skolos and Wedell to San Diego, where they led a gallery tour at the opening reception and the next day presented a public lecture about their methodology, followed by a workshop on collage as a process for poster design.

Jan Tschichold said that Russian Constructivist El Lissitzky "was one of the great pioneers. . . . His indirect influence was widespread and enduring. . . . A generation that has never heard of him . . . stands upon his shoulders" (*Meggs' History of Graphic Design*, sixth edition, 325). There's no doubt that students with awareness of whose shoulders they're standing upon are better equipped. Knowledge of who came before, their contributions, and the context within which they worked nourishes a broad perspective, imparts a sense of pride, fosters an appreciation of the scope of the field, and helps students consider where they might fit in and how they might contribute to the continuum.

One of the most enlightening lessons of graphic design history is that graphic design doesn't operate in a vacuum. It's as vulnerable as any other field to sways in cultural attitudes, advances in technology, and shifts in political and social conventions. One of my early students told me that her coworker looked puzzled when she said that she was taking a graphic design history class. "But the computer hasn't been around that long," the coworker said. Such misconceptions can easily be cleared up when students are armed with the tools to enlighten others about graphic design's long and productive past and how graphic designers like Milton Glaser continue to contribute to society in meaningful ways.

Susan Merritt teaches at School of Art + Design, San Diego State University. She is coauthor, with Jack Davis, of The Web Design WOW! Book, *which was published in 1998 by Peachpit Press and is the author of the ancillary materials for* Meggs's A History of Graphic Design, *which include an instructor's manual and student study guides, published by John Wiley & Sons.*

IMAGE CAPTURES: CHANGE THE CANON

Steven Heller

I just lifted onto my lap the heaviest—also, I suspect, the largest—graphic design history book ever produced. I don't know how many pounds (or stone) it weighs, but carrying it from bookstore to home demands Olympics-grade weight-lifting prowess. It also stands taller than virtually any book in my, and perhaps any, library, and so there is no shelf on which I can even store it. This is a new evolutionary development in the history of graphic design history.

The book is *The History of Graphic Design, Vol. 1, 1890–1959* (Taschen) by Jens Muller, edited by Julius Weidmann. It is an impressive work produced by a respected design historian (who is also the author of *Pioneers of German Graphic Design*). But it is nonetheless such an unwieldy volume, similar to those plump scholarly Oxford or Webster dictionaries that are so huge that in order for you to to turn the pages, they have to sit on a podium. In fact, this is not one, but Taschen has published books that come with their own podiums. Yet that is not the gist of this essay. What concerns me of late is the frenzy—a cross between the gold rush and an Easter egg hunt—for images to fill a rash of design histories, chronicles, and documentaries devoted to our field's discovery and preservation.

Since Philip B. Meggs published the first edition of *A History of Graphic Design* in 1983, which he purposefully called "A History" not "The History" knowing that more books would follow, I have, among other practitioners, scholars, and collectors of graphic design and illustration (i.e., commercial art) histories, torn through extensive masses of primary and secondary printed matter, scouring bookstores, flea markets, auction houses, and archives, storage bins, indeed whatever and wherever artifacts have been squirreled, filed, and yes, forgotten, in search of unknown or barely considered materials that in some way fill in the blanks or create new categories and genres of graphic design history. What has resulted is a mixed blessing. There is a lot, lots of lots, that is worthy and unworthy of consideration.

Unknown work by lost or anonymous makers have indeed been uncovered, documented, and introduced, thus expanding an admittedly limited male, Eurocentric, white, exclusively educated canon. Some deserved the elevated status; others are simply curiosities. But enlightenment never hurt anyone. Designers are not the only benefactors of this new material, either. Graphic design is intertwined with so many commercial, social, political, ethnographic, and

"... one of the jobs of today's design historians and documentarians is, rather than pick the low-hanging fruit, to reach beyond to find well-known designers' lesser or unknown work, analyze it ..."

technological areas, that each discovery opens doors in major and minor areas of interest. That's all good.

There is a tremendous increase in redundancy in books and exhibits. The same canonical images which make museums and archives considerable profit in reproduction fees are invariably going to be used again and again, and with good reason. Back when design history was in its infancy, these (mostly posters, which have long been highly collectable) were earmarked as iconic. How is it possible to discuss Russian Constructivism without "Beat the Whites with the Red Wedge" or American corporate identity without Paul Rand's "IBM" eye-bee-m rebus? It is possible to leave them out, but some critics will invariably and reasonably ask why. It is possible to reproduce lesser or unknown works by these two designers and few will not say, "That's a rare find, congratulations!" But publishing mostly unknown material begs the question: "Is this work up to the standard of the canon?"

I've faced this issue with some of my books, where editors argued I have to show such-and-such or so-and-so simply because it would be either misleading or mistaken not to, when I would much prefer to add more new or lost material to the mix. It is invariably more exciting for a writer or researcher to convey the story of this material than rehash well-told tales. But this causes a quandary of sorts. In Jens Muller's sweeping survey of over sixty years, his mandate is to show the familiar icons if only for accuracy. Also, publishers are forced to assume that audiences for such books are new to the field, so this may be the first sighting for many of them. Still, one of the jobs of today's design historians and documentarians is, rather than pick the low-hanging fruit, to reach beyond to find well-known designers' lesser or unknown work, analyze it to determine its value to the individual's legacy and history in general, and find those obscure items that may stimulate inspiration and further discovery—even if it's, well, not as good.

Admittedly, many of my own books, articles, and exhibitions rely on famous objects, but I always struggle for "diversity"—for those pieces that when I find them send me into a state of euphoria, like when Amerigo Vespucci found around 1502 that Brazil and the West Indies did not represent Asia's eastern outskirts, or some other apt analogy. And there are certain risks involved. For my recent book *The Moderns: Midcentury American Graphic Design* (Abrams), coauthored with Greg D'Onofrio, we made a conscious effort to include designers who had not been as widely covered under the "modern" umbrella, including women, persons of color, and those who were not entirely orthodox in the modern methods. We too clawed through stacks, drawers, and boxes of things that have not been republished in current design histories. The challenge was to balance the known while capturing the unknown. Never-having-been-seen-before alone was not a good enough criterion, but finding new artifacts on which graphic design history can evolve from its accepted standard should be the goal. Whether heavy or light, fat or thin, a book with too much redundant imagery does not keep our historical legacy vital. Let's capture the lost, ignored, and wild.

CH3

I asked a select group of teachers and instructors of graphic design history similar questions about how they view design history as a discipline (As facts of a broad narrative? As a collection of anecdotes that give a general overview? As part of a cultural, social, political, etc., tapestry?) and what the benefits are for the student.

ANGELA REICHERS

Program Director of the Graphic Design Department at University of the Arts

How do you view design history?

I say it's definitely a cultural sociopolitical tapestry with many narratives. We pick and choose the threads we want to follow, however. In the United States, design schools pretty much follow a classic Western art tradition for basic history, lumping Asian art, African art, women's art, outsider art, etc., into separate and often nonrequired classes. In my experience, the canon still covers a somewhat narrow spectrum despite the fact that there is room, and I would say demand, for a wider view.

What do you want your students to learn from or take away from history?

That everything is connected. Everything came from somewhere. We can connect the dots back through time and always, always find fascinating links and relativities. And that design is both a mirror and a shaper of culture, reacting to manufacturing advances, social conditions, technology, music, fine art . . .

Is history a series of object lessons for teaching contemporary practice?

I see history as an additive process without a total sum ever in sight. Or like building with LEGOs: the same pieces and ideas and theories in the hands of different people always yield different results. We aren't accountants; there is never a single right answer to a design problem. Some solutions are much better than others, of course. So while history influences contemporary practice, it becomes more like a tool kit than a series of object lessons.

"I see history as an additive process without a total sum ever in sight. Or like building with LEGOs: the same pieces and ideas and theories in the hands of different people always yield different results."

Is there a right and wrong way to look at or contextualize design history?
No, as long as we are clear about the motives and goals of what we are putting forth. "This course covers the history of design in Europe and America." Or "This course discusses the history of design in Asia." I do think it's wrong to assume that any history is superior to another.

Can design history be taught as an island or as part of a broader survey?
I always like the atomized history approach: design is part of life and doesn't need to be isolated on its own in the classroom . . . other fields of knowledge as well can be blended into the study of design, with surprising results.

Is design history purely Western? How is diverse culture injected into a Western historical survey?
A. Only to Westerners. B. At great protest and with great reluctance.

BETH KLEBER

Founding Archivist of the Milton Glaser Design Study Center and Archives (opened 2003) and the School of Visual Arts Archives (opened 2007)

How do you view design history?
Design history is all of that—art history, social and political history, industry and business history. It is among the most immediate manifestations of what is going on in the world at any given moment, so context is essential.

What do you want your students to learn from or take away from history?

I'd like them to examine how design innovators reinterpret ideas and themes from the past within a new political/social climate and context, and how they might have been exposed to those ideas in the first place.

Can design history be taught as an island or as part of a broader survey?

I should hope it already is taught within a broader historical survey, though perhaps it isn't being labeled as such. It doesn't make sense to assume that artistic and cultural developments happen in a vacuum.

Is design history purely Western? How is diverse culture injected into a Western historical survey?

Of course design history encompasses non-Western cultures. As dissemination of information and sharing of images became so widespread over the course of the twentieth century, it became easier to see how designers could absorb the influence of other artistic styles and cultures. Now we're awash with images from every place and period, but the mission of any kind of historian is to preserve context, both physically and intellectually.

GREG D'ONOFRIO

Teaches the History of Graphic Design at the School of Visual Arts and Cooper Union in New York City; Coauthor of The Moderns: Midcentury American Graphic Design

What is to be gained by teaching graphic design history?

We can improve and inform our practice by having an awareness of graphic design history. When we establish and broaden our visual vocabulary and visual literacy, we learn to interpret and make meaning from information presented to us. Graphic design history goes beyond understanding the foundational movements, milestone events, pivotal ideologies, pioneers, and even styles that have shaped our comprehension. Instead, the cultural, social, political, or technological circumstances that inform design provide us deeper historical context and meaning to why something looks the way it looks—these connections are paramount in understanding its rich, broad, and meaningful history. As an educator who's interested in teaching students how to use history to make contemporary connections, this involves teaching an awareness to help them understand the context from which a design surfaces.

Learning to foster a unique perspective while discovering a greater understanding is at the core of my graphic design history teaching.

Which methods work well to accomplish this?

The teaching methods I rely upon focus on history, theory, and form and include a combination of chapter readings and primary sources, slide lectures, off-site visits and classroom exercises that allow students to see slowly and closely real graphic design objects. This method of object-based teaching in conjunction with historical narratives has been most useful in helping students gain valuable insight into critical periods of graphic design. Seeing slowly (and closely) helps students to appreciate and analyze the visual form of objects and the content of a design—encouraging their historical empathy and extended interest in the physical object. For me, this has proven to be a far better solution than "only" looking at thumbnails in a book or via the projector.

Exposing students to original design artifacts is both inspirational and educational and helps to tell a distinct and accurate point of view about graphic design, typography, and some of its pioneers—mostly since there's so much that's never been published before. As much as possible, I challenge my students to take advantage of the many (mostly free) resources available: libraries, auctions, exhibitions, galleries, antiquarian bookstore, scholars, collectors, and private and public graphic design collections. I mostly struggle with finding a balance between the students who want to look briefly at slides and see many images vs. those who wish to look at less and take their time with each piece, up close and personal—this is rarely constant and changes from semester to semester, depending on class size and student ambition. Nonetheless, I've learned that looking motivates students' relationship with history and learning to "see and observe" while building your visual design vocabulary helps further study and exploration.

Which examples of teaching have proven successful or not?

I expect my students to demonstrate knowledge and familiarity re: pivotal movements, styles, and design pioneers. Apart from teaching a broad understanding of various graphic design movements, we also examine particular subjects, themes, and technological innovations of the period. In additional to gaining an understanding and appreciation on the importance of the history of design, I challenge my students to discuss, analyze, research, and write succinct paragraphs—this often includes presenting effective and appropriate verbal and written ideas (both independently and as a group). My class assignments have less to do with styling (i.e., creating or making form) and more to do with reading, research, and writing. Additionally, assignments and class discussions are about being curious and asking questions and help us observe and talk about design—essential skills to becoming a better designer or communicator. Encouraging students to become more visually fluent and proficient in reading and writing will help them develop an original spirit and philosophy while creating their own benchmarks of quality.

Is history a series of object lessons for teaching contemporary practice?

I believe a series of object lessons can benefit the classroom, yet we must be mindful that teaching design history only by the way something looks falls short. It's not enough to show the object and judge it only by how it looks—it's also about what the artifacts can teach us and how they can help us better understand graphic design history. A primary responsibility of the teacher (and student) is to better understand how the object's use can far exceed its role as inspirational "eye candy." When we do, we uncover something deeper and more meaningful, and it's at this moment that artifacts become valuable tools to design practice, education, and research. Standard graphic design history slide lectures are good, but to better understand the design, you need to see/interact with the real object—and to fully comprehend how it was perceived or used by its audience(s), you need to see it in its original context.

How do you view design history?

My lectures are designed chronologically as a broad narrative and when appropriate a collection of narrow points of reference to tell a richer story or elaborate on specific context and connections. A standard seminal graphic design history book is used in conjunction with thematic or categorical lectures. Yet, this approach has its limitations—mostly because it's painstakingly difficult to teach graphic design history rigorously in one fifteen-week semester. One of the problems facing graphic design history educators is finding a balance between teaching a standard chronological survey and going beyond the canon to explore a much deeper (and wider) time line. Instead, a series of courses taught back-to-back in consecutive semesters would allow both instructor and students to explore both deep and wide.

Is design history purely Western? How is diverse culture injected into a Western historical survey?

Perhaps, but teaching design history from a Western perspective is not as problematic as its exclusion of women and people of color (even if throughout history the industry lacked diversity and was dominated by white males for years). There are too few books about forgotten graphic design histories and/or underrepresented figures, or lesser-known works from iconic figures. And furthermore, what's familiar is not always the most appropriate and are rarely diverse. Design history has been written by a select few, and perhaps outlier opinions could help shed light on diverse views or the neglected and overlooked participants. I'm not sure how this will play out, but the timing seems ripe to extend existing perspectives and to explore new narratives and unchartered territories . . . but those new, distinct voices need to emerge.

JAN BALLARD

Teaches Graphic Design, Typography, Corporate Identity, and Publication Design at Texas Christian University, College of Fine Arts, Department of Graphic Design

How do you view design history?
As the instructor, I value an overview of how the field has evolved. Graphic design is communication in all its forms. Students fail to see that critical connection and concentrate on digital delivery as design-defined. The time line of communication is both image and word, but in the context of the audience and environment. I teach typography—What would a Phoenician alphabet be without the discussion of trade and seafaring commerce in the Mediterranean? What would the Roman alphabet be without the discussion of politics and the Roman Empire? The much-copied posters of San Francisco without mentioning the promotion of rock concerts?

What do you want your students to learn from or take away from history?
History repeats itself. To know history is to understand opportunities to reach an audience.

Is history a series of object lessons for teaching contemporary practice?
In short bursts, yes. Students may concentrate only on the deliverables, though. The real connection is the discussion and understanding to view the designer as facilitator of information. Designers should be able to solve any problem.

Is there a right and wrong way to look at or contextualize design history?
The study to regurgitate dates is wrong, but often the standard academic approach. The use of lessons as case studies in problem solving builds skills as historical evidence of the practice.

Can design history be taught as an island or as part of a broader survey?
Both. A broad sequential survey is good overview. I always incorporate comparative case studies in my classes: Alvin Lustig and Chip Kidd for publication; Toulouse-Lautrec and Erik Nitsche for posters; Ivan Chermayeff and Egyptian hieroglyphs for logos.

Is design history purely Western? How is diverse culture injected into a Western historical survey?
Unfortunately, this is true in published texts. I do point out that bias in my lectures. For contemporary designers, I try to pull work from Latin America and Asia, since the university has outreach in those areas.

LOUISE SANDHAUS

Former Program Director and Current Faculty in the Graphic Design Program at California Institute of the Arts (CalArts); Author of Earthquakes, Mudslides, Fires and Riots: California and Graphic Design 1936–1986

How do you view design history?
Ideally, history is made coherent to students by providing some sort of armature onto which they can hang ideas that have manifested in design artifacts. That may be a time line against a backdrop of cultural, social, and political events. For me, however, the history of production, distribution, and consumption is the narrative that most readily gives "sense" to design.

What do you want your students to learn from or take away from history?
That they, as designers, are part of a continuum. That *they* as individual designer or design visionary or as team leaders—however their practice manifests—can add to the knowledge of design. The other option is to simply repeat what's already been done—often for a context that no longer exists—or simply repeat the current trends. The hope is that students can learn something from those practitioners and works of design that have endured and that we continue to share. They endure

"You never know what's going to ignite a spark in a student—something said or an example of work that enables them to see the work that they're doing in another way."

because they're remarkable in some way. Not just good design, but enduring lessons for design—the reason we still talk about that work today.

Is there a right and wrong way to look at or contextualize design history?
Everything is relative, of course. We learn different things about ourselves and our past through different lenses. You never know what's going to ignite a spark in a student—something said or an example of work that enables them to see the work that they're doing in another way. BUT providing NO context suggests that design emerges out of a vacuum.

Morally, on the other hand, I feel a personal imperative for students to see that the world around them is a product of design. Decisions are made about why things look the way they do and have manifested out of a set of values. These decisions have consequence in that these artifacts shape our sense of ourselves and how we're expected to behave.

Can design history be taught as an island or as part of a broader survey?
Not as an island, because the context provides relevancy and meaning, but how far do you go? A historian can only know so much.

Is design history purely Western? How is diverse culture injected into a Western historical survey?
In part it depends on what we're calling or what we mean by "design" (lower case). Planned? Human contrivance? People have always designed things, everywhere in every culture. But design as specific, recognized practice—as the field/practice/profession we know today—is the product of industrialization and modernity—Western cultural instantiations.

PAUL MARTIN LESTER

Clinical Professor, School of Arts, Technology, and Emerging Communication, University of Texas at Dallas

How do you view design history?
In the broadest possible way.

As part of a cultural, social, political, etc., tapestry?
Bingo. The wall hanging metaphor is apt because of its link to practical instruction. How can an animation student feel educated about her profession without a detailed study of the Bayeux Tapestry? Political, economic, religious, cultural, historical, and ethical factors influence everything. They should be part of any discussion about design.

What do you want your students to learn from or take away from history?
At my shop, students are as diverse in their interests as they are ethnically. They want to be illustrators, typographers, graphic designers, fabricators, sculptors, painters, data visualizers, filmmakers, photographers, interactive creators, game coders, makers, and writers, animators, and/or educators. Some are gifted; others should find a different major. Some will find their dream careers; others will settle for working for their uncle. Regardless of their present and future interests, my students should possess a passion for stories and storytelling. The best histories connect us to those who have come before by helping us see and understand the common humanity we all share. A cave artist 20,000 years ago who painted his hand on a cold stone wall is telling us an important message for today—it is important to be proud of what you create. History informs the present in a much more forceful and obvious way than the present.

Is history a series of object lessons for teaching contemporary practice?
Rather than stand-alone, inspirational stories, historical influences should be infused within every assignment so that the connections between theory, discovery, practice, and analysis becomes embodied within the consciousness of each student.

Is there a right and wrong way to look at or contextualize design history?
Without being judgmental, yes ;). Wrong: History as a finite event. An invention. A singular purpose. A date. A person. Right: History as process and as a collaboration between cultures over time.

"Try this idea: teach a post-Roman design history survey or lab course that removes all influences from Anglo/Caucasian men."

Can design history be taught as an island or as part of a broader survey?
Design history should be integrated within every lecture and assignment. Imagine a project in which you ask students to create an illustration concerned with President Trump's tweets. With the island or ahistorical concept, the work would probably all show some variation of Trump's hair in the form of the Twitter logo (although maybe a dull gold instead of blue). In other words, a contemporary style—which is okay. However, with a broader, historical perspective, the students' work might be influenced by various art movements that were discussed in previous lectures. Imagine the illustration influenced by art nouveau, art deco, Dada, de Stijl, Bauhaus, pop culture, punk, New Wave, or hip-hop? Islands should be reserved for super-rich Brits. Stay on the major landmasses.

Is design history purely Western?
No. As a part of a set of two courses that concentrate on pre- and post-Roman Design, it would be appropriate to feature non-Western and Western art. However, I would still be uncomfortable omitting Asian, Middle Eastern, and Mesoamerican influences (among others) within a post-Roman (Western) design course.

How is diverse culture injected into a Western historical survey?
Try this idea: teach a post-Roman design history survey or lab course that removes all influences from Anglo/Caucasian men. You would be forced to research and present the work from designers who receive little recognition, but who have influenced the field in countless ways.

RICHARD DOUBLEDAY

Fulbright Senior Scholar at Tsinghua University, China, and Associate Professor at Louisiana State University

How do you view design history?

I would speculate that it is formed by the rich history of visual communication and its formation crafted from a canon of works of design. Whatever way it might be viewed, I believe this canon is of utmost importance to the study and teaching of graphic design practice and the history of graphic design. The conception of the graphic design canon also imparts scholarship past and present. Eventually, this history is documented, researched, and interpreted in their historical and cultural contexts. Graphic design as an activity and the history of visual communication date back to the cave painting at Lascaux, pictographic scripts, and the development of early writing. However, the field of graphic design only began recording its history in 1969 with Herbert Spencer's *Pioneers of Modern Typography* and Dover Publications' *The Golden Age of the Poster* and *The First World War in Posters,* and above all, Philip B. Meggs's *A History of Graphic Design,* the first comprehensive survey on design history. So, I think we are still only at the beginning stages of recording and fully understanding our history.

What do you want your students to learn from or take away from history?

I want my students to learn that the history of graphic design is a record of the development of visual communications from its origins in prehistoric paintings in caves, the earliest writing, to the invention of movable type and printing, to the work and influence of modern and contemporary graphic designers. I would refer to Meggs's *History* to establish a solid foundation of historical knowledge—as an important entry point into an evolving history—and then students can decide which areas they would like to pursue.

For example, as part of my history course, students are responsible for writing a research paper intended as an investigation into the history of writing, visual language, and the culture of communization in which we live and work. This is the major writing project for Survey of Graphic Design History.

The research project is an extended investigation of a subject in design history, whether it is a design movement, designer, typographer, the story of the influence of an epoch in the history of visual communications such as the fifteenth-century invention of printing or the early twentieth-century Surrealist movement, or a contrasts of two epochs, design movements, or typographic epochs. The investigation will enable the student to gain a deeper understanding of the spirit of that time and the social, political, and economic life of the culture of communications.

The research should involve an in-depth study of the subject using at least three written or library online sources—not the Internet. The study can analyze the chosen subject, contrast the subject with other influences, and feature the successes and failures of the subject, and its place in the history of visual communications. A full apparatus of footnotes, bibliography, and correctly labeled illustrations is required. Oftentimes, I give them the liberty to design and lay out their papers. I want my students to investigate stylistic movements; the wide range of design theories and practices; political, social, and economic influences; and the effects of digital technologies that inform the accelerated, multidimensional, visual communications environment in which we live.

Text readings, lectures, written essays, exams, and a semester research project support students in thinking, analysis, and development of their own critical awareness and understanding of graphic design history and visual communications. The course projects are designed to support students in design thinking, learning research methods, developing writing skills, and in the development of a personal vision of graphic design as a visual language of communications. The careful examination of graphic design history, as Meggs described: "The ultimate goal of design history study should be more effective practice. Its contribution should go beyond the use of design history as a vast data bank of forms and solutions to problems that can be accessible to the contemporary designer, expanding his or her vocabulary of possibilities. Graphic Design history is a history of ideas. Eric Gill's 1928 Gill Sans typeface was based on the idea of using the proportions of Roman inscription letter forms in a sans serif type design. Its geometric contemporary, Paul Renner's 1927 Futura was designed in enthusiastic embrace of industrialism, standardization, and scientific rationalism. Gill, however, sought to retain values from humanist tradition. Understanding such divergent viewpoints leads to greater awareness of the nature of form and its meaning, and brings conceptual understanding to professional practice."

I believe the canon of design should more inclusive of major cultures of non-Western art (Africa, Asia-Pacific, Oceania, Central and South America) and women graphic artists. In the end, these topics would be folded into my historical map and evolving course outline.

One such example in non-Western design practice is the rise of modern Japanese graphic design. From my Western perspective, there appears to be a lack of research during this period as well as a record of recent developments in contemporary Japanese graphic design. Comparatively, the documentation of modern and contemporary design practice in Japan has been unexplored thus far. A more rigorous investigation and in-depth study and inclusion of these non-Western historical events in the existing graphic design canon would not only provide new knowledge among nations in the understanding of cultural differences, but the role of non-Western value systems and the dynamics of social and ethical behavior in the design profession.

Is history a series of object lessons for teaching contemporary practice?

The terminal point of is it a thorough understanding of design history for successful contemporary practice.

Is there a right and wrong way to look at or contextualize design history?

I believe a design educator should be well informed and have an in-depth knowledge of the history of graphic design, beginning with the concept of a classic canon, then shifting with current social and political events.

Is design history purely Western? How is diverse culture injected into a Western historical survey?

They may need to be treated differently, but only as long as Westerners gain a better understanding and appreciation for non-Western culture as well as from a global perspective—multicultural social and ethical principles in the practice of graphic design.

Let me give you one example from the current work I am developing as part of my Fulbright research in China:

The ascent of a new aesthetic of graphic design came into existence with the rapid expansion of greater China's economy. Deng Xiaoping's 1978 Open Door Policy gave impetus to the economic transformation of modern China and set in motion a new chapter in contemporary Chinese graphic design. The value of design and creativity has attracted attention from the Chinese public and is one of the instrumental factors and significant resources to lead in the new information age. With China's rapidly growing economic environment, graphic design will undoubtedly play an increasingly significant role in fostering socio-economic growth and affect innovative change and expanding its role in the creative service industry. As China has risen to become a global economic superpower, including its reciprocal influence with Hong Kong, Taiwan, Macau, Japan, Europe, and the United States, a movement has emerged to combine its five-thousand-year-old Chinese artistic and calligraphic traditions with principles of Western artistic traditions and design education. The country has become an extraordinarily rich region for cooperation and crosscultural dialog in graphic design. There is a remarkable opportunity to research and document the evolution of a modern design history and cultural legacy in the presence of *China's ongoing economic* transition and global *growth* for the foreseeable future.

Do you have a way to expand knowledge of the non-Western canon?
This research will first examine the development of modern Chinese graphic design beginning in the Republic of China to the Cultural Revolution in order to reveal modern Chinese graphic design activities' profound effect on contemporary Chinese graphic design. This historical paradigm contains a framework of modern design thinking and a set of ideas that bridge contrasting methods and together have shaped contemporary design education and practice. I will focus on three historical periods of design activity during the twentieth and early twenty-first centuries. The first period is from 1900 to 1949, the second period is from 1949 to 1979, and the third period is from 1979 to the present. The goal is to trace this modern design activity and examine traditional print materials and work of influential graphic designers advancing the field forward from the 1900s to the present to try to unveil a materializing "Chinese" visual language and unique cultural identity as they relate to graphic design. A primary goal of this research is to document Chinese graphic design innovation and Chinese graphic designers who have played an important role, imparting a singular aesthetic vision, and who have made notable contributions to its development and advancement over the past one hundred years. The aim of this exploration is to document the development of the visual language of modern graphic design communication and examine how design practitioners have mixed Western design theory with the five-thousand-year-old fine art traditions of China. The aim is to examine and form modern design ideas and cross-cultural concepts of East and West—the underlying social and cultural values that define a developing contemporary visual language and the new history that is modern Chinese graphic design are explored in consideration of its aesthetics, culture, and design in their historical and sometimes political context.

R. ROGER REMINGTON

Vignelli Distinguished Professor of Design, Vignelli Center for Design Studies, Rochester Institute of Technology

How do you view design history?

I prefer to approach teaching design history as a deep dive into the specifics and details of people, process, and products. While I try to set this in an historical context, the broad view is less important than the particular. Since we have unique, world-class designer archives here, the overarching theme is "activating the archives." Students do not memorize slides or images from books or online. Instead, they learn from immersing themselves in the actual graphic design artifact. This is a very special opportunity and makes the study of design studies at RIT rich in content. Studying graphic design history is a must if we want our students to be professionals.

What do you want your students to learn from or take away from history?

An understanding of the field of graphic design. Where it came from, who were its pioneers, what did they accomplish, and how does this all fit into a broader context. My students especially appreciate working from original-source materials and the anecdotal information from a teacher who has known many design pioneers. Becoming literate about the history of graphic design is important. This means thinking critically and being coherent in writing and speaking about content. Students emerging from my courses must have had the history of graphic design "brought alive."

Is history a series of object lessons for teaching contemporary practice?

Yes, there must be a bridging of graphic design history content into the needs of the contemporary designer. It must be relevant.

Is there a right and wrong way to look at or contextualize design history?

I feel that there are many ways to approach design studies, but memorizing images is not the most effective way.

Can design history be taught as an island or as part of a broader survey?

See my first answer. I organize graphic design history content as sequential, as retrospective, as theoretical, by style, in a thematic way, in a micro/macro way, as problem solving, by media, and finally by person/process/product.

Is design history purely Western? How is diverse culture injected into a Western historical survey?
This is a challenging issue. My approach is to focus on the West because that is where I come from and the context in which my information is transferred. It is the area of my own research, and from that extensive knowledge base emerges the core of my expertise. Whatever is presented must be substantive, detailed, accurate, contextual, and meaningful.

RUSSELL FLINCHUM

Associate Professor in the Department of Graphic Design and Industrial Design at North Carolina State University's College of Design

Should design history be included as a requirement for all design majors?
I am in favor of a design history requirement. In fact, I owe my job to the fact that NASAD (the National Association of Schools of Art and Design) requires industrial designers with a BID degree to have successfully completed a class in design history. Design history has become the lingua franca via which we communicate with other designers. When I first arrived here, I stated rather righteously in a meeting of the PhD faculty that "no one should graduate from the College of Design without knowing who Josef Hoffmann was." And yet discussing Vienna at the turn of the previous century is already slipping through my fingers because design history really means "contemporary design." I mean that in the sense of "tell me what I need to know to inform me how we got to today so I can be a good designer today." So I've had to give up my penchant for the nineteenth century and am actually beginning surveys with 1919 and the founding of the Bauhaus, so we have a shot at making it to 2019. But the most important change is that this is no longer going to be offered in their senior year, but as freshmen or sophomores. That is where the greatest potential for a contribution exists. The students come to us with brilliant portfolios, but only a fraction have what I consider an adequate historical background.

What method is best for the designer who is not going to be a design scholar?
I'll surprise no one by saying that the goal for a designer who is not taking the scholarly path is to familiarize themselves enough with the

territory that they can navigate for themselves. It is structured around major figures and major events, but I insist on doing some serious visual analysis along the way. This is my principal concern, that people are losing the ability to describe in detail what they see. They seem mute. They seem comfortable with the idea that the work of art is the image on their screen. I was lucky enough to be educated at the tail end of connoisseurship and will tell you I believe we'll be desperate for connoisseurs in the future. When a Bugatti goes for $125 million at auction, you can bet there is connoisseurship involved, not just of the vehicle, but also of its previous restorations. Many mass-produced items change significantly over time with little notice of these incremental changes. Which do you show, the first production model or the last? I also believe in showing the typical next to the greats. Growing up in Winston-Salem, the first Eames seating I saw was at elementary school, certainly not in peoples' homes.

Is the art historical method relevant, or is there a model unique to design that includes ethnography, technology, and sociology?
I come out of an art history background at a time when there was no PhD program in design history in the United States. I was very lucky to be well prepared in the groundwork of the field when I hit CUNY in 1985, because it was bewildering. I suddenly went from fact-based studies to a theoretical minefield. And then there were these "Americanists," a new breed, as well. These were the days of *October*, and people seemed terrified of saying the wrong thing in Rosalind Krauss's class. I didn't know any better and perhaps didn't care, because I was stunned that a room of thirty of the brightest people in the field were terrified to even venture a guess at an answer to her questions. I like to quote Charcot on this one, where he stated, "Theory is good, but it doesn't make things not exist." I was very lucky to have Marlene Park as my dissertation advisor, who worked mainly on public art and women sculptors and was very open to the idea of an exhibition on Henry Dreyfuss. Marlene was amazingly knowledgeable, which she attributed to a time "when they paid us to sit in Avery Library and read." Ethnography I definitely see being applied with good results, the history of technology is the Achilles' heel of most design historians, and sociology . . . I feel like someone is always there to take care of that. It can be great, like Karal Anne Marling talking about Mamie Eisenhower's sense of style. But this is not what I do best nor does it especially interest me.

What should the student ideally learn or take away from this study?

That Bucky Fuller was correct when he spoke of "anticipatory design"; we still aren't thinking as big as the nineteenth century did. That some creative challenges are unprecedented, but most really aren't. That the solution probably does lie in the correct statement of the problem. That the impact of a new technology is generally overestimated at its introduction and underestimated over the long term. That the analog world was perfectly capable of amazing things, like spy satellites. And that the cast of characters overlaps, collides, eludes, and otherwise behaves in more of a Brownian motion that the tightly limited narrative of historians.

What do I really want? I want people to think for themselves, and one of the ways to do that is to refuse to tell them what to think or what *you* think. I want them to read the original material instead of learning someone's august opinion secondhand.

How do you measure the result?

I'd like to state I had no problem with such measurements until I landed at NC State, where data are taken VERY seriously. It's usually a mixture of identification (that helps determined who studied) and essays (to see who listened in class). Now I have to rethink all of this as I turn to teaching freshmen and sophomores instead of graduating seniors. What will be most valuable to them in the next two or three years? What will be valuable in thirty?

I asked someone I admire in administration a theoretical question: "How should we measure the comparative achievement of a student who came in with no familiarity with design and makes a B versus someone who's been prepared throughout high school and makes an A?" Her response was, "That's a good question."

How do you personally make history more than remembering key dates, people, and things?

I start by explaining to people that dates are like coat hooks; they seem unimportant in September, but by golly you sure want them in November. I start with big dates, like the World's Fairs and World Wars. I talk a lot about biography, and luckily have a good recollection for quotes; my favorite is still Bassett Jones referring to New York as "the center of organized discomfort." It's as true in 2018 as it was in the 1930s, when he penned the sentiment. Nobody knows he lit the 1939–1940 New York World's Fair and was one of the foremost mechanical engineers in an age that still revered such figures (Gano Dunn, anyone?). Nobody knows much about the origins of human factors, for that matter.

"At the end of this, I'll turn it all on its head and say, 'What kind of architect would you be if you'd never had a class in architectural history?'"

So my own inquisitiveness is reflected in my classes, where I will talk about the challenges I'm facing in researching a specific topic. *You have to realize your impact might not be felt for years.* You might not have any impact. But once students finish my class, I hope they have a feeling that people have remained people even as the built domain has begun to outstrip our comprehension.

What drew you into history, and what made you stay?

I have never not been interested in old things, and returned to my parents' home many years ago to find my room exactly as I had left it at nineteen, and was kind of amazed . . . I had curated my room. It was a *Kunstkammer*, with railroad locks and paperweights, ashtrays and ingots. I had superb teachers in high school and college. Honestly, I chose art history because I made better grades and there were pictures in the books (I have a better memory for images than anything else). On one level, I'm still an archivist, a job I held for fifteen years; I love preserving what I think will one day be valuable, and not because of inherent worth in terms of material. On another level, I love the work of a master like John Keegan, who came out and said Clausewitz was *wrong* about war being a continuing of diplomacy through other means. Arthur Schlesinger Jr. was someone I knew enough that we had an appreciation for each other. In his last public speech, he spoke about the essential nature of history, and his jarring line that is so misunderstood: "Each generation must rewrite history." He didn't mean it in the sense of an endless revisionism where no truth is permanent; he meant that history must be told in a manner that is comprehensible to this new audience. That is what I am struggling with today, as a newly tenured associate professor at the age of sixty. How do I make what I "know" to be important relevant to someone one-third my age? Ultimately, it leads to the question, "Do I think this is important because I know it, or because I truly believe it to be essential knowledge for future practitioners?"

At the end of this, I'll turn it all on its head and say, "What kind of architect would you be if you'd never had a class in architectural history?"

SUSAN MERRITT

Design Teacher at the School of Art + Design, San Diego State University

How long have you taught design history?

I proposed a graphic design history course at San Diego State University's School of Art + Design in 2000/2001 as a special topics class. That meant the course could go into the schedule right away and be taught for up to three years while applying for permanent status. I taught the first session in 2001/2002 as an elective seminar, which allowed me to keep the group small while I developed the course. Up until then, history had been informally covered in our graphic design studio classes or not at all. I relied on the third edition of Philip B. Meggs's *A History of Graphic Design*, as it was the most comprehensive text available at the time. By 2005/2006, the course had made its way through the curriculum process and into the university catalog as a required lower-division class and in 2007/2008 was redesignated upper division with two lower-division art history courses as prerequisites. I taught the class until 2018, when I retired from the university. So, seventeen years.

What has been the students' response to what you've taught?

Student feedback on the positive end of the spectrum ranged from "the class opened my eyes," "it helped me better understand studio

Student Work, Typographic History Project by (This page) Brent Davis. (Opposite) Keith Tran

assignments," and "the most important class I've ever taken" to "too much information for one semester" on the opposite end. I agree. Graphic design history should definitely be a two-semester course. I received one of the most memorable student responses during a trip to New York City. While walking to the subway, a young man passed me, stopped, turned around, and said, "Professor Merritt?" I recognized him as a former student, but I hadn't seen him for years. "I was so surprised to see you," he said, "I just had to say something because you changed my life. I was so inspired after taking your graphic design history class that I decided to go for it and move to New York. I've been working here as a graphic designer for ten years." The history class is a perfect forum to demonstrate what's possible through the lives and work of others and against that backdrop to encourage students to expand their perspectives, travel, go to where the good jobs are, and continue to learn. Moments like that encounter in New York make teaching so worthwhile.

How inclusive do you go into the history? What amount of detail is enough detail?

Philip B. Meggs's *A History of Graphic Design* was the seminal text when I started teaching graphic design history. I continued to lean on Meggs while expanding content to include more of my own research from study trips to special collections and archives, museum exhibitions, and design studios in the United States and abroad.

To me, it's all important. I struggle with streamlining. Some students appreciate that I present the full spectrum of visual communication beginning with early writing systems and alphabets, while others would rather I focus only on the nineteenth and twentieth centuries.

"Linking graphic design history to studio instruction complements the design history class and is an effective way to extend exposure and add another layer of meaning to hands-on assignments."

But the fifteenth through eighteenth centuries are so pertinent to the foundation of graphic design, specifically type, printing, and book design, that whenever I consider collapsing content, I convince myself to hold on to that material. I'm sensitive to the fact that students have a difficult time understanding the relevance of what they consider ancient history, so I often interject contemporary examples that demonstrate how people, technologies, or visual approaches were influenced by prior occurrences.

Linking graphic design history to studio instruction complements the design history class and is an effective way to extend exposure and add another layer of meaning to hands-on assignments. Beth Weeks, an adjunct professor, and I developed projects for Typography I and Typography II—both required classes—that involved examining historical type specimen books and other archival materials in the university's special collections. Essays by historical and contemporary designers served as copy for typographic exploration. I also slipped historical content into projects in Typography III and IV, two upper-division electives.

How do the history of art classes intersect with the design history sections?

There are many more art history courses than there are design history courses, which puts design students at a disadvantage. The problem, I decided, was in the degree being offered. At the undergraduate level, SDSU's School of Art + Design only offers a BA in Art, which is a liberal arts degree. In 2001/2002, I proposed a professional degree, a BFA in Graphic Design, to complement the BA in Art with emphasis in graphic design. Sadly, it was never fully implemented due to an unexpected state budget crisis, lack of faculty support, and a flux of directors, six to be exact, some more in favor of the BFA than others. The new degree would have required more units in design history in accordance with the National Association of Schools of Art and Design (NASAD), the agency that accredits our programs. While NASAD puts design history on an equal footing with art history ("art/design history"), many institutions, including SDSU, do not yet recognize design history as

a viable subject or an equivalent option to art history. At SDSU, art majors are required to take twelve units of art history, two lower-division and two upper-division courses. The graphic design history class that I taught was not allowed by the School of Art + Design to substitute for one of the art history courses under the guise that the professor was required to have a PhD. Recruiting a design historian with a PhD to teach only one class would be a challenge, if we could locate such a candidate at all. Having more available design historians would elevate the subject, fill a growing need, and nudge academic programs toward a balance in course offerings that better prepares graphic design students for professional practice.

Should art historians teach design history?

An art historian with the right credentials might be an acceptable candidate to teach design history, especially if the person's education and research focus were in design, although a qualified design historian would be preferable.

Do we need more design historians?

Yes, we need more design historians with advanced scholarship and research and a terminal degree that qualifies them to teach in colleges and universities. Candidates who have an undergraduate degree in

Typographic History Project
by Rebecca Valenzuela

Typographic History Projects
by (Left) Tim Bunda
(Right) Natalie Hall

design and professional practice experience could also teach both history and theory, as well as studio classes. Those who have broad knowledge across design disciplines might even be able to cover the history needs of multiple design programs within a school, such as graphic design/visual communication, interior, fashion, and product design.

What do you see as the main distinction between the two academic disciplines?

Art and design are two separate disciplines, and their histories reflect the people, influences, and innovations that contributed to their distinct development. Although their histories experienced moments of overlap and shared influences, the historical events that each discipline emphasizes are predicated on point of view and relevance to their practices.

Take Albrecht Dürer as an example. Students learn about Dürer, the artist, in an art history prerequisite class where they study his paintings, drawings, and prints. To remind my students who Dürer was and make the leap to graphic design, I discuss several of his paintings and prints that include writing. The text on these works reveal Dürer's shift away from Gothic to roman lettering following his extended stays in Venice during the Italian Renaissance. Then, I focus on his applications of geometry to structure, which were influenced by *Euclid's Elements*, a copy of which Dürer acquired while in Italy. Instances relevant to graphic design include Dürer's structural analysis of the capitals found at the base of the Trajan column in Rome, his detailed instructions for properly drawing these letterforms using geometry, his method of constructing a black letter alphabet based on a grid system of stacked and rotated squares, and an array of other design applications laid out in his 1525 book *Underweysung der Messung mit dem Zirckel und Richtscheyt* (A Course in the Art of Measurement with Compass and Ruler). One of the first books I wanted to examine after I started teaching history of graphic design, I tracked down a Latin edition of *Underweysung der Messung* set in roman type at the Grolier Club library in New York and later discovered a German version set in black letter at the Getty Research Institute in Los Angeles. These two volumes exemplify the practice at the time of choosing type based on language. Type is the bedrock of graphic design and an essential topic in the study of its history. Advances in handwriting techniques, the emergence of type and printing, the influences behind typeface characteristics, and typography, the arrangement of type for communication and visual effect, are germane to the evolution of graphic design and, in my opinion, the main distinction between the two academic disciplines.

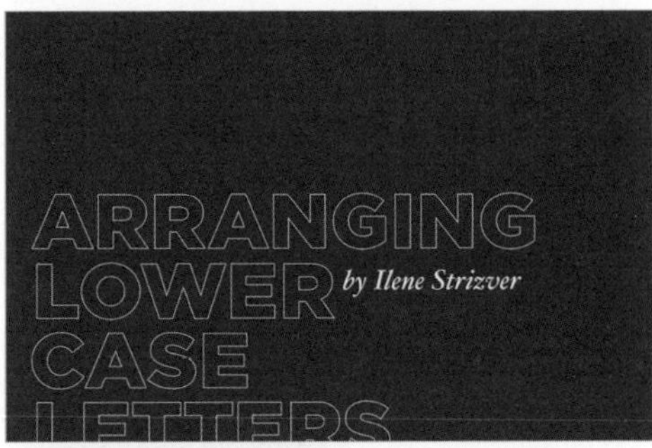

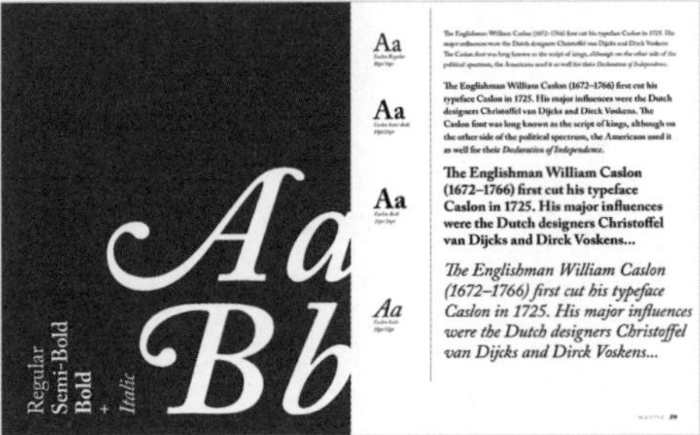

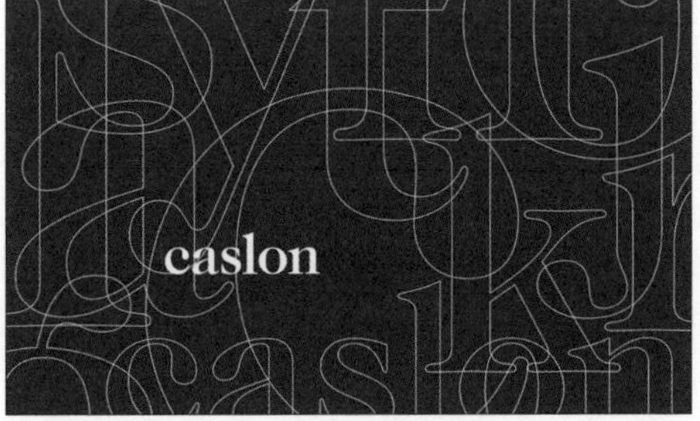

Typographic History Project by Luis Hernandez

CH4

HOW MAKING A MOVIE ABOUT DESIGN HISTORY CHANGED HOW I TEACH

Briar Levit

In making the documentary *Graphic Means* over a period of three years, I spent a lot of time thinking and talking about graphic design workflow as it relates to tools and technology. The computer has been a great and revolutionary tool that has thoroughly changed our field. Graphic designers went from existing as one person of many to create a piece of design to becoming the designer, production artist, typesetter, and, possibly, photographer and illustrator and more, all in one. And while this added control of typography and access to tools has allowed us to do more than ever before, it also means just that—we have to do more than ever before. This has drastic effects on our output. As writer and publisher Adrian Shaughnessy says in the film, "If you eliminate all thinking time, design really suffers."

So when *are* we getting that "thinking time" in? While I do require my lower-division students to learn and follow certain steps of the design process, I realized I was still guilty of allowing that thinking time to be truncated. And so my research and personal work in making a film about graphic design production history truly began to inform my pedagogy in a significant way. Here's how my own research into design history has changed my approach to teaching studio classes.

More Thinking Time = Better Design

Portland State University is on the quarter system, which means our classes are ten weeks, plus one week for finals. It's a whirlwind, to say the least. When I started teaching, it was standard to have three projects for nearly all studio classes—quite a feat for a ten-week period. My first step in allowing more thinking time was the most obvious and the easiest—I simply removed one project from all of my studio classes (those I teach and those I have the lead on). While this could have created some friction among my colleagues, as we want to make sure students have enough work to select from for their Sophomore Portfolio Review, there was none. In fact, most cheered as they imagined what this added time would allow their students to achieve. It was plain to see that two good outcomes is much better than three mediocre ones.

I will say, it can be a double-edged sword—more time. Students may feel a bit too comfortable and not feel as much urgency in doing the work. As an answer to that, I have increased graded weight of process/critique in the overall grades. This makes the process just as much a part of the journey, which is a message I'd like to send in the early part

"... I also blame us, the educators, for not finding more ways to develop those eyes that were once developed by hand drawing grids and rules, and pasting individual headlines, drop caps, and columns of text. Now, a student enters a headline, sets the point size, and calls it done."

of a design student's education. Sometimes grades are the only language students understand, so I'm happy to use them to make my point.

Now, I'm guessing some of you might find this a bit tedious in terms of grading or feel that in the "outside" world, the final piece is the most important. But I would argue that this is worth trying, at least for first- and second-year students, as a sort of training wheels that will come off in the final years of school.

Sketching Is Still Critical

Another approach I'm taking that is inspired by my hours of talks with designers of the Analog Design Era is a strictly hand-sketched first round of concepts. Now, I suppose I'm outing myself as being outrageous for not requiring this before. But as I mentioned, I had ten weeks, and three projects to complete, so I *would* require sketches but would have the first round done as digital roughs, and the sketches brought to be shown alongside those, but not investigated in detail during critique. This meant that sketches could be sloppy, underdeveloped, and limited in number if I didn't require a minimum number. Those days are gone, and I'm seeing marked improvement. I'm sure you are shocked!

Projects now consist of approximately four formal critiques, the first of which is hand-drawn sketches. These can be drawn in one to three colors using colored pencils, pens, or highlighters. Students are also allowed to use an implement like an Apple Pencil or other stylus, but it's important that they not use type, vectors, textures, etc.—the idea must flow through a writing implement that can be rendered quickly and not cause distraction with the bells and whistles of the digital software. Finally, the sketches must be printed out, so that notes and additional sketches can be added during the critique by the student and their peers.

What does this requirement do? It requires them to come up with many concepts rapidly at the very start of the project. By drawing with an implement that is not a trackpad, mouse, or keyboard, they are not distracted by type, color, and other graphic elements that can derail the brainstorming process and cause a student to focus disproportionately on one concept over the many they are supposed to be generating.

While students are not required to have perfect rendering skills, the sketches must be at least readable to the rest of the class as they present them in small groups. Notations on color, type, or image are welcome additions to make sure they are able to describe the concept to their classmates when the time comes.

When the students finally present their sketches, they should have many very deliberate concepts, as opposed to what often happens when they jump on the computer too quickly, which is a variation of the same idea with the elements moved around a bit until the layout feels pretty good. By the time they move to the computer, they are using the machine for what it is—a tool—and simply plugging in elements of their design as shown in their various sketches.

Dry Transfer Typesetting

Teaching typesetting is both easier with the computer, but also more difficult. We have all the tools at our fingertips (not the case before, and something that meant many designers learned to spec type on the job), but we also have a tool that tricks us into thinking that everything is done for us, when often it is not. Students and many younger designers simply don't have the eye for detail that was once a hallmark of the discipline. Perhaps some are to blame themselves, but I also blame us, the educators, for not finding more ways to develop those eyes that were once developed by hand drawing grids and rules, and pasting individual headlines, drop caps, and columns of text. Now, a student enters a headline, sets the point size, and calls it done.

One of my interviewees, Gene Gable, a former type shop owner, talks about the fact that letterspacing really clicked for him when he learned to use the Photo Typositor. This massive piece of equipment utilized typefaces on long strips of film that were stored in rolls. The typesetter rotated the rolls to expose one letter of type at a time with the built-in camera and darkroom, onto a piece of light-sensitive paper. This meant that they would need to be especially careful about how much space they allowed for each additional character as they progressed.

In keeping with my desire to slow down and avoid the slickness and distractions of the computer, I really wanted to find a way to do this with my students. It makes so much sense as a way of learning about letter and word spacing to me! Sure, we can require our students to draw letterforms and make sure spacing is taken into account, but if we want to have an exercise in which we are focusing specifically on spacing (not also on the actual drawing of letterforms, which is a whole other monster), I realized that dry transfer type can be a great stand-in for the Photo Typositor, which is no longer something you can find in operation.

The thing I love about this exercise is that there are some added bonuses. Students get a little history lesson here on just how incredible our computer tool is and how these details are still something that they should care about paying attention to, regardless of the many features offered. Entering a headline at the right point size is not the end of the job. Details need to be inspected and adjusted. It's also a moment in which you can help them understand how designers of just a generation or two ahead of them worked. And perhaps the best part is that students go absolutely nuts over dry transfer type. Some don't even realize how much they were dying to get off the computer and see something created with their hands, but an exercise like this can really help that click for them.

For a page layout or even a design history class, you might take this exercise further and have students create something akin to a paste-up mechanical to help them really experience firsthand the level of detail that was required to create a whole page in position not long ago.

Writing to Synthesize Ideas

My mentor during the process of making *Graphic Means*, Doug Wilson, director of *Linotype: The Film*, joked that documentary making is really just spreadsheet making. I quickly learned how true this was—I became a true mistress of spreadsheet making. But I also became a much stronger writer, and organizer of ideas, while making the film. And now that "designer-as-author" is no longer a concept that exists on the fringes of our discipline, but is something that is accepted, and something that we at Portland State University like to encourage, I think it's more important than ever to help students develop these skills.

I'm folding writing into my classes more than ever. I've always required a brief written rationale for each project to make sure students were not only making deliberate choices in their work, but to make sure they had the vocabulary and ability to discuss it cohesively.

Rationales remain a requirement. They serve as a way to allow students to review the work they've completed and essentially "sell" it to me in written form. In addition to those, however, I'm requiring more written and presented proposals. What I mean by this is a written document or prospectus that outlines the potential concepts/directions for a project before the student begins the work. A requirement like this forces the students to do their research up front, and to get very deliberate about their ideas. It also mimics more closely the way a studio or agency often proposes their ideas to a client—sometimes in a digital deck/presentation, or sometimes in an actual physical presentation, which might also include a printed proposal.

I try to help make the writing less intimidating by offering sample outlines for proposals—whether for a prospective magazine, brand, or thesis project. Students can use the outline as a jumping-off point and add to it, or skip the areas that aren't relevant to their work. Additionally, I use class time for writing, and for peer feedback of the writing and presentations, which signals to the students that this is, in fact, an important part of the process. This is not an afterthought, or busywork, but a part of what it means to communicate your prospective idea and have it approved.

Sharing My Research Methods

Another thing making *Graphic Means* has given me is a sample from which to pull examples for my thesis students in their own research journeys. Certainly before I made the film, I had my own BA thesis project and MA work to draw from, but I admit, these periods were feeling further from me and were made when I felt less realized in my personal approach and interests as a designer and researcher. When I embarked on making a documentary, I was extremely motivated to make my concept happen—one I'd been pondering for some time—and I was the only one (in the beginning) who could do that.

The massive nature of the project put me into many roles, some of which I had never had and never expected to have—director, producer, script editor, musical supervisor, etc. I know in this era of entrepreneurship and designer-as-author, many of my students will take on similar multirole projects themselves. Their thesis is their chance to try this in a safe way. So when I teach thesis, I share my experience in project planning the nitty-gritty calendar details, seeking out and working with collaborators, and presenting concepts to potential financiers from Kickstarter donors to corporations. I can also draw from my own methodologies in collecting my research. What should one consider when including interviews in a project? How does one make sure they are triangulating their research to cover all bases? How does image research and rights work? These many little hats I wore all come in handy as I advise each completely unique student thesis project.

Conclusion

I knew making *Graphic Means* would eventually inform my teaching, but I don't think I realized in just how many ways it would—from graphic design methodologies, to project management, to writing, it's affected the way I teach all of my classes. I don't expect the workflow in our industry will be slowing down anytime soon (or ever), but I do hope that in slowing down how I teach process, my students will learn to truly appreciate the ways these steps can elevate their outcomes and that they will find their own ways to execute them within our industry's rapid workflow.

Briar Levit is an assistant professor of Graphic Design at Portland State University and teaches Introduction to Typography and Communication Design, Page Layout, Information Design, and Thesis. She cut her teeth as a designer at Discovery Channel Retail and soon after as art director at Bitch *magazine in the early 2000s. Most recently, she has focused on her film* Graphic Means, *which tells the story of technology in the mid-to-late twentieth century and how it affected the discipline of graphic design. She is currently starting work on a companion book to the film.*

INDEPENDENT STUDY: DESIGN HISTORY OUTSIDE THE CLASSROOM AND OFF THE GRID

James Sholly

Indiana may not be the first place that comes to mind when considering the expression "hotbed of design." But in my nearly thirty years of experience working as a graphic designer in Indianapolis, I have never seen my location as a hindrance, limitation, or liability to producing creative and thoughtful work. And more to the point—it may have even served as a motivation to work harder.

The studio operated by my brother and myself is called Commercial Artisan. In 2005, we were struggling to come up with a concept for a self-promotional piece that we could use to bolster our roster of clients. The traditional approach of selling ourselves and showing our trendiest design work seemed embarrassing and banal. We imagined how much more interesting it would be for us to write about someone we admired and show the design work that inspired us.

It wasn't difficult to discern the "who?" part of our discussion. Gene and Jackie Lacy were graphic designers, illustrators, and artists who lived and worked in Indianapolis from the 1950s to the 1990s. We were familiar with them because they were also my in-laws. Their work, for both corporate and cultural institutions, was rooted in modernism but also softened by a charming humanist touch. Logos that they designed were still in use in central Indiana in the 2000s, but both the Lacys and their work were virtually unknown anywhere else.

Working with Gene and Jackie's daughter, we set out to chronicle their story. Gene had died in 1990, and Jackie had recently been diagnosed with dementia, which created a sense of urgency for uncovering the details of their lives and sussing out what remained of their work—much of which was stashed in weathered portfolios under beds and in closets.

This led to the publication of the first issue of *Commercial Article*—a thirty-two-page journal sent to friends, family, and colleagues that served as the only record of two Midwestern lives lived creatively, but whose legacy was dissolving into obscurity. In an introductory letter, I make the point that work by designers like the Lacys is disappearing every day and suggest that there could be an initiative to document the designs of lesser-known figures in unexpected places like Indianapolis.

This experience prompted us to wonder who else in our Indiana backyard was producing significant work that was either unrecognized or had vanished from memory. Putting aside our halfhearted desires to self-promote, we opted instead to assume the role of amateur historians and take on the challenge of uncovering and preserving these stories ourselves. We used our first issue as a template and model for the method we would employ moving forward.

To allow a designer's work to shine, we keep the layouts intentionally simple using only Helvetica and a grid that changes minimally from one issue to the next. The dimensions always end up being about 6×9 inches, but formats may be accordion-folded, saddle-stitched, perfect bound, or unfolded into a flat poster. We've always endeavored to utilize printing to create a sense of this being a series so our readers think of new issues as essential objects to be collected.

Over the course of ten issues, *Commercial Article* has documented the lives of Indiana figures from graphic, fashion, product, industrial, architectural, and environmental design disciplines. A few of the designers we've been fortunate to learn about are . . .

Avriel Shull has become a central Indiana cult hero. A graphic artist turned self-taught master builder, her midcentury modern home designs regularly command top dollar and incite bidding wars among her devotees. She's as well known for her progressive design abilities as she is for her beauty and the verve with which she lived her short life.

George Philip Meier and Nellie Simmons Meier were a couple whose transatlantic lives could have emerged from a glamorous early talkie. He was a fashion designer for the elite society women of early twentieth-century Indianapolis, and she was a "scientific" palmist, whose clientele included Walt Disney, Eleanor Roosevelt, Carole Lombard, and Amelia Earhart. When they weren't in Paris, they were at their home "Tuckaway," a base of operations that has become a legendary Indianapolis time capsule.

Norman Norell was an international design giant and Coty Award–winning legend. Following stints as a costume designer for film and the stage, he turned his attention to fashion. His collections were revered by designers as diverse as Bill Blass and Stephen Sprouse (both from Indiana), but he remains largely forgotten by the public today.

Leslie Ayres drew the proposals that sold civic leaders on the building designs that would come to define downtown Indianapolis. A master renderer and architect himself, Ayres possessed a Fred Astaire–like elegance and brought both moderne *and modern style to the buildings he designed.*

Opposite:
(Left) Cover of Commercial Article 01 featuring graphic designer Gene Lacy in his 1955 Indianapolis office.

(Top right) Gene Lacy painting featured on a self-promotional poster for the "Max the Printer" printing company, 1970.

(Bottom right) Gene Lacy at work in the downtown Indianapolis office that bears his name, 1955.

We look for connections between our subjects to try to determine if there's a particular Indiana design ethos. They all appear to be driven to succeed, despite having to overcome geographic and, in some instances, gender biases. They all seem to be sophisticated with an acute understanding of what was occurring in their disciplines during the time in which they worked. These traits may not necessarily be unique to Indiana designers, but as a designer from Indiana myself, I suspect that a perceived underdog status may have compelled them to work harder to achieve their goals.

Delving into the lives of these design figures can help develop one's latent detective skills. Always looking for a hidden photo in an archive. Hoping someone's great niece held on to that elusive sketch. Tracking down the location of a previously uncredited building design. The more information that's uncovered, the more thrilling the hunt.

Just as exciting is the response from the community when they discover how much outstanding design comes from their home state. Indiana, long regarded as prime flyover real estate, has suffered from its reputation of being (at the generous end of the spectrum)

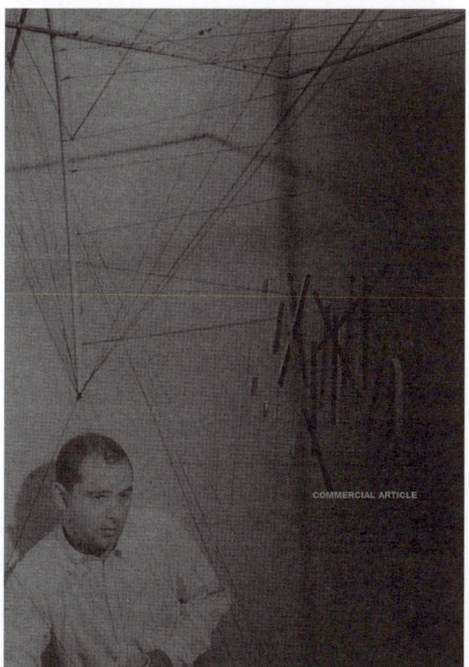

Above:
(Left) Cover of Commercial Article 03 featuring modern home designer Avriel Shull. Shull was a fierce self-promoter who arranged for LIFE magazine to cover her 1951 wedding.

(Right) A teenage Avriel Shull painting a mural to brighten the Norways Sanatorium in Indianapolis, 1950.

unsophisticated. Learning that Indiana designers produced masterful design work on par with design being done by acclaimed figures in other places is a source of tremendous civic pride.

Most people in Pendleton, Indiana, probably don't realize that Walter Dorwin Teague is regarded as the father of industrial design. Or that Noblesville's Norman Norell designed dresses worn by Jacqueline Kennedy and Michelle Obama. How many in Vedersberg know that the work of Jane and Gordon Martz was selected by Alexander Girard for MoMA's *Good Design* exhibit? Information like this has opened the eyes of our readers and prompted others to pursue design preservation efforts of their own.

Roland Hobart was the subject of our ninth issue. Hobart is an Austrian artist and designer who came to Indiana in the late 1960s. In 1973, he won a contest to design the first "Urban Wall" in downtown Indianapolis. His nine-story super-graphic composition was painted

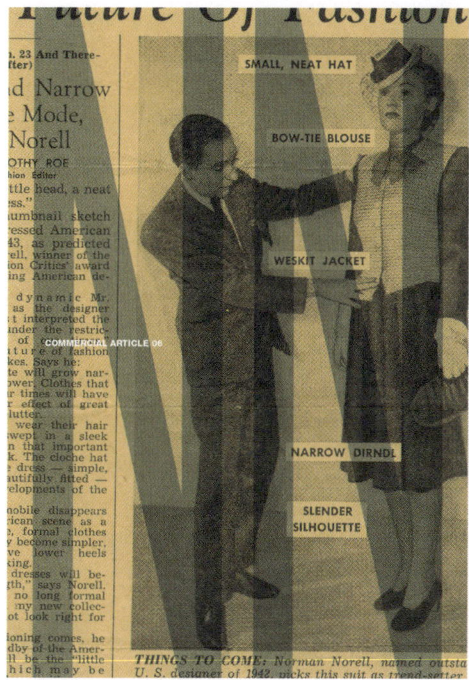

Above:
(Left) Cover of Commercial Article 06 featuring the fashion giant from Noblesville, Indiana Norman Norell.

(Top right) The stories behind the signs and symbols of Indiana are told in Commercial Article 10 (cover, 2017).

(Bottom right) Cover of Commercial Article 09 depicting Austrian import Roland Hobart's 1973 Urban Wall in downtown Indianapolis.

MARSHALL STUDIOS MODERNISM: JANE AND GORDON MARTZ

1922 Mrs. Jesse Talbott Marshall goes into business in Indianapolis making hand-painted parchment lampshades.

1924 Gordon Martz born February 20.

1926 Mr. and Mrs. Nicholas T. Marshall, son and daughter-in-law of Jessie Marshall, join the business. Nicholas Marshall begins making hand-turned wood lamp bases.

1929 Jane Marshall born January 19. Marshall Studios incorporates.

1932 Jessie Talbott Marshall passes away. Nicholas Marshall returns to Marshall Studios from a period studying architecture at the University of Illinois.

1938 Marshall Studios begins producing equipment for the photography industry. Nicholas Marshall makes and produces commercially the first color slide viewer, the Marshall Studios Vuescope. Additionally, the Marshall Slide Binder is produced. Later, Nicholas designs and produces a color film

Jane Marshall set out for Gulf Park College in Gulfport, Mississippi, in the summer of 1947. Two years later she transferred to the New York State College of Ceramics at Alfred University. It turned out to be a fortuitous transfer for the history of Indiana ceramics, but why the change in schools? Gordon Martz, Jane's husband of more than 50 years, answers that question: "Jane went to Gulf Park because she wanted to. Jane was forced to go to Alfred because her father wanted her to learn ceramics [which] he then would introduce . . . into Marshall Studios."

Ceramics for a Modern World

That may be oversimplifying the beginnings of the transformation of Marshall Studios, originally opened as a handmade lampshade company by Jane's grandmother. But it's a good start for the story of how Jane and Gordon Martz turned a Veedersburg, Indiana, lampshade factory into a nationally acclaimed producer of modern ceramics.

Jane Marshall grew up in a family business — a handmade, hand-painted lampshade firm in Indianapolis called Marshall Studios — started by her grandmother, Mrs. Jessie Talbott Marshall, in 1922. When Jessie Marshall died in 1932, her son, Nicholas Marshall, quit architecture school at University of Illinois to take over the business with his wife, Grace. Nicholas was an inventor whose patents included the Vuescope for viewing slides and other photography related items, and he added these to the Marshall Studios' catalog. He also added plaster and hand-turned wooden lamps to the company's offerings, but lampshades remained the meat and potatoes of Marshall Studios. Born in 1929, Jane Marshall was just twelve years old when the Marshalls moved their business and their home to Veedersburg, Indiana, because wartime rationing had

made city life challenging i
1940s. The Marshalls move
a farm outside the small to
and found factory space in
building constructed by th
Veedersburg. The townspe
became a good source of
labor. One of Nicholas Mar
inventions, the densitomet
measured the density of p
graphic emulsion, was pur
by the federal government
priority basis, ensuring tha
became an essential indus
therefore stayed busy ever
these years when home dé
businesses, which didn't c
to the war effort, suffered.

World War II had an eno
impact on the home front.
bodied young men all but
peared; women entered th
force in high numbers to k
factories and businesses g
while the men were at war.
Marshall Studios, though,
didn't cause the same turn
workers that was common
where. The firm had wome
workplace from its incepti

LEFT Catalog photograph of M221 and M194 ceramic lamps, 1974 / **LEFT TO RIGHT** The Vuescope, a device used for viewing slides, and one of several photography-related

Introductory spread from Commercial Article 04 featuring Jane and Gordon Martz and their Marshall Studios homewares business.

on the sides of two buildings and was among the city's first public art offerings. But through the decades, Hobart's wall faded and decayed until it was barely recognizable. With no funding available for restoration, the wall appeared to be doomed. But with our publication as a persuasive tool, concerned citizens and preservationists were able to tell Hobart's story to civic leaders in an effort to secure funding for the wall's return. Restoration efforts have been slated for 2018.

Commercial Article was included in *Graphic Design: Now in Production*, a major museum exhibition exploring the state of contemporary graphic design and organized by Walker Art Center (Minneapolis) and Cooper Hewitt Smithsonian Design Museum (New York). And issues now reside in the collections of research institutions like the Fashion Institute of Technology and the Indianapolis Museum of Art. At the Indiana Historical Society, archivists are currently using our research to support programming for Indiana's upcoming bicentennial celebrations.

I've personally had the opportunity to discuss independent publishing and Indiana design history, and to provide issues of *Commercial Article* to

by Connie Zeigler

during wartime, ownership of a family farm, a factory space which was available, and affordable labor. Catalog #3 produced.

1948 A fire in the photographic department destroys all of the dies and equipment, and it was decided to discontinue manufacturing photographic supplies.

1949 Jane Marshall begins attending Alfred University to study art and industrial ceramics.

1950 Jane and Gordon are married on June 15.

1951 Gordon Martz graduates Summa Cum Laude from Alfred University. Jane and Gordon Martz move to Veedersburg, Indiana, and become the third generation of Marshall family to join the family business. Jane and Gordon add contemporary designed stoneware lamps and accessories to the Marshall Studios line.

1953 The Marshall Studios M101 lamp is featured in Edgar Kauffman, Jr.'s 1953 "Good Design" exhibit at the Museum of Modern Art in New York. Catalog #4 is produced in the fall of 1953.

1955 "Family Share Business" article published in the Christian Science Monitor, January 19.

1956 John A. Marshall and his wife, Carolyn M. Marshall, trained in business administration from DePauw and Drake University, join Marshall Studios.

1957 Catalog #8 produced in April of 1957.

1958 "US Home-Based Crafts Increase" article featuring the work of husband-wife artisans including Jane and Gordon Martz, Frances and Michael Higgins, and Mary and Edwin Scheier; published in the Christian Science Monitor, August 19.

ess was started by a - Jessie Marshall; by 1947 owned by a woman — rshall, Jessie's daughter- rhaps because the hand f lampshades was a handi- work especially appealed company was more open women workers.

se during the war, like most manufacturers in those rshall Studios was staffed with women. When the men rom service at the end of ther manufacturing busi- the U.S. returned to single- ale workplaces. Marshall Studios continued to employ women even after their men returned from the war. The firm also employed the disabled, including both Nicholas Marshall's aunt and uncle. Wheelchair ramps were part of the Marshall Studios landscape long before they were demanded by the Occupational Safety and Health Administration (OSHA). Jane Marshall, who would turn 18 the year the war ended, grew up around this modern-style workplace with both men and women workers and the able and less-able bodied. Her worldview arose out of a family and a business where it was okay to be different.

While Jane was coming of age in small town Indiana, Gordon Martz grew up in a big city — Chicago. He was a somewhat sickly child who found enjoyment and escape in art, and although he was color blind, he didn't let that affliction keep him from artistic pursuits. In grammar school, Gordon was such a good artist that he became the art editor of his school's newspaper, a position he kept throughout high school. He was so talented in this area that his teachers would excuse him from English class to work on the artistic elements of the newspaper. At the time, Gordon didn't mind that. He was becoming familiar with the language of art, but he later realized he'd missed out on some of the fundamentals of his own language — a realization that guided him in his first college choice a few years later.

When World War II heated up, Gordon was drafted in 1943. Because he was both a talented artist and gifted at drafting (a class he'd taught one summer during high school), he was stationed at Mitchell Field on Long Island, New York, to work as a draftsman stateside during the war. Before he was discharged in 1946, and luckily for the future of Indiana ceramics, Gordon visited a USO in New York where he tried his hand at working clay. As he recalls it, "everyone gathered around to see what I was doing, which wasn't much, but the director fired my pieces and I was inspired." Despite his obvious talents, Gordon never considered art as a career. After his discharge, he enrolled in Elmhurst College in Illinois because he thought a liberal arts college was a pragmatic choice where he could learn both a foreign language and the fundamentals of English that he'd missed out on during his years of skipping English class. But within a year, he transferred to the New York State College of Ceramics, at Alfred University. He'd decided to follow his inspiration and make it his career.

Jane Marshall was also trying her hand at pottery about this same time. In 1947, she started college classes at Gulf Park College for Women, near Gulfport, Mississippi. Jane thrived at the school far from her Veedersburg home. Her classes included the typical Liberal Arts fare, but there was also a whiff of southern genteelism, such as her class in posture training. Jane also took a fair number of arts-related courses, including piano, fine arts, and (of course) pottery. Jane excelled in all but her physical education courses.

During her time at Gulf Park, she maintained a regular correspondence with her mother. Although her letters didn't survive, Jane kept every one her mother sent. Some of her mother's letters suggested, not so subtly, that Jane might find a husband to bring home. But neither Jane nor her mother was expecting Jane to follow a completely traditional path of marriage and motherhood alone. A line in a letter from Grace Marshall to her daughter in November 1947 nudges Jane toward a hoped-for future career and contribution to the family business: "We enjoyed your letter about the pottery today VERY much [emphasis is in the original] – and are especially glad that you still like pottery! It has always seemed to us that this would be about the most satisfying thing a person inclined along these lines could do, and you most certainly are inclined."

That nudge was probably unnecessary. Jane, who had been gifted in art and encouraged by her family to pursue that gift since she was a young girl, was aware of her family's desire that she come back to Veedersburg to add pottery lamps to the Marshall Studios catalog. She had no way of knowing that she'd return there with a husband who was also a gifted potter, or that together they would influence modern design in households and offices across the United States through their ceramics.

Jane finished her first year of study at Gulf Park, and then, because her father wanted her to, in 1949 she started at Alfred University. According to Gordon Martz, she was upset about making the change, but was obedient to her father's wishes. Once at Alfred, however, she enjoyed her work as a design student. At Alfred, Jane would expand her knowledge and experience in ceramics as part of her father's plan to have her bring a new dimension to the family business.

Alfred had a co-ed student body of 800 when Jane Marshall started classes there in 1949. Probably fewer than half of these were enrolled in the ceramics program, so it was inevitable that Gordon Martz and Jane Marshall would meet. But what happened at that first meeting? "I walked in while she was working in the evening and criticized a sculpture . . . and didn't make a good first impression." Not much of a meet-cute. But their relationship aptly started over a shared interest in ceramic design, one that would last through their decades-long marriage.

(Photo: Rick Soloway) / Jane and Gordon Martz as pictured in a Catalog No. 7, late 1950s / Even the Marshall Studios hang tags were a modernist "Treasure" to enjoy / **TOP** A selection of some of the artfully-designed catalogs and price lists that displayed the Marshall Studios wares / **BACK COVER** A catalog photo displaying a wide range of Marshall Studios products

students enrolled in graphic design programs while visiting universities. It's particularly rewarding to see people become excited by our subjects and know that students, researchers, and individuals investigating the state's design history now have access to stories and work we've uncovered.

By taking history into our own hands, our hope is that we've created a compelling resource for civic, educational, and design communities that celebrates Indiana designers who would remain otherwise forgotten.

James Sholly is owner of the Indianapolis-based graphic design studio Commercial Artisan and its offshoot publication, Commercial Article. *His work (for cultural institutions, not-for-profits, and corporations) has appeared in* Eye, Print, Emigre, Communication Arts, *and other publications and competitions over the course of a thirty-year career.* Commercial Article *documents the histories of design figures from Indiana whose stories have been underserved, overlooked, or forgotten.*

PAUL RAND, CRITICAL THINKER/CHANGES HIS MIND

Nathan Garland

> *"It ain't over till it's over."* —YOGI BERRA

Paul Rand, my friend and mentor, was decisive. His strong opinions were legendary and expressed in everything he did and said. Many of his ideas and images remained constant, but others were amended or reversed at will. He reserved the right to change his mind.

Paul scrutinized whatever he saw, heard, thought, or did. All art, design, and writing were suspect. His own ideas were examined at least as much as anyone else's. Everything he did was in a perpetual state of review and, if necessary, revision. Quality was the goal. The question was always the same: what was best? Three examples of this pattern follow.

First: The IBM logo

In 1956, Rand modified the IBM logo but was not satisfied. It seemed too assertive.

He was also concerned that the sequence of the letters from left to right, or narrow to wide, were out of balance. In addition, both the solid and the outline versions of the logo were being used and were found to be confusing. He thought he should improve it, so he did.

Paul said the stripes tie the letters together and "suggest speed and efficiency." I believe the stripes also activate the surrounding white space as if woven into the background. The logo is lively and legible at first glance. It draws the eye but eludes capture. Its ability to endure may be the dual result of its simplicity making a strong first impression and its complexity inviting repeated viewing. Steven Heller believes that the stripes also provide a mnemonic function.

The change was not requested by the client. It was Paul's idea. He was able to implement his redesign not just because he was the corporation's senior graphic design consultant; he also had real "clout," as he was in close touch with "the top guy." Paul often said that both access to and the trust of senior management were key to a designer's effectiveness.

The Eye, Bee, M poster was designed by Paul Rand in 1981. Playing with the IBM logo

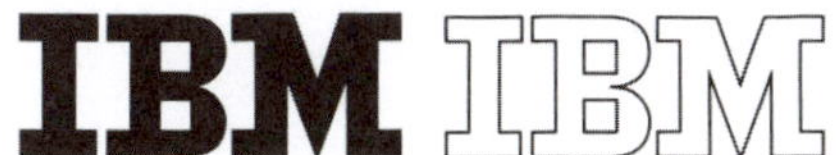

as a rebus meant that Paul gave himself permission to break his own rules. When first shown, some corporate managers feared it would lead other designers astray, but Paul maintained control. Ultimately, both the poster and the logo became classics.

Second: Univers

Paul thought Univers was a bad font when first released. He told several classes of his Yale students to avoid it. Many of those students followed that advice for years. Later, he used Univers frequently—as the primary typeface for Cummins as well as for his book *Paul Rand: A Designer's Art*.

Third: His Last Book

Paul asked me to read the manuscripts of each of his three Yale Press books and comment. He wanted feedback. Did I get it? Would readers get it? His last book, *From Lascaux to Brooklyn*, was perhaps his most misunderstood—a challenge to write and read. It was published in 1996, but he was not satisfied. A bit later, on June 14, he handed me a two-page addendum to the book, which he believed finally got it right. He died on November 26.

In the addendum, Paul states, "The Greeks considered all subjects a form of discourse, and therefore almost all education is a form of language education. . . . Aesthetics is the language of appearances—what things look like—of art, design, of the beautiful, and the ugly. Without aesthetics, talk about art is not about art. . . . Confusion and misunderstanding in the arts is the result of the absence of a common language."

(Opposite) Paul Rand IBM Rebus, 1981.

(Above Left) The two-striped version of the logo was designed in 1962. The eight-line version was specified for most uses. The thirteen-line version was designated for such fine applications as engraving.

(Above Right) The solid and outline versions were done in 1956.The solution was the less static, two-version striped logo of 1962.

Validation

Paul embraced Pragmatism, as it taught him that the truth could change. The philosophy of William James, Charles Peirce, and, most significantly to Paul, John Dewey offered a theoretical grounding for Paul's evolving thoughts and actions.

Sources:

Conversations with Marion and Paul Rand.

Paul Rand: A Designer's Art, by Paul Rand (pages 39 to 42).

THE LEGIBILITY WARS

Steven Heller

"What did you do during the legibility war?" asked one of my more inquisitive design history students.

"Well, it wasn't actually a war," I said, recalling the period during the mid-1980s through the mid-to-late-1990s when a few designers were trying to make a distinction between old and new through illegibility. "It was merely a skirmish, or rather disagreement between a bunch of young designers, like your age now, who followed New Wave, postmodern, PM, PoMo, Swiss Punk, and other antimodern cliques, and who felt it was necessary to replace existing design methods with something freer and more contemporary. Doing that meant attacking the so-called old guard modern designers, who believed design should be simple, clean on tight grids, and Helveticized."

"Do you mean bland?" he quizzed further.

"Maybe some of it! Yet in retrospect it wasn't such a big deal," I insisted. "Still, it was when technology was making a lot of contorted options possible. Aesthetic standards were changing, and younger designers wanted to try everything, while the older, especially the modern ones, believed everything had already been tried."

"I read that Massimo Vignelli called a lot of the new digital and retro stuff 'garbage,'" he said. "What did you say or do about it?"

"Well, I was more or less on the modernist side and wrote about it in an *Eye* essay, 'Cult of the Ugly.' This article was not against illegibility per se, just the stuff that seemed to be done badly. I justified biased distinctions not between beauty and ugly, but good ugly and bad ugly or what was done with an experimental rationale and with merely style and fashion as the motive."

"So you were a reactionary?" he probed.

"I guess so," I responded with guilty annoyance. "But you had to understand the times. The modernists were fighting for their principles in a few academic articles and seminars, but mostly among themselves. I was caught up on both sides but chose to go on record against the larger problem of illegibility, which I defined as ugly. Later, I surrendered to the forces of inevitability and the realization that there was no war to be won, no battle to be fought or skirmish to be had. It was just inevitable that the new computer technology would stimulate new ways of doing things." "Other than a few designers," he asked, "did anyone care?"

"I don't know," I muddled. "But not too many 'anyones' cared about graphic design other than those of us who were involved. Still, it was part of our history."

“Illegibility was a flaw turned into a code used by ’80s graphic designers like psychedelia was for ’60s poster artists. . . . Illegibility was like batting around modernists before the kill.”

That’s exactly why I am writing this personal re-explanation of what the so-called legibility skirmish was all about, where it ended up, and what, if anything, it means today to practitioners, teachers, and scholars. So, where to begin?

Modernism of the 1920s was a revolution in art that replaced outmoded traditions with radical methods of producing art, architecture, design, music, dance, and literature inspired by science and technology—as well as psychology. We still admire the output and celebrate it in countless exhibits and books. Collage, asymmetrical typography, and anarchic layout were raw and exciting—a new language, too. But ultimately, the next stage, Swiss modernism, was hijacked for political and institutional uses. The modernist vocabulary became a means of communicating to and from the global corporate world, which gave way to modernistic styling, perceived as formulaic and triggering alternative styles. The Swiss style’s characteristics included very readable sans serif type—you all know which they were—generous amounts of white space, geometry, and emphasis on simplicity. So, one consequence of the Swiss method is that it ran the gamut from exquisite to bland.

It was the formulaic side that was being critiqued by a new generation of designers who believed design had to have more flexibility than flush left Helvetica and serve more than just corporate identities. So, in 1984, when Apple’s first TV commercial announced that the Macintosh was the next major design tool, young designers embraced the power of the computer, in part to make use of primitive techniques like pixelating, overlapping, underprinting, and serendipitous digital flaws. Illegibility was a flaw turned into a code used by ’80s graphic designers like psychedelia was for ’60s poster artists. Designers were also being a tad sadistic—like cats playing with mice, illegibility was like batting around modernists before the kill.

But legibility is not the same as readability. The sin is not the former, but the latter. It can be argued that when something is illegible, it is unreadable, but in fact, it is readable for those who crack the code.

In the early 1920s, Dada and Surrealist typography broke many of the classical rules of printing but could be read by anyone with the patience to solve the puzzles or pass roadblocks to unfettered comprehension.

In the mid-'80s and '90s, *Emigre* magazine, the voice of the new type and digital typography edited by Rudy VanderLans, was dedicated to showcasing a coterie of avid contra-modernists who railed against dead style in favor of a so-called postmodern or po-mo approach that, in part, questioned the very form and function of type and imagery and the role played by the grid in making type read well. Again, illegibility was only a small part of the questions and answers. But altering these standards often meant taking license both in practice and theory. Katherine McCoy, who ran Cranbook Academy's graphic design program, saw this legibility/readability construct as part of a linguistic evolution. "Visual phenomena are analyzed as language encoded for meaning. Meanings are deconstructed, exposing the dynamics of power and the manipulation of meaning."

Illegibility, such as it was, played out in *Emigre* and niche magazines like David Carson's *Ray Gun* and *Speak*, *Shift*, *Blur*, and *Lava*, among others. But even the complex layering of type, picture, and doodads that gave an impression of illegibility were never entirely indecipherable. For those who had no patience for deciphering, if it wasn't clean, then it was considered illegible. With the first of Rick Poynor's two *Typography Now* books (Edward Booth Clibborn Editions, 1991), the argument about whether or not this was a legitimate type of revolution was given credence. There was enough "new typography" to prove a real generational movement. Poynor's *Typography Now Two: Implosion* (1998) curiously brought closure to the illegibility versus legibility debate, since even the most radical were readable. And his *No More Rules: Graphic Design and Postmodernism* (2003) summed up the whole phenomenon as a complete historical epoch from 1980 to 2000. In fact, illegibility long ceased being a defining postmodern issue years before the last regular issue of *Emigre* (#69) in 2005.

The real revolution was technology, which starkly increased the power of women in design, and the number of women experimenting with illegibility and readability was considerable. April Greiman had been entrenched in modernism until 1984; when the first Macintosh was introduced, she embraced it with gusto. While most graphic designers were skeptical or afraid of its mystery, Greiman established herself as the pioneer, specifically of digital comingling collage of video and still photography with type. Her mixed media work was called New Wave in the design press, but it defied imposed labels. "She had been rocking the modernist boat for a few years when she undertook a major assault upon the design community's sensibilities and preconceptions of what constitutes design in 1986, in an issue of *Design Quarterly*," stated the American Institute of Graphic Arts in 1998, when she received its Lifetime Medal of Achievement. Published by the Walker Art Center, Greiman was the subject and designer of *Design Quarterly* #133. It was thus an opportunity not only to present her digital work, but as the AIGA noted, "to ask a larger question of the work and the medium: Does it make sense? Reading Wittgenstein on the topic, she identified with his conclusion: 'It makes sense if you give it sense.'" Illegibility was simply an outcome of other perceptual experiments. Greiman trashed the standard thirty-two-page format, which she remade into a poster that folded out to almost three by six feet. On the front is a pixelated image of Greiman's naked body amid layers of text and image; it also included notations on the digital process all composed within Macintosh and MacDraw. "Beyond considering whether digital technologies made sense, the *Design Quarterly* poster seemed to embody the disillusionment of a nation deeply wounded by the Vietnam war and shaped by the growth of feminism, spiritualism, Eastern religion, Jungian archetypes, and dream symbolism."

Digital typeface design was a significant postmodern outlier, and no one captured the essence and evolution of the 1980s and 1990s better than Zuzana Licko, the designer of such early digital fonts as the pixel Lo-Res and dot-matrix Matrix. Dozens of her faces both precise and grungy, classical and novel, helped to typographically define graphic design that can in some instances pinpoint PM's moment of conception and in others, like Mr & Mrs Eaves, have the timeless look that defies the stereotypes and clichés of either ism. This type was not illegible. It was type! Type is legible by definition. Users could do whatever they pleased with it. And while some layered and distorted it, others used it straight up and easily readable. The fact that messages needed to be read was never a question. Only how they'd be read was of concern—and who would read them. I contend the illegibility skirmish was about designers talking to other designers. It was a natural outgrowth of a profession in transition.

Today, all kinds of design theatrics coexist separately or together. Rather than one or two dominant styles, there are multiple personalities in graphic design, and a lot more on video and digital screens. The experimental versus classical debate discourse may occasionally flare up—as will the difference between readability and legibility—but the polarization that spiced up the earlier argument is over. In its wake is the sense that graphic designers are freer from hard-and-fast rules, but rarely is the issue more radical than that.

CH5

For over two years, I wrote a column for *Print* magazine that covered history through artifacts of major and minor significance. These were often used as jumping-off points for design history classes. Here are a selected few.

MISE EN PAGE

Steven Heller

During the nascent years of modernism in the early 1920s and 1930s, certain eminent designers in Europe and the United States delighted in telling other designers how, and what, to design. These self-appointed prophets were so convinced they had discovered graphic design's holy grail—rightness of form—they wanted everyone in eye- and earshot to revel in their revelations. To spread the Word (and image), they frequently issued sermons from the mount in the form of verbose manifestos and detailed manuals. Most proved inconsequential; a few, such as W. A. Dwiggins's *Layout in Advertising* and Jan Tschichold's *die Neue Typografie* (The New Typography), both published in 1928, endured. The former laid out rigid rules of contemporary advertising design, while the latter foretold progressive mannerisms and styles that did, in fact, take hold.

But it was another, more commercially oriented book, appearing a few years later, that defined the new mainstream aesthetic of the period and became, arguably, the design bible of all design bibles. Alfred Tolmer's *Mise en Page: The Theory and Practice of Layout*, published in 1932 in separate English and French editions (Dwiggins's and Tschichold's books at that time were only published in English in the United States and in German in Germany, respectively), codified the most widely practiced of all the early twentieth-century design styles. Advertised in the leading design journals, and sought after by European and American advertising artists, *Mise en Page* (the French term for layout) was a lavishly printed primer of that strain of design then called *moderne*, and subsequently dubbed art deco.

Tolmer's tome was an ambitious and alluring treatise on contemporary style. His goal was to position deco in history and provide formal guidelines, while at the same time encouraging opportunities for inventive design options, thus luring some business to his firm. With slip-sheets, tip-ons, embossed and debossed pages, and fold-outs, the book itself was a model of eclectic mastery, a template for all designers who wanted to be on the crest of a stylish wave.

Cover of English edition of *Mise en Page*, 1932.

In *Mise en Page*, Tolmer co-opted fundamental aspects of apolitical modernism for commercial application. Photomontage, then considered the foremost progressive design conceit (Moholy-Nagy called it "mechanical art for a mechanical age"), is given considerable attention in Tolmer's hierarchy. "Photography gives concrete form to the subtlest thoughts," he wrote. "It has the gift of imparting the dullest, most mechanical and impersonal things the sensitiveness and poetry which admits them into our dreams." These words may be more flowery than those found in the typical modernist manifesto, but they are no less committed to a cause. And they exemplify how Tolmer fervently and singlehandedly smoothed the edges off orthodox modernism, making once-radical design concepts palatable for business and the masses.

Tolmer, who died in 1957, is not as well known today as Dwiggins or Tschichold, but he played a significant role in the French printing and advertising industries. He was the third generation of the prestigious Parisian printing house Maison Tolmer, which produced some of the most stylish graphics in France for luxe publications and packaging, fashioning a diverse array of exquisitely conceived printed commercial products, from elegant boxes to advertising posters and publicity brochures. In addition to overseeing the output of his family's firm, Tolmer edited art books and catalogs and illustrated covers for magazines and children's books: a true design auteur.

While his writing was a bit strained (maybe a result of bad French-to-English translation), he did his utmost to present solid intellectual arguments for why modern/*moderne* design was the perfect form for the age. Tolmer began by posing the idea that writing and design were one and the same. "The art of lay-out," he wrote, "is born at the moment when man feels the urge to arrange in an orderly fashion the expression of his thoughts. The first writing is a decorative setting in itself, a symbolic décor closely connected with the décor that is purely ornamental."

This vivid presentation of *moderne* design appeared at exactly the right moment. The visual genre was introduced to the world in Paris at the *Exposition Internationale des Arts Décoratifs Industriels Modernes* in 1925, and the new, ornamental sensibility quickly became the vogue for all the applied arts throughout the industrialized and commercialized world. A style of affluence at the outset, deco trickled down to the bourgeoisie, skirting the ideological overlays of its mingled modernist traits. Cubist, Futurist, Constructivist, de Stijl, even Bauhaus elements were absorbed by *moderne*; rectilinear geometries and sans serif typefaces combined with stark ornamental patterns such as sunrays, lightning bolts, motion lines, and other symbols of Machine-Age progress.

Between the world wars, design entrepreneurs like Tolmer understood that, given the ebbs and flows in European and American consumption brought about by the financial roller coaster of the world markets, this kind of high style was needed to position goods. Styling was touted by marketing and advertising experts as a tool of allure that encouraged sales in everything consumable.

For all its popularity, *Mise en Page* was not always easy to obtain. The book earned a reputation that far exceeded its initial French edition printing of 1,500 copies and comparable English language editions simultaneously published by prestigious London design publisher Studio Books and New York–based William Rudge (the publisher of the original *PRINT*). Each edition reportedly sold out within three months of release, but designers who never laid their hands on the original were given some access to it through excerpts in leading trade magazines like the German *Gebrauchsgraphik* and French *Arts et Métiers Graphiques.*

Mise en Page's astute sampling of modernistic methodologies convinced contemporary designers they were essential: with Tolmer's boost, deco lasted more or less until the outbreak of World War II, when an austerity binge hit Europe. Elements of deco were incorporated into subsequent styles, but for the most part simplicity ruled design. In 1966, following a retrospective exhibition, "Les Années '25', held at the Musée des Arts Décoratifs" in Paris, the allure of deco artifacts triggered a rash of pastiche. Today the original artifacts are treasured as midcentury gems in exhibitions (like one in 2003 at the Victoria & Albert Museum that traveled to the Museum of Fine Arts in Boston in 2004), and updated versions of this stunning decorative mannerism are routinely injected into contemporary design.

ABSTRACTION

Steven Heller

Before the Abstract Expressionists seized control of American university art departments during the post–World War II era, nonobjective art had influenced an earlier generation of graphic designers who were inspired by the progressive artist/designers of Europe's early twentieth-century avant-garde. There was excitement by the potential of blending fine and commercial art, and the designers saw their mission was to modernize how graphic design and illustration were practiced and perceived. As it happened, passions for and against modernity caused huge rifts between traditional and progressive practitioners, which was nowhere more volatile than among American realist illustrators who were committed to romantic and sentimental fashions of the 1930s, 1940s, and 1950s. And although graphic designers were not as stubborn about maintaining an aesthetic dogma, traditional and modern designers also argued over the efficacy of abstraction as a means of graphic communication.

The schism between modernity and tradition occurred at the turn of the century, when, as an offshoot of the Russian Revolution, progressive art movements such as Suprematism, Cubo-Futurism, and Constructivism were raising the banner of geometric/abstraction. A revolutionary alternative to bourgeois decorative styles, these and kindred movements triggered the radicalism of graphic designers who believed that abstraction was the gateway to enlightenment, which for a time it was.

Early twentieth-century American graphic design history was partly defined by the resistance to and acceptance of abstraction. Initially kept at arm's length, since the primary role of graphic design was to sell and convey a client's messages, mainstream American commercial artists viewed abstraction as antithetical to their mandate, which was clarity. Still, graphic design has never existed in a cultural vacuum, and so it was inevitable that modern art would influence and even dominate the field in various ways through work by young designers and art directors who bucked rules and conventions and found ways to make the abstract more viable.

It took a longer time to catch on in the United States, where agencies and studios feared that abstraction (which was tantamount to anarchy) might shock and dismay their clients. But ever since the Armory Show in 1913, abstraction had appealed to a growing number of artists and designers. Some belonged to organizations like the American Abstract Artists (AAA) in New York, founded in 1936 to exhibit their work and engender support. The graphic designers who belonged to AAA, rather

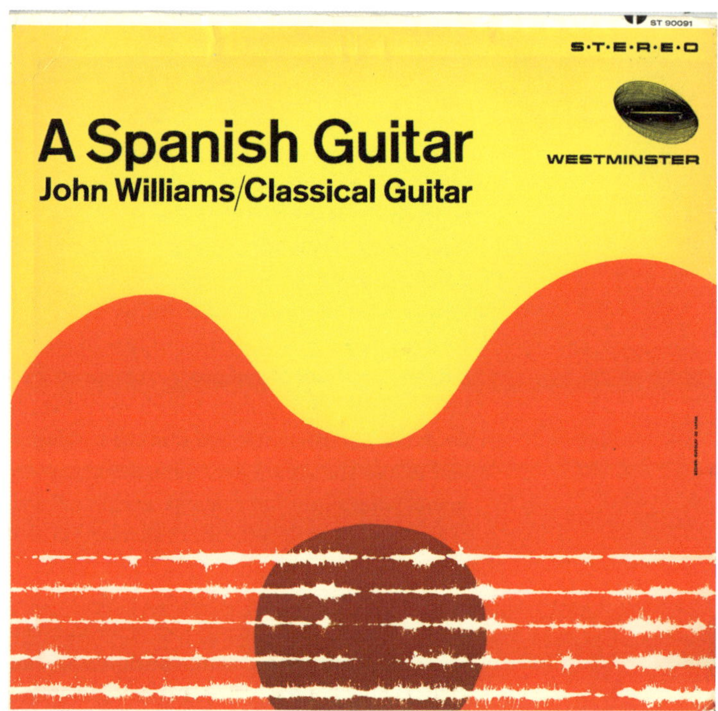

Rudolph de Harak uses an abstract motif to suggest the shape and strings of a guitar.

than inject abstraction into their design work, instead found an outlet by painting on the weekends. Of course, ultimately, it took a few intrepid designers to push the barriers that introduced abstraction into the American design lexicon.

In Europe, designers like Richard Lohse and Max Bill had long advocated abstraction in their art, although it spilled into their graphic design. In the United States Paul Rand and Lester Beall, among others, were recognized for introducing hybrid contemporary styles, mixing Cubism, Futurism, de Stijl, and other abstract avant-garde aesthetics together in a design stew that has passed the test of time. What the Germans call *gesamtkunstwerk* or the "total work of art" was a philosophical concept arguing that fine art and commercial design could together be a complete work where the languages of art and commerce existed as one. Adherents believed it was existentially important for art of all kinds to be integrated in daily life, and those fellow travelers within the graphic design world (designers like Alvin Lustig, E. McKnight Kauffer, and George Guisti) used abstraction in designing their book covers, advertisements, and posters.

These are common methods today, but when first introduced, they threatened the status quo. It became the job of leading design trade journals published in many countries around the world (most notably the Zurich-based *Graphis*) to promote the capacity for abstraction to transcend the commonplace and amplify rather than conceal a client's message. The trade journals may have been complicit in spreading the gospel of abstraction, but rarely at the expense of the ultimate goal of the graphic design profession—conveying that message.

Print was one of the journals that celebrated convention but also pushed the envelope. *Print*'s February / March 1957 edition was unique for giving an entire issue over to Bob Cato, the respected record album art director/designer, to produce what a brief editorial statement called "a highly personal document" devoted to "Sources of Inspiration." Abstraction was one of these sources. Cato addressed how many different factors influenced contemporary design and how for over half a century, abstract art and design had gradually merged into a shared visual language resulting in methods and styles that continued into the midcentury modern movement (and continues in various ways today),

Rudolph de Harak applies geometric abstraction to suggest the sound of many trumpets.

but it also raised the question about how commercial art that was required to communicate messages without ambiguity could engage in ambiguous abstraction.

Although abstract work requires deciphering, even the purest abstraction is not entirely incomprehensible. Meaning exists in everything, and although translating an abstract code may be challenging, once the key is in the door, it unlocks the secrets. Nonetheless, abstract design was only appropriate for certain kinds of clients where the messages are more cerebral than tactile. For instance, automobiles are not ideal subjects for abstraction, whereas pharmaceutical products are.

Abstract graphic design practice owes much to Picasso and Gris, of course, who used typography in some of their own paintings. Paul Klee was also a beacon on the hill for many. Yet for this special *Print*, the first inspirational example shown is Piet Mondrian's *Broadway Boogy Woogy*: "No matter how many times you see his work," wrote Cato, "the completely new world that he uncovered through painting constantly gives inspiration to painters, architects, typographers and designers."

George Guisti uses an abstract design to interpret Rachmaninoff's symphony.

Alvin Lustig's divider page is designed under the influence of Russian Constructivism with a dynamic, geometric abstract design.

"In graphic design, rebirth is often met with caution, if not suspicion and resistance, yet abstraction allowed commercial artists more creative options for expression."

Jackson Pollock defined abstraction as "energy and motion made visible." Abstraction in graphic design meant starting totally and passionately anew. "I want to be new born," wrote Paul Klee, "knowing nothing, absolutely nothing, about Europe; ignoring poets and fashion, to be almost primitive. Then I want to do something very modest; to work out by myself a tiny, formal motive, one that my pencil will be able to hold without technique." Although this quotation is not exclusively about the power of abstract art, it implies that new ways of seeing and communicating were erupting in all the arts.

In graphic design, rebirth is often met with caution, if not suspicion and resistance, yet abstraction allowed commercial artists more creative options for expression. While there are those designers content to follow the standards and rules, others saw abstract methods that could imbue client work into a kind of personal expression. In the long run, abstraction created a bounty of visual tropes: overlapping, transparent color; random geometric forms; and amorphic shapes. Abstraction as a style method also enabled designers to leave cumbersome literalism behind and make commercial art that stimulated the conscious and subconscious on many levels. By the 1980s, abstraction was so vernacular that its original avant-garde-ness had evaporated into professional/corporate cliché but remained an integral option for many designers. When the digital typographic wave hit during the late '80s and throughout the '90s, abstraction took a different turn. Rather than building on geometry, it became anarchic (and grunge). Arguably, it was truer to Abstract Expressionism. Today, abstract coexists with retro with anarchic with classic. It is part of a large scheme that marks the utter diversity that constitutes the graphic design playroom. Its influence is its continuum. It came and never really left.

A TYPE CATALOG LEGACY

Steven Heller

The end of mass-market commercial letterpress printing in the second half of the twentieth century was also the death knell of metal and wood type founding as a flourishing industry. After five hundred years, the moveable type revolution gave way to photocomposition and then (if you don't count press-type) to digital typefaces in various programmatic incarnations, which reduced the need for factory-foundries. "Physically, the only remaining vestige of an American foundry," wrote Maurice Annenberg in *Type Foundries of America and Their Catalogs* (originally published in 1975 in an edition of five hundred and reprinted in 1994 by Oak Knoll Press), "could be an old worn type catalog. "

A commercial printer who had an early interest in studying and chronicling the history of his profession, Annenberg (1907–1979) collected a substantial library of rare printing manuals, journals, and type specimen books that serve among the raw materials of design history—and are today both treasured and fetishized. "The artists and designers of the present century," Annenberg wrote over forty years ago, "now find these catalogs extremely valuable in tracing old alphabets to be used as a pattern in creating 'new' typefaces using the photo distortion camera."

When his extensive research into America's foundries and their catalogs was first published, Annenberg noted that printing arts librarians reported that the pilfering of vintage catalogs had increased tenfold during the 1970s over previous decades. Type and graphic designers realized that their value as an original resource for exotic and eccentric fonts was garnering new appreciation, resulting in the emergence of classical revivals and contemporary retro graphics. Type vendors like Morgan Press and Tri-Arts sold antique nineteenth-century wood and metal types, while Dover Publications, among others, published clip art books filled with copyright-free reproductions of pages containing full or partial alphabets and a wide range of printing ornaments taken directly from the original foundry specimens.

Decades earlier, sample books were routinely given freely to customers as part of their printing toolkits offered by foundries, which in addition to type included presses, binding, and folding machines, and other hardware. These books were so heavy that sales agents often complained about having to carry so many. New ones were kept for a while; old ones were discarded since they took up so much space. Eventually, large books gave way to sheets and brochures. Few at the time could predict that the specimen books would eventually become rare, expensive artifacts. (In fact, twice during the early 1970s, I was given the opportunity to sift through the stores of catalog and specimen libraries from two failed printing companies that had no further need for their respective hoards. One of them simply left the material in a flatbed truck parked for a week on a street in lower Manhattan.)

Yet not all these materials were summarily trashed. Columbia University in New York purchased the American Type Founders (ATF) library in 1941. Begun in 1908, the 1923 ATF catalog summed up the importance of their archive this way: "The collections in the library include type specimen books and broadsides from 1486 to the present time. . . . The Typographic Library and Museum assumes the duty of collecting and preserving the memorabilia of printing and printers of all nations."

Type specimen books are wellsprings of all kinds of sociohistorical (and even political) documentation. The late nineteenth century, for example, was the early era of what could be seen as "capitalist modern" printing in most industrialized nations of the world. Type foundries were integral to the publishing of information, but also to selling goods and services through advertising and packaging. Type was not just a means, as it was in Gutenberg's time, for efficiently propagating religious teachings or, later, in making government decrees and bureaucratic declarations. Nor were books and magazines the primary customers as literacy increased. The rise of industry and spread of commerce created a need for an entire printing industry, and, of course, distinctive type designs played a large role in articulating the importance of business and the joys of consumption.

Type itself became a competitive business, and the majority of late nineteenth and early twentieth-century catalogs were designed to sell. Typical of the kind of sales text in specimen books is the following from an obscure New York foundry, Adorinam Chandler & Co., which Annenberg stated "is obscured in type founding history and the only tangible legacy is his type catalog," which announced in a preface that "The ornamental types exhibited in this specimen are cast in stereotypical plates, and the letter separately fixed to wooden bottoms. . . . Printers are left to judge for themselves, whether it is not a saving to buy this, instead of giving forty-two cents per pound for type metal." And the following, from the 1893 Boston-based Dickenson Type Foundry book, admonished type that was "cast from Copper Alloy Metal," the "Lightest and most durable in the world," that "The arrangement and printing of these pages is the result of necessary haste, but we bespeak the leniency of their printer when considering these imperfections in connection with the large labor involved."

"Type specimen books for some young designers are vestiges, while for others they are gems of legacy. The era of these kinds of elaborate bibles of typeface design is long over . . ."

A.M. Cassandre's Bifur typeface from a Deberny and Peignot type specimen, 1929.

PRINT designed to influence us is "somewhat like love—one does not *judge* it, one submits to it." And then Cassandre, esthetic Parisian, goes on to say that advertising "is not a game, but a natural phenomenon like night and day—one of the most beautiful results of contemporary activity." The poster

Catalogs made clear to customers that while their faces may not be the latest fashions, they were reliable. From the Western Type Foundry in Chicago and St. Louis in 1909 comes this: ". . . whenever you see the name WESTERN TYPE—it is as good as the type made by the foundries 20 years ago. . . . Better material was never made than that which goes into WESTERN TYPE."

The problem with publishing specimen books was keeping up with the newly designed faces. The Inland Type Foundry preface from 1906 asserted: "The printing of a specimen book requires time, and the Inland Type Foundry produces new faces with such rapidity that a new edition was scarcely off the press until it was, to some extent, obsolete, as one or [more] faces had been produced while the book was going thru the press." It added that "The experiment was tried of issuing supplements, but this was found unsatisfactory. Often they were received by people

(Opposite) Agency Gothic from an American Type Founders catalog, c. 1935. (This page) Gothic blocks and sans serif shadow face specimen c.1940.

who thought them to be ordinary circulars and threw them in the wastebasket." The answer the realized was a loose-leaf volume for updates—so innovative that Inland wrote: "We particularly request that you designate some person who shall receive these supplements and shall have positive instructions to place them in the book as soon as they come to hand . . . [and] promptly send us the name of this person."

One specimen book generally looked a lot like another, though each handled samples differently. In *Alphabets to Order: The Literature of Nineteenth-Century Typefounders' Specimens* (Oak Knoll Books, 2000), type historian and printer Alistair Johnston analyzes the typographic/ word juxtapositions in scores of catalogs. For example, the line "HAMBURGH Beautiful Sierras" was on the same page as "ARTISTIC SELECTION / The Modern Sciences 2567." In another, from Chicago's Union Type Foundry, was the line "MONOPLE RARE / CHANCE TIDBITS / 23 MERE 62," which seems like an arbitrary selection with a touch of absurdist modern poetry.

One of my favorite combinations was an 1894 ad for Inland with the headline "This Is Not Pi" set in a rash of different faces. For those who don't know the term, PI is when a case or chase is accidently dropped and all the types are a mess of mixed-up sizes. This ad is reminiscent of the Futurist and Dada typographic mischief that began more than a decade later.

Type specimen books for some young designers are vestiges, while for others they are gems of legacy. The era of these kinds of elaborate bibles of typeface design is long over; digital times require digital samples with "test-drive" capacity and other type manipulating software (like http:// metapolator.com/home/). Some digital foundries continue to produce paper specimen sheets and posters, if only to pay homage to the past, and to leave an analog collectible behind. Still, like the bibles they were, paging through a vintage type book is a mix of religious and ecstatic experience.

BOOK AND THE TIME MACHINE

Steven Heller

In *The Time Machine*, H. G. Wells predicts that by the twenty-first century, books will be replaced by audio rings. In Ray Bradbury's *Fahrenheit 451*, futuristic firemen burn books to extinguish knowledge. And in *Star Trek: The Next Generation*, the crew of the Starship Enterprise inhabit a paperless twenty-fourth century where books are relics. In fiction, the book's future looks dim. In fact, it remains a vessel of cultural achievement. Digital media will not supplant the book. Print is not dead.

But ever since Gutenberg introduced moveable type, print has indeed been mutable. The book has been a laboratory for writers, artists, designers, and typographers, from ancient scribes to contemporary fontographers. Although circumscribed by a cover and inside pages, the book is no more constrained than any other medium and no less vast than any other art form. The very rules and regulations that govern book design and production incite rebellion. Efforts at altering the book's basic form have changed publishing paradigms and readers' perceptions.

During the late nineteenth century, when book publishing was spurred on by increased literacy throughout populations in the world's industrialized nations, artists and designers used the book to influence popular opinion and taste. For those who saw the potential of mass communications, the book was an unparalleled tool. Periodicals were immediate, albeit ephemeral, but the redoubtable book had long-term impact. Its objectness made it a permanent fixture. Its heft made it

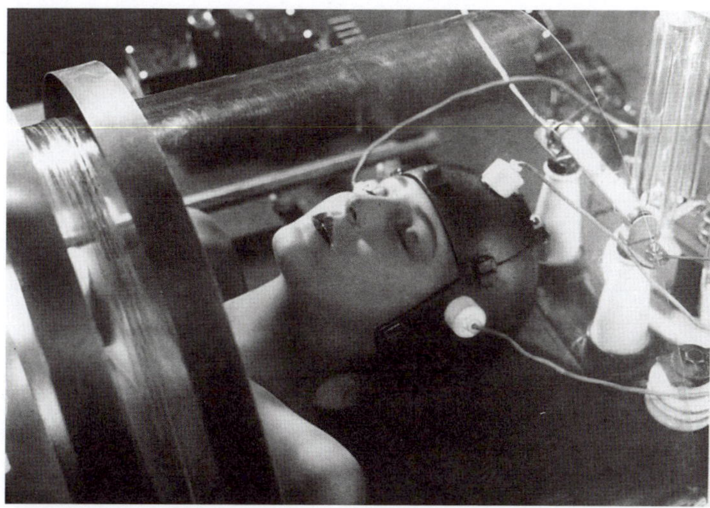

The book has been pronounced dead many times. Many alternatives have been attempted. Could this mind control machine be viable?

The future has already been decided. This is El Lissitzky's design for Mayakovsky's *For the Voice* (1923), a progressive alternative to the layout and makeup of interactive poetry. Those tabs on the side, which iconically indicate the distinct poems, prefigure the computer icons we rely on today.

difficult to ignore. But so not to be a doorstop, a book also had to be visually compelling.

The designer's role was to attract the reticent and support the loyal reader by complementing the narrative with visual content. Some book designers drew inspiration from history. In the 1896 *The Works of Geoffrey Chaucer*, designer and philosopher William Morris revived medieval illumination and introduced new cuts of old humanist typefaces. Other designers embraced modernity. In the 1908 version of *Ecce Homo*, architect and designer Henry van de Velde replaced antiquated graphics with art nouveau ornamentation. While a majority of commercial book publishers were content to produce pages of uninterrupted text, enlightened publishers viewed the total integration of type and image as the highest form of printed art.

The history of book design has been well chronicled by Joseph Blumenthal's *The Printed Book in America* (David R. Godine) and *The Art of the Printed Book, 1455–1955* (David R. Godine), Adrian Wilson's *The Design of Books* (Chronicle Books), and *John Lewis's The 20th Century Book: Its Illustration and Design* (Herbert Press), making a summary unnecessary here. However, addressing exactly what it is that constitutes creative innovation in book design, the subject of this unique exhibition, is necessary to appreciate how the designer has contributed to the evolution of the medium.

If an idea is the heart of a book, writing is its blood, and design is its circulatory system. Elements of design cannot be underestimated. A book that is merely composed according to a template, rather than designed with forethought and imagination, may be adequate for reading yet lacks the quality that makes it a complete experience. While a great text will conjure mental pictures, a great design—the marriage of type, typography, and image—will give the reader added levels of perception that encourage cognition and appreciation. Even the most rudimentary design components—the texture of the paper, the kiss of a fine cut of type, the style of the running heads or feet—are much more than aesthetic niceties.

By the late nineteenth century, the designer's job was to package a book's contents using complementary illumination, illustration, and typography. By the early twentieth century, as art itself busted strict academic conventions, design became an integral part of the content, as well. Filippo Marinetti's 1914 Italian Futurist manifesto, *Zang Tumb Tuuum,* turned book composition on its ear by introducing on the same page multiple typefaces in varying weights and sizes (an arduous task for even the most skilled compositor). The type was further arranged so

In 1927, Fortunato Depero's *The Bolted Book* symbolized the advent of the mechanical age and was a portent of what the next age of bookmaking could be.

(This page) Books may or may not transform into multisensory experiences. But that's nothing new. Books like *Words in Freedom*, designed by Bruno Munari in 1933, were bound in tin.

(Oppossite)
F. T. Marinetti, a poet and author, made use of onomatopoeia to give the sensation of sound to the reader. *Words in Freedom*, 1919.

that it approximated the roar of the machinery and engines described in the text. Lazar El Lissitzky's 1923 Russian Constructivist classic, *For the Voice*, a collection of Mayakovsky's poems designed to be read aloud at public gatherings, transformed text type into pictograms, which gave the reader additional cues to follow for both inflection and meaning. And Fortunato Depero's *Depero: Futurista* (referred to as "the bolted book" because it was bound with two metal bolts) kineticized type so that reading the text was like experiencing the movement of a high-speed vehicle. These books were not neutral containers, but stages upon which words and images performed.

Innovation in book design is not, however, defined solely by radical departures from the norm. Many book designers sought to replicate classical forms. For example, the American type designer Frederic Goudy's 1918 *The Alphabet and Elements of Lettering* is based on central axis composition born of seventeenth- and eighteenth-century Italian and French book traditions, but not indentured to them. This book was composed with his own typefaces and ornaments (influenced by the past) in an effort to achieve balance, harmony, flow, and contemporaneity. Similarly, Eric Gill's 1936 *An Essay on Typography* paid homage to the standards established by seventeenth-century Venetian printers yet was imbued with a contemporary spirit fitting his time and place. Likewise, W. A. Dwiggins, who provided a link between the turn-of-the-century Aesthetic Movement and later trends in modern design, designed and illustrated a 1930 limited edition version of *The Time*

Les mots
en liberté
futuristes

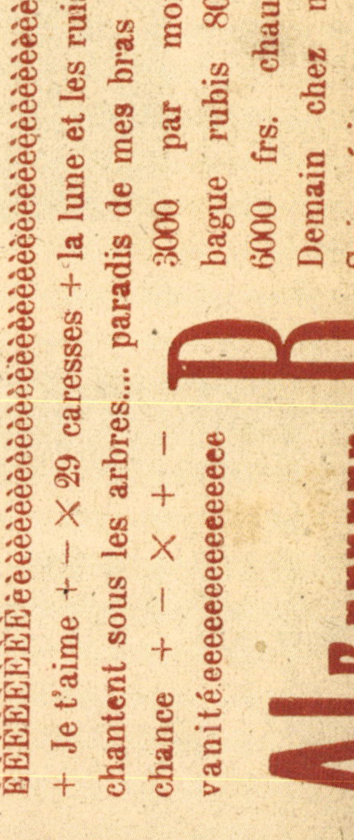

EDIZIONI FUTURISTE
DI "POESIA"
Corso Venezia, 61 - MILANO
1919

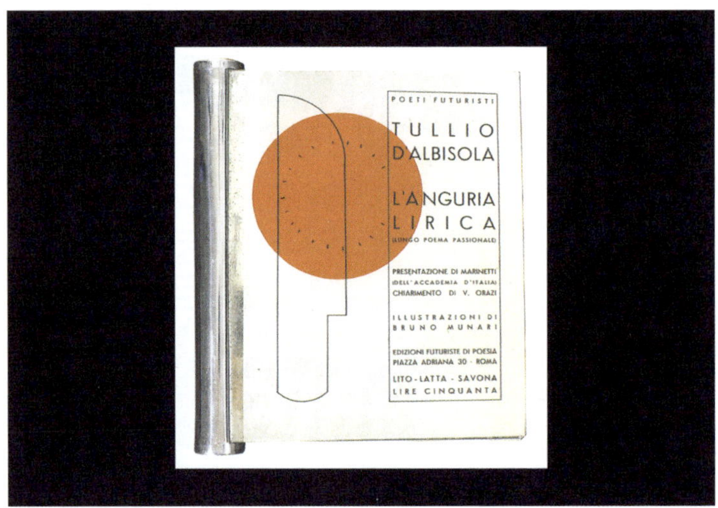

This metal book is a masterpiece of futurist making. It was as much a portent of the future as ebooks are today.

Machine, where he observed tradition but introduced contemporary graphic elements that interpreted the futuristic (and apocalyptic) nature of the text. By upholding tradition, though not slavishly replicating old-fashioned templates, book designers such as these bridged the past and present. But what about the future?

"Tradition, to be a creative force, must be constantly under construction," wrote designer John Begg in the catalog for the 1951 exhibition *Books of Our Time*. "It must be moving, even going too far on occasion, rather than never going far enough." The demands of the twentieth century indeed required demonstrative changes (or forced obsolescence) in commerce. Yet only one book was bold enough to wed experimental ideas to commercial requisites. Jan Tschichold's 1928 *Die Neue Typographie* was a design manual that vigorously rejected past verities. In Germany, where it was originally published, antiquated design standards were imposed on all printers. The spiky medieval Gothic typeface Fraktur that was used in most German printing made it impossible to design books in a modern manner. In 1925, as guest editor of an otherwise staid trade magazine, *Typographische Mitteilungen*, Tschichold introduced German printers and designers to new trends in European avant-garde typographic experimentation. He demonstrated that decorative ornament was unnecessary, central axis layout was unsuitable, and antiquated typefaces were unresponsive to contemporary needs. Compared to Marinetti's cacophonous Futurist books, *Die Neue Typographie* was undeniably disciplined.

"If the book is endangered, it is not because people are reading or buying fewer books, it is because pushing the boundaries is a costly gamble."

But as a synthesis of Italian, Dutch, German, and Russian avant-garde experiments, Tschichold developed a design system that could be flawlessly followed by any printer or designer while still offering surprising variations. *Die Neue Typographie* pushed the boundaries of functionality and radically altered convention.

Yet Tschichold was considered a purist—rigid when imposing the rules of modernity on books (and graphic design in general). A. Tolmer, a contemporary Parisian typographer, was not as inflexible, and in 1931, he wrote and designed *Mise en Page*, a style guide for designers who were not yet sold on the austerity of the New Typography. While Tschichold fought to rein in unruly eclecticism, Tolmer celebrated it as tool for attracting the reader (and consumer). His followers were commercial artists who preferred ornament to economy. His notions sampled the avant-garde but smoothed out the edges. *Mise en Page* was a twentieth-century illuminated manuscript, full of complex printing novelties (embossing, metallic foils, and die cuts), designed to show the full range of contemporary reproduction technologies.

Tschichold and Tolmer represented two distinct paths of twentieth-century book design. The former used design as frame for content; the latter used design as an end in itself, where text was but one component of a larger experience. The history of mid- to late-twentieth-century innovative book design can be summed up as a conflict between these two preferences. Although the results of the latter appear to the more innovative, in fact, innovation in functional design is decidedly harder to achieve.

Tolmer's *Mise en Page* removes constraints and gives an illusion of freedom. It further prefigures other books that are rooted in a play principle. What might be referred to as art-based books, such as Tullio d'Albisola's 1934 *Parole in libertá futuriste*, Richard Hamilton's 1960 *The Bride Stripped Bare* by Marcel Duchamp, Dieter Roth's 1964 *Snow*, and Tom Philips's 1980 *A Humument: A Treated Victorian Novel*, represent a high level of experimentation and play—what John Begg might describe as going "too far on occasion." But the functional book has many more obstacles to overcome. In such books as Paul Rand's 1945 *The Tables of the Law* by Thomas Mann and Alvin Lustig's 1949 *Native Arts of the Pacific Northwest,* design purposely is not conspicuous, but rather frames the text and pictures to encourage optimum readability. Books like these, which must address a mass audience rather than initially satisfying the creator's muse, have pushed the book further along in its commercial evolution.

To arbitrarily play with the form would be irresponsible. Nevertheless, to extend the boundaries within the requisites of the various material is indeed responsible—and necessary. Books like Ladislav Sutnar's 1950 *Catalog Design Progress,* Herbert Bayer's 1953 *World Geo-Graphic Atlas,* Erik Nitsche's 1965 *Dynamic America,* and Bradbury Thompson's 1980 *Washburn College Bible,* reveal a highly sophisticated vocabulary that has become the cornerstone of modern functional design. Sutnar's book organizes largely disparate material into a unified whole. Bayer's book makes concrete and readable vast amounts of complex data. Nitsche's book incorporates principles of film to direct the reader's eye on the page. And Thompson's book makes a cluttered morass of scripture into an elegant tapestry of ideas.

Books continued to evolve throughout the twentieth century. Richard Eckersley's 1986 *The Telephone Book,* Abbott Miller and Ellen Lupton's 1991 *The ABC's of . . . The Bauhaus & Design Theory,* and Skolos and Wedell's 1992 *Ferrington Guitars*—each book revealed that conveying information clearly is the key to success. As manifesto or entertainment, book designs that ignored or defied conventional functionality tested the limits of creativity and the standards that govern them. Such book designs as Massin's 1964 *The Bald Soprano,* John Cage's 1973 *M: Writings 67–72* and Bruce Mau's 1995 *S,M,L&XL* have exerted a huge impact on how the paradigms of type and image now allow for more reader interactivity. Even functional designers approach the structure and form of books differently in the light of this new thinking.

The book is going through a simultaneous experimental revival and a conservative retrenchment. On the one hand, progressive commercial publishers agree that for a book to compete in today's market, it has to sound some of the same bells and whistles as high-tech media. On the other, most mainstream publishers are concerned with holding the bottom line and are, therefore, unwilling to invest the money (and charge the higher cover price) needed to go the extra distance to make a book truly unconventional. If the book is endangered, it is not because people are reading or buying fewer books, it is because pushing the boundaries is a costly gamble.

Yet during the past decades, some novel book designs and packages, like Skolos and Wedell's *Ferrington Guitars*, Bruce Mau's *S,M,L&XL*, Nick Bantock's 1991 *Griffin & Sabine*, David Carson's 1996 *Cyclops*, and Jonathan Barnbrook's 1997 *Damien Hirsch* (a veritable catalog of pop-ups, pull-outs, slip-sheets, and die cuts), not only receive additional critical notice, but reach a wide range of bibliophiles who appreciate the book-as-object. When a designer is encouraged by a publisher to step over the edge, the effect is often to enrich the standards of the field and expand the reader's anticipation.

The book designer's role as form-giver and content-provider, brought on by new technologies, makes the book fertile ground for creativity. These abilities, coupled with an understanding and respect for tradition, increase the potential for further innovation. Despite predictions to the contrary, the book is still viable. Yet as boundless as it may be, the definition of a book may demand revision. The digital "readers" are making inroads, and the iPad just may be the corner that will be turned in the future of the book.

Nonetheless, let's return to the fictitious twenty-fourth century. As a respite from seeking out new worlds, Star Trek's Jean-Luc Picard sits in his captain's seat with a rare, leather-bound relic in his hand. Even in the most futuristic science fiction projections, the book continues to hold a place of honor.

CH6

VISUAL LITERATURE 101

Warren Lehrer

Every year, on the first day of my Writing and Designing the Visual Book class at the "Designer as Author" MFA program at the School of Visual Arts, I give a talk on Visual Literature. I am continually revising and updating the talk, and I also present versions of it, in various lengths, as part of visiting artists' gigs at other colleges and universities. A majority of the time, I'm presenting this talk to graphic design students; sometimes it's to students studying book arts, new media, oral history, creative writing, or digital humanities.

At the beginning of the talk, I try not to define what I mean by Visual Literature—as my definition is broad, and my hope is that the talk itself, and the wide range of work I show, ends up answering the question as well as posing new ones about what this deeply historical and very alive field might consist of. In the context of the SVA class or the Artist/Writer Workshop class I teach at SUNY Purchase (both studio courses), this introductory survey functions as a kind of superconcentrated Vis Lit 101, containing historical and contemporary examples of different subgenres, followed up throughout the semester with lots of show-and-tell.

As much I love turning people on to things they never knew about, I wish more students—especially graduate design students—were familiar with the work I'm showing them. The fact of the matter is: **while the field of graphic design and its historians proudly equate the origins of graphic design with cultural productions of early twentieth-century poet/painters, radical language artists, utopians, and revolutionaries, it defines contemporary graphic design practice primarily as a commercial enterprise based largely on a corporate service model.** Even today, with all the talk of authorship, collaboration, storytelling, and *design for good* echoing around graphic design pedagogy, most

All images from Visual Literature 101 Keynote slide show

students graduating with undergraduate (and graduate) design degrees know very little about:

- visual poetry from ancient pattern poetry to the works of William Blake, Stéphane Mallarmé, Guillaume Apollinaire
- modern poets and typographically conscious writers like E. E. Cummings, Gertrude Stein, Kenneth Patchen
- the Concrete poets, Situationists, Letterists, Samizdat, and Fluxus artists and writers
- the relatively recent but robust history of artists' books, graphic novels, contemporary novels employing all kinds of design/typographical elements and structures
- graphic agitationists and agitprop activists from Bread & Puppet and Gran Fury to Shepard Fairey and Occupy Design
- word and text-based "fine art" from paintings to sculptural installations and public works
- practitioners of design fiction and speculative fiction
- writer/programmers of web-based, interactive, and electric lit
- media and performance artists using the tools and methods of graphic design.

Teaching in programs that embrace notions of design authorship and define graphic design as a field of professional art practice that "gives shape to culture," and "communicates ideas and feelings through words and images," makes it **imperative to broaden the scope of what we expose students to and what we consider graphic design and its history to be.** Yes, it is necessary for design students to understand branding, advertising, packaging, data visualization, and other mainstream aspects of the field, but I also think it's high time to include, acknowledge, and teach visual literature as an important, formative (albeit fringe) branch of design practice and history.

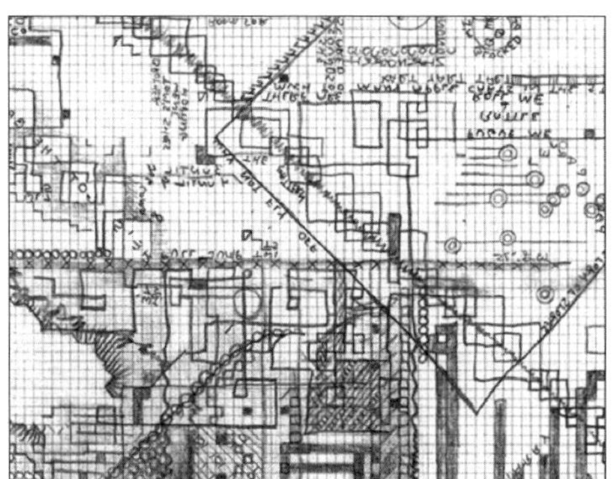

Steve Heller asked if I would share my introductory Vis Lit lecture for this book. I don't use any notes when I give these talks, so I wrote it down for the first time. It took up a hundred letter-sized pages! Too long. So for this publication, I've decided to collect as many of the images from the talk as I could (presented here as thumbnails), dispense with my description and analysis of each work, and simply (or not so simply) paraphrase the thrust of each section. If you would like more detail, feel free to invite me to come give a talk.

I interweave some of my own story into the history of visual literature, beginning with an admonition I received from a painting teacher of mine in the 1970s. After looking at some drawings I had made that included letterforms and words, he shook his head and said, "Words and images are two different languages, two different worlds, and shouldn't be combined." Feeling like I'd been given a mission in life, I bought a type specimen book and hand-lettered an alphabet book titled *Type Dreams. 1977.*

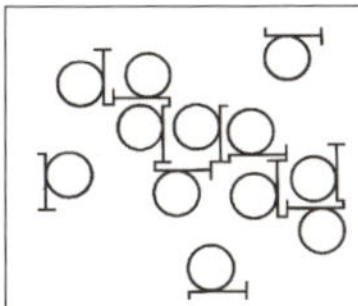

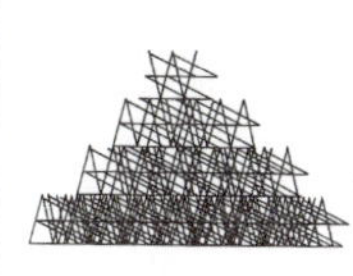

Looking back at it now, I realize there was precedent for mixing words and images in the world I grew up in—within comics, newspapers, and advertising.

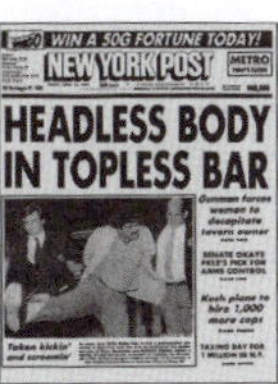

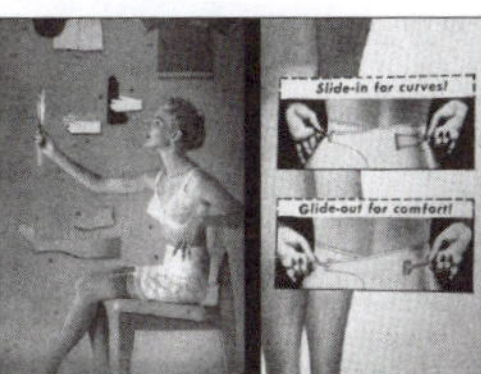

Looking back even further: human beings started documenting their lives by painting images on the walls of their caves (considered the origins of both art and writing). Written language evolved from pictorial modes of representation and (starting with the Phoenicians) morphed toward *phonetic* alphabets. That transition marks the split between written language and picture making. I suggest that graphic designers and practitioners of vis lit are always trying to bring those two worlds back together. We touch on **semiotics** and different modes of representation and discuss the difference between processing words, icons, and images.

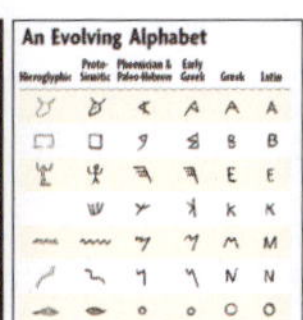

Ryuichi Yamashiro's 1954 concrete poem/poster for a Japanese tree planting campaign helps us consider the living legacy of pictorial icons in some contemporary languages as well as the persistent urge to reunite the alphabetic with the pictorial. Illuminated by hand with incredible artistry (and sometimes gold leaf), intertwining text, color, shape, and image, **sacred manuscripts** like the *Book of Kells* and the *Koran* inspire awe and spiritual revelation.

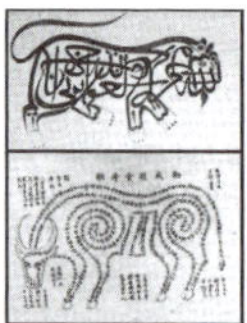

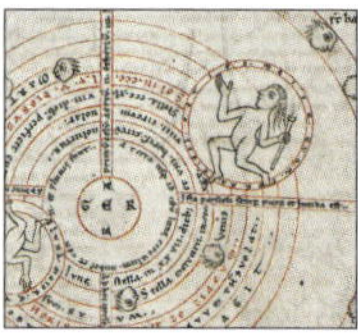

There is a long history of **Pattern Poetry**, dating back to antiquity and found all over the world, that has been (for the most part) overlooked by the keepers of literary, visual art, and design canons. We look at a number of cxamples including *Phaistos Disk* (1700 BC), a series of poems written by the fourth-century Latin poet Publilius Optatianus Porfirius, and analyze the metaphorical hierarchy of *Four Angels*, written and scribed by a sixth-century German Benedictine monk. Part game, part metaphysical experience, many pattern poems are composed in multiple directions, run top to bottom, side to side, and diagonally, and very often contain supplementary text hidden within the body of the poem, intended to be discovered by the reader.

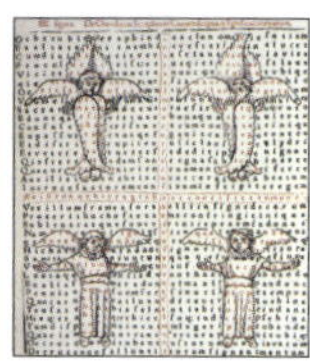
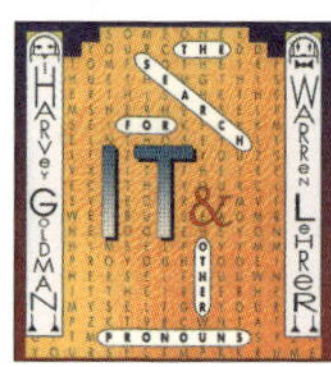

We mostly think about the positive effects of the invention of movable type: how it helped democratize storytelling, made the means of production less painstaking, and paved the way for more people—outside the clergy and aristocracy—to have access to books. But the **Gutenberg Revolution** also had effects that may not be so positive, like de-emphasizing the role of oral storytelling and paving the way for even greater mechanization. So that even today, in this twenty-first century digital age, the interior of most (printed and electronic) books (of fiction and nonfiction) look pretty much the same, no matter the subject: monolithic columns of text. After framing this rather cynical view,

I make the case for neutral, "transparent" settings of text as argued in Beatrice Warde's essay known as *The Crystal Goblet*.

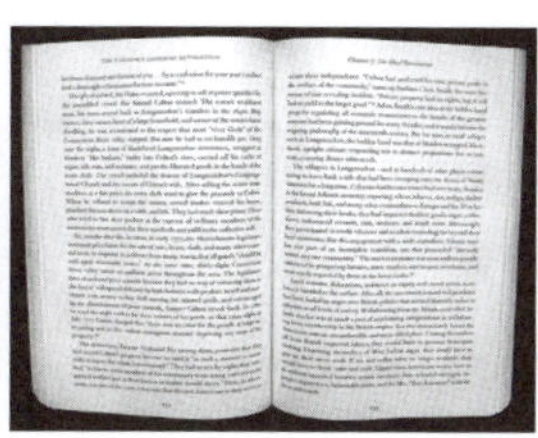
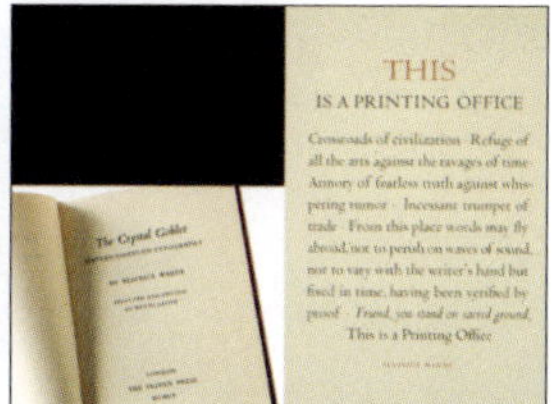

In contrast to Warde's (and classical) notions about the proper way to compose text on a page, many writers, artists, and thinkers coming out of World War I embraced more expressionistic and experiential approaches as they questioned the efficacy of Western traditions and institutions including: so-called rational thought, class-based societal structures, museums, newspapers, "the academy," even the use of the sentence as the basic unit of writing. I show a sketch by the Italian **Futurist** F. T. Marinetti that attacks the column of text with agitated words and fractured letterforms and Guillaume Apollinaire's poem about rain that rains down the page. I talk about French **Symbolist** poet Stéphane Mallarmé's essay *The Book, Spiritual Instrument,* written at the end of the nineteenth century, which envisioned a new kind of book: "*Why—a burst of grandeur, of thought or of emotion, eminent, a sentence pursued in large letters, one line per page, in a graduated arrangement—wouldn't this keep the reader in suspense throughout the whole book, appealing to this power of enthusiasm—all around, minor clusters, of secondary importance, explicatory or derivative—an array of flourishes.*" Living up to his essay, Mallarmé's poem "Un coup de dés jamais n'abolira le hasard," published in 1897, eschews ordinary punctuation and linear structure, equates silence with blank space, approaches the two-page spread as a singular visual proscenium for lines that seem unshackled from any column. The book-length poem is a score; the reader is the performer. In his *Words in Freedom* manifestos, Marinetti rails against Mallarmé (who was thirty-four years older) as being too tied to lyricism and traditional structure and imagines a kind of writing that creates experience on the page, free of traditional syntax, making full use of a typographical palette that utilizes mathematical and musical symbols, juxtaposes multiple voices on a page, and celebrates the onomatopoetic.

We analyze the visual metaphors and vernacular references underpinning a poem by Apollinaire titled "Lettre-Océan" (here on the bottom right). The poem presents two points of view, an exchange

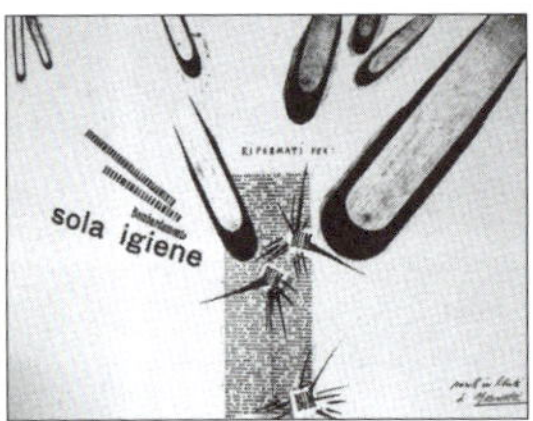

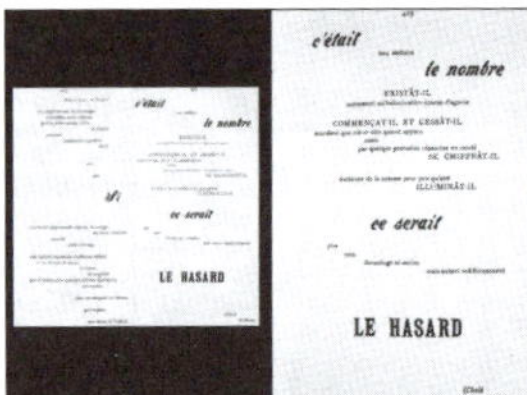

between Apollinaire, in Paris, and his brother Albert, in Mexico. Its visual structure is influenced by the format of a postcard, radio transmissions from the top of the Eiffel Tower, a telegraph's ability to instantaneously communicate across oceans, and the relationship between Europe and a country it once colonized. Apollinaire's hand-drawn sketch and the resulting printed pages show this to be an example of a text that is conceived as a visual/textural composition.

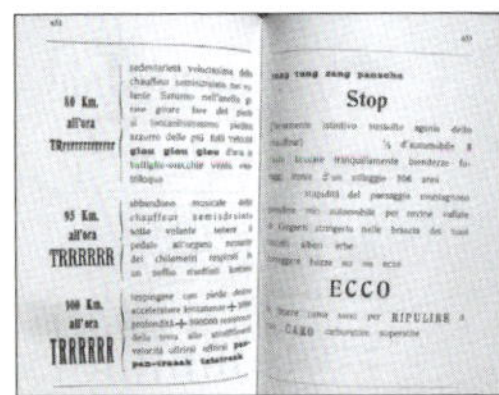

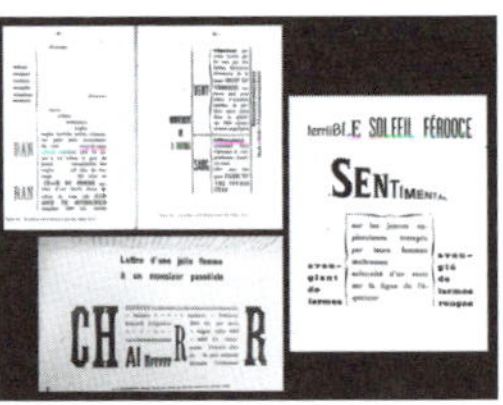

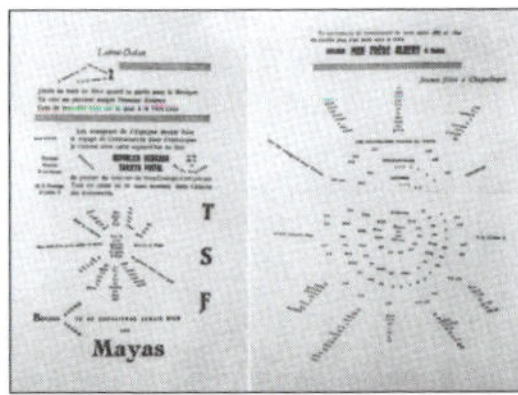

At around the same time as the Futurists were exploding and reinventing language, music, and art in Italy, **Dada** sprung up in Zürich, Switzerland, and Paris, France, even in New York City, doing similar kinds of things, except the Dadaists were more antiwar, even more puckish, into irrationality, nonsense, and chance processes. We look at Tristan Tzara's recipe for making a Dada poem, Hugo Ball's sound poem "Karawane," and Kurt Schwitters's "Ursonate."

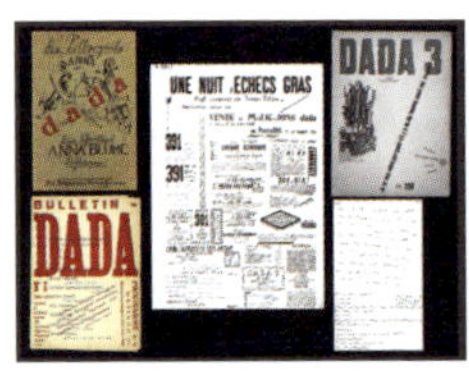

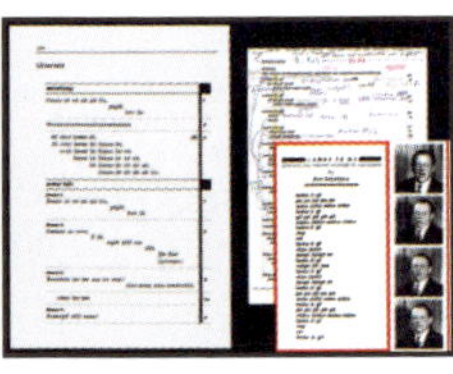

The numerous radical art movements that spread across Europe in the early decades of the twentieth century, including **de Stijl**, **Vorticism**, **Cubism**, Russian **Constructivism**, **Synchronism**, **Surrealism**—along with many individual artist/writers—pioneered their own versions of modernist vis lit including the Russian Futurist writer, artist/typographer Ilia Zdanevich, known as Iliazd. Less political than most of his peers, Iliazd's *Zaum* poems and plays focused more on interior, emotional life and universalist themes. In his typographic compositions, words snaked down and around pages, spacing between lines could curve and wobble, words and sound constructions could form puzzle-like constellations, and individual letters could take on character traits of their own. Blaise Cendrars and Sonia Delaunay's 1913 accordion book *La Prose du Transsibérien et de la Petite Jehanne de France* describes the experience of traveling the Trans-Siberian Railway during wartime. Delaunay's prismatic, abstract shapes and kinetic composition surrounds and infuses Cendrars's apocalyptic scenes of war, hunger, devastation, fragmented memories, and imaginary trips to tropical paradises. I recite a passage from Gertrude Stein's *Patriarchal Poetry*. Though she didn't focus much on typography, Stein's groundbreaking cubistic writings, written mostly in Paris, were no doubt influenced by her friendship with visual artists like Picasso and Braque.

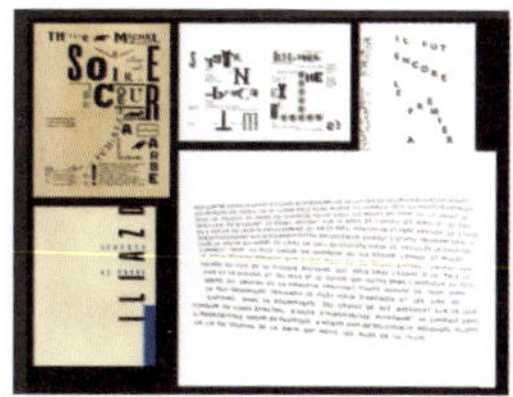

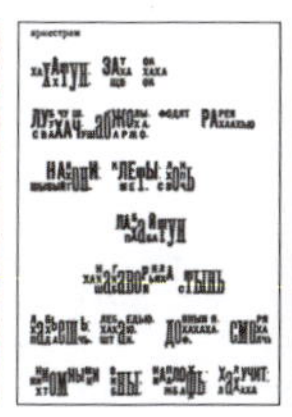

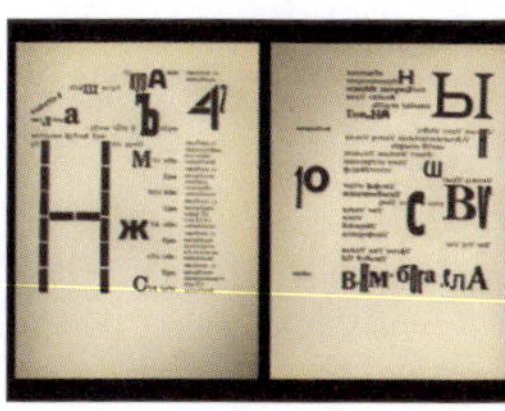

Lest we think that all typographic, structural, compositional, and playful innovations within visual literature sprung solely out of the twentieth century, I show examples from eighteenth- and nineteenth-century publications including a songbook/parody published in 1770 by Charles-Georges Doucet Coqueley de Chaussepierre, composed of nonlinear sentence fragments and punctuation sprinkled throughout its airy pages. Published in nine volumes from 1759 to 1767, Laurence Stern's *The Life and Opinions of Tristram Shandy, Gentleman* is written as an autobiography of a fictional narrator and is famous for its literary parody, meandering digressions, double entendres, descriptions of sex, purposeful misspellings, meta and graphic devices including superlong dashes indicating pregnant pauses, asterisks used in place of expletives, subversive uses of arrows, fleurons and other dingbats embedded throughout the text, doodley lines diagramming the shape of a story, "missing" chapters that reappear in subsequent volumes, text printed on top of a solid black rectangle evoking the voice of a character after his death, and blank pages for readers to write their own responses. I show pages from the first edition as well as a 2011 edition published by the London-based press Visual Editions. In Lewis Carroll's 1850 sketch of

The Mouse's Tale, the mouse says to Alice, "Mine is a long and sad tale." Thinking the mouse said *tail* and not *tale*, Alice imagines the rest of the poem in a twisting tail-like shape.

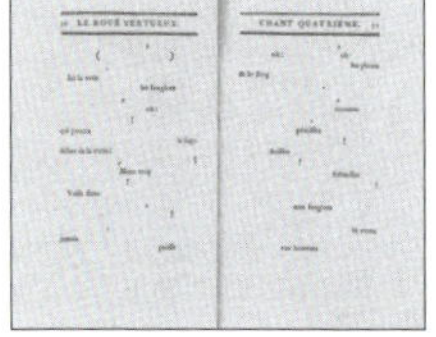
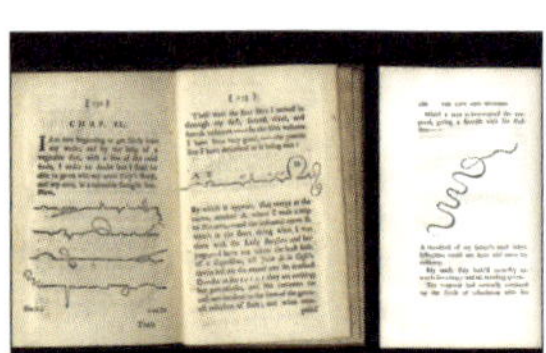

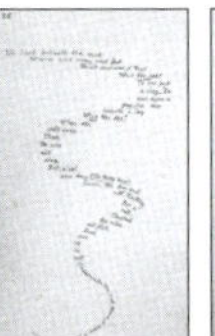

Back to the twentieth century. I recite E. E. Cummings's richly vernacular 1925 poem, "Jimmie's got a 'goil." We witness how Cummings controls the pacing, takes licenses with punctuation and capitalization; hear how oral and funny the writing is. I show pages from Kenneth Patchen's 1943 and 1949 novels *Cloth of the Tempest* and *Sleepers Awake*. Usually no one in the group has heard of this great American innovator who incorporated music, painting, drawing, and typographic expression into his poetry and novels and became a central influence on Beat and Concrete poets and generations of antiwar writers. Yet Patchen is barely a footnote in the literary canon. Perhaps graphic design will give him his due and take a fresh look at his diagrammatic word pictures and long-form works that anticipated Deconstructionist approaches to typography and writing (minus the veils of academic pretense).

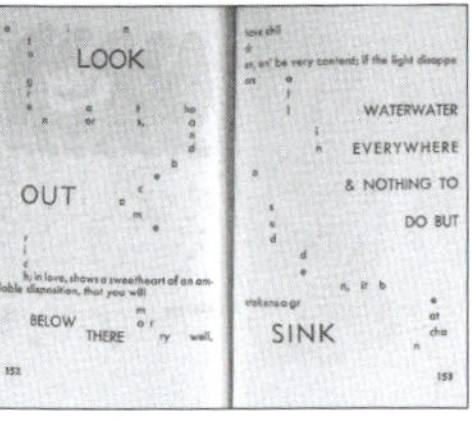

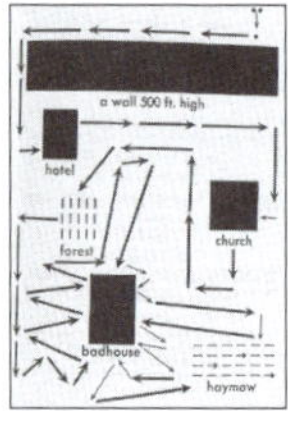

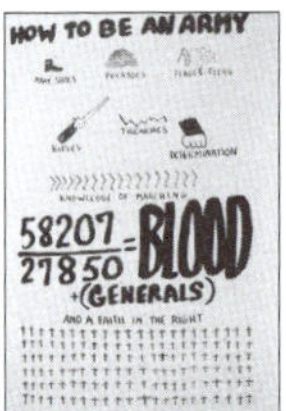

Jack Kerouac claims to have typed his defining stream of consciousness novel *On the Road* on a continuous roll of paper. We look at the scroll, compare it with the true story of how he wrote the book, and the way the final printed book looks. It's also instructive to look at William Burroughs's **"Cuttings"** method used to write his seminal 1959 novel *Naked Lunch*, and J. G. Ballard's unpublished "hypothetical novel" *Zero Synthesis,* pieced together from articles he wrote as a copywriter for *Chemical and Engineering News.*

French graphic designer Robert Massin broke the traditions of playscripts in his 1964 page staging of Ionesco's absurdist play *The Bald*

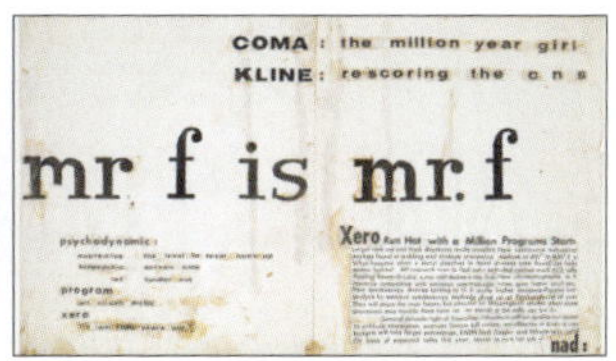

Soprano using high-contrast photos of actors from a London production, casting characters in different typefaces and expressive means to reflect whispers, shouts, revelations, and simultaneous talking (not unlike a fourteenth-century manuscript with animated dialogue flowing from mouths of a teacher and student). In 1961, Massin collaborated with Raymond Queneau on the *Cent mille milliards de poèmes,* in which each line of poetry appears on a separate strip, forming a near infinite "exquisite corps" of verse. They were part of **Oulipo**, an alliance of writers and mathematicians who created works using constrained storymaking techniques.

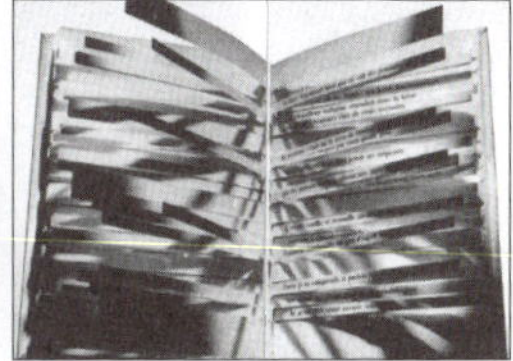

Beginning in the early 1950s, a movement of abstract visual artists emerged in Brazil with similar interests in math and gamesmanship. They called their work Concrete Art and were soon joined by poets who called what they did **Concrete Poetry**. There's a direct lineage to ancient pattern and shaped poetry, but with decidedly more emphasis on the typographical, "concrete" aspects of the composition. Concrete poetry soon became an international phenomenon (known by many

silencio silencio silencio
silencio silencio silencio
silencio silencio
silencio silencio silencio
silencio silencio silencio

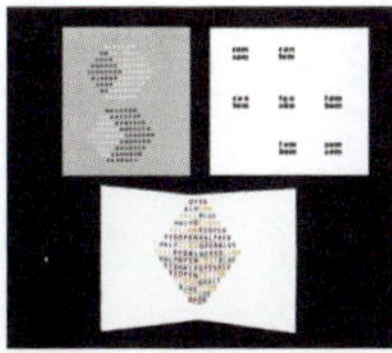
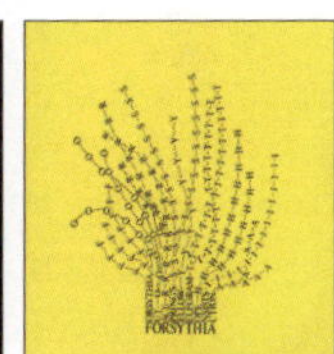

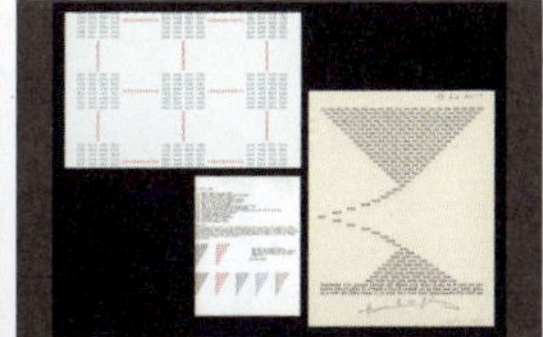
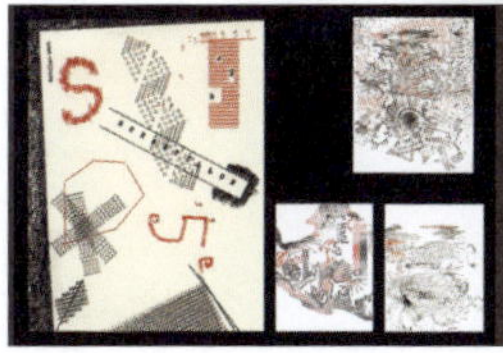
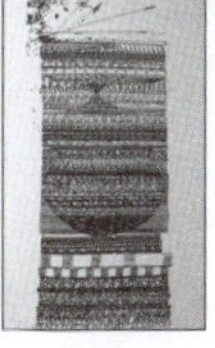
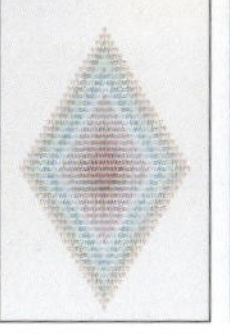
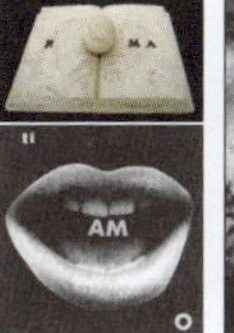

names), documented in anthologies by Mary Ellen Solt and others. The typewriter, rubber stamps, and 3-D materials were principle tools.

The influence of El Lissitzky and Vladimir Mayakovsky's 1923 poetry book *For the Voice*, and other works of figurative and abstract typography by modernist designer/printer/artists like Piet Zwart and H. N. Werkman, is apparent in "experimental" books, films, and prints by contemporary designer/artist/printers like Romano Hänni (Switzerland), Frances Butler (USA), Judith Poirier (Canada), Karel Martens (Netherlands), and David Wolske (USA).

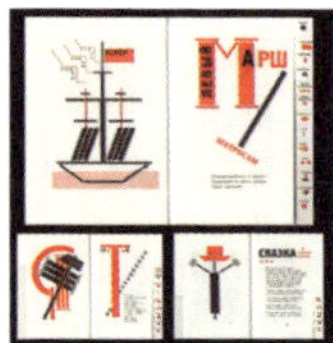
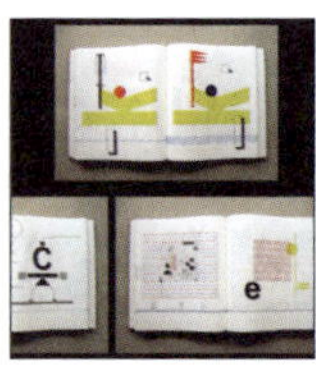

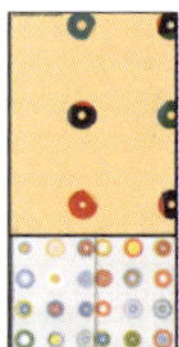
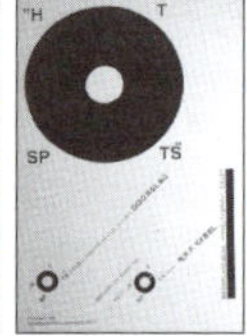

I find it fascinating to look at and *read* the works of **modern and contemporary painters** and other fine artists who incorporate letterforms and words in their art, such as Stuart Davis, Ed Ruscha, Mel Bochner, Laila Rezai, Wayne White, John Baldessari, Bob and Roberta Smith, Jean-Michel Basquiat, Jean Dubuffet, Hanne Darboven, Cy Twombly, and Mira Schor. Some reflect the language in our landscape and of our world; some explore the elemental gestures of language.

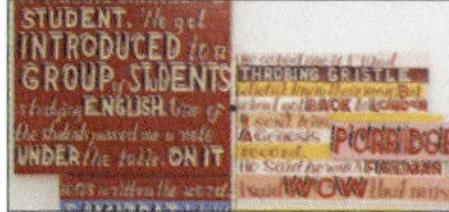

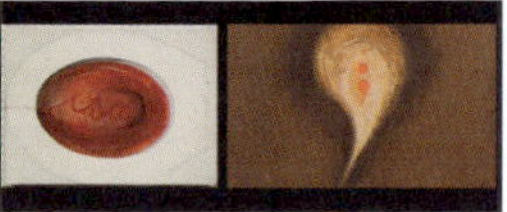

Artist journals, **diaries**, and **notebooks** make for some of the most authentic and poignant examples of vis lit. Examples here are from Frida Kahlo, Jonathan Borofsky, Javier Vazquez, and a documentary book by the photographer Peter Beard mashing up Karen Blixen's, her cook Kamante's, and his journals.

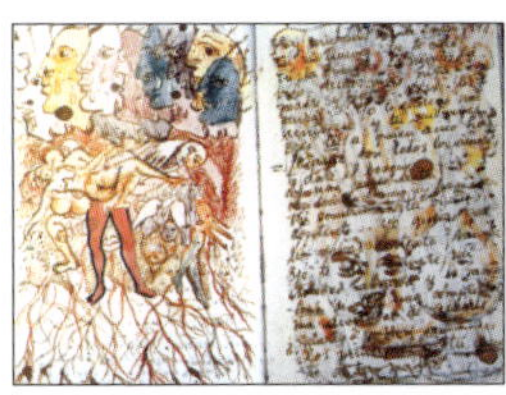
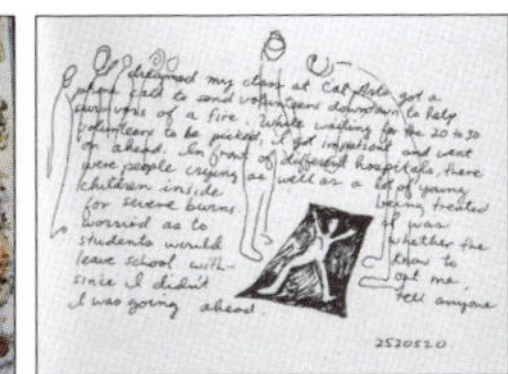

Fluxus is an international movement of "poly-artists," sort of a 1960s version of Dada, whose anti-high art **happenings**, typographic experimentations, objects, and ephemera frequently questioned the barrier between art and life. Their street level FLUX Shop in NYC sold **"Multiples"** such as *Total Art Match Box* or *FLUX Year Box* filled with objects and pamphlets containing visual poetry and performance suggestions. Some Fluxus folks made **Mail Art**, a movement onto itself that bypassed the commerce of art and facilitated exchanges of lovingly made correspondences between friends and likeminded people.

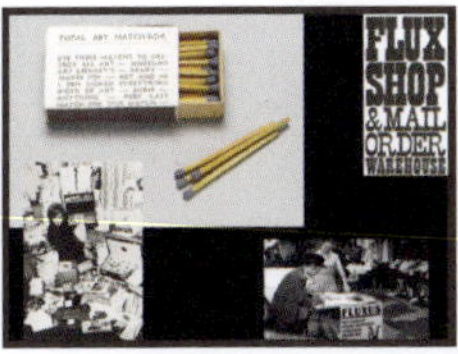

Design Fiction and **Speculative Fiction** is a relatively recent branch of design whose practitioners also produce conceptual objects and products as a form of cultural critique, science fiction, and speculative imagination.

Which brings me to **artists' books**, not to be confused with *Livres d'Artistes*, which typically pairs a famous painter with a famous poet to make a "finely printed" book or portfolio in a limited edition usually with an image on one page and the poem safely on the opposite page. What's referred to more often as artists' books began in the 1960s by artists interested in making books that were inexpensive to produce, publish, and purchase, and explored the form of the book as a dynamic, time-based medium. From 1962 to 1978, Ed Ruscha produced sixteen

“Among other things, artists’ books have served as a laboratory for artists and writers to explore deeply personal and taboo subjects; notions of identity, place, and performance; and nonconventional forms of writing and storytelling . . .”

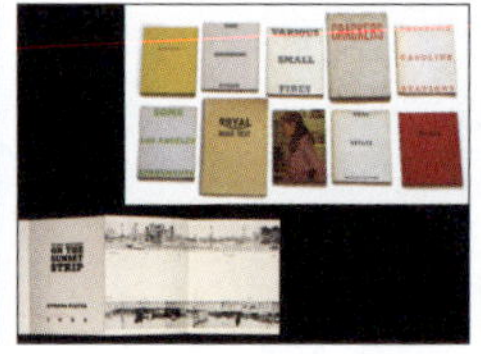

small artists’ books that each documented something from his environment in Los Angeles, from potholes to fires to every building on the Sunset Strip.

Among other things, artists’ books have served as a laboratory for artists and writers to explore deeply personal and taboo subjects; notions of identity, place, and performance; and nonconventional forms of writing and storytelling (be it fiction, metafiction, documentary, memoir, even telling stories entirely through pictures). They explore different physical, formal, structural concerns like sequence, word/image relationships, pacing, erasure, recombination. . . . Practitioners shown below include: Tom Phillips, Jonathan Safron Foer, Dieter Roth, Warren Lehrer, Ruth Laxson, Paul Zelevansky, Keith Godard, Jack DeWitt, Linn Underhill, Johanna Drucker, Scott McCarney, Michael Snow, Rebecca Lown . . .

A HUMUMENT
A TREATED VICTORIAN NOVEL
TOM PHILLIPS
FRENCH FRIES
DRIVE THRU
ENTRANCE
FRENCH FRIES
THE POTATO IN AMERICA
A Hundred Years of: LEX FLEX
BOOM
THE FIRST FRAGMENT
FINGER FOOD
JACK DE WITT
TABLE OF CONTENTS...
INTRODUCTION:
IT BEGINS:
A SOME INTENTIONS:
A READING:
B OKAY OKAY:
OUT DRINKING:
C MY BIG MAC:
NOTHING MORE:
D TRUMP:
HOT PERFORMANCE:
E THIS IS OF:
INTEREST:
F WOMAN WHO LIKED:
SOL LEWITT
GEOMETRIC FIGURES & COLOR SOL LEWITT
OF EIGHT POINTS
PHOTOGRIDS
STRUCTURE OF THE VISUAL BOOK
Keith A. Smith
IN CASE OF EMERGENCY

Artist book makers such as Kevin Osborne, Janet Zweig, Jennifer Cole Phillips, Phil Zimmermann, and Clifton Meador explore and exploit the haptic qualities of books, reading at different speeds, noncodex bindings, and sculptural structures.

Experimentation with book form is also not exclusive to the contemporary era. Looking to the earliest examples helps us reconsider the definition of what a book is/can be. One open-ended definition: *a series of leaves bound together.*

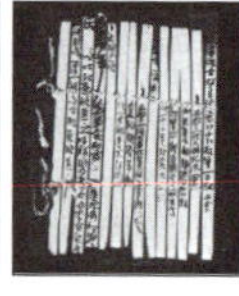

Sometimes the obsession with books leads to brilliant work. Sometimes it can devolve into nostalgia or fetish, and it makes you question the attachment.

Our public landscapes are (for the most part) controlled by commercial and governmental entities. But artists, writers, and public art organizations have also inserted themselves in the landscape through **public works**. Sanctioned and unsanctioned textworks (signs, poetry, alternative messages, political statements, provocative ideas) can be seen on city streets, scoreboards, billboards, benches, rooftops, barns, vacant storefronts, bus shelters, carved in ice, perched on horizons. Artists include Richard Tipping, Ilona Granet, Jenny Holtzer, Barbara Kruger, Ligorano/Reese, Randy Burman, Purchase College Community Design, Mark Mendel, Robert Montgomery, and Stefan Sagmeister.

Public interventionist designers/artists like Candy Chang, Steve Lambert, Mathieu Tremblin, and Cause Collective solicit community participation and publish their crowdsourced findings online, in books and real-time computation.

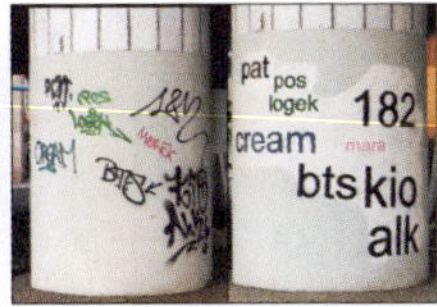

While large-scale public textworks (like Gordon Young and Why Not Associates' *Comedy Carpet* in Blackpool, England) are well funded and done by "professionals," many poignant examples are created by people who are self-taught (including graffiti "writers," "outsider artists," and "visionaries").

Political movements have used human bodies as carriers of visual messages (for good and evil) at protests marches, fascist spectacles, public actions.

Text-based installations in museums, galleries, vartist spaces, airports, and vacant spaces create environments that envelop and interact with readers. "Truisms" spiral down LED strips (Jenny Holtzer), two computers argue then apologize (Janet Zweig), a

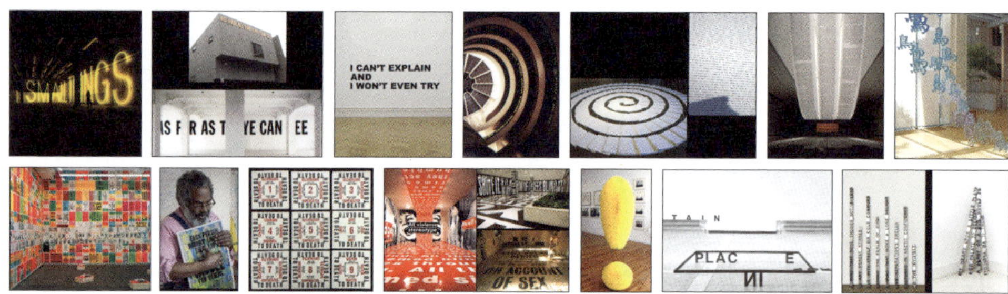

definition of (bird) rises off the floor toward the ceiling (Xu Bing). Also Barbara Kruger, Lawrence Weiner, Steven Doyle, Amos Kennedy, and Roni Horn.

The fundamental skills needed to be a good writer are plenty and deep and require daily practice. If you're a visual writer, you've got even more variables to work with. Most compose their writing within two-dimensional space, some into three and four dimensions. Joseph Egan and Hunter use anamorphic illusions to blur dimensions. Some **theater and performance artists** such as Laurie Anderson, Jaume Plensa, and myself incorporate text in their theater and performance works, as sets, projections, costumes.

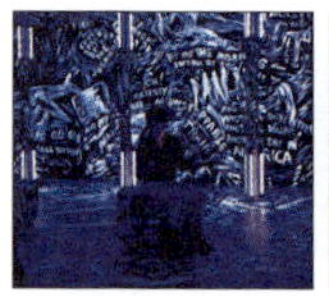
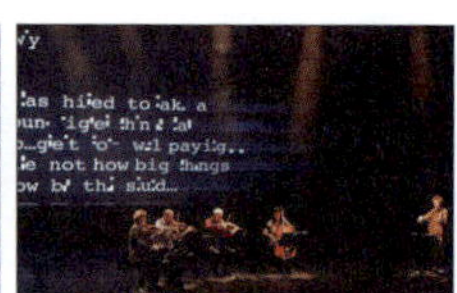

Wearable texts. David Dunlap paints suits with poetic text about dreaming and work. Lesley Dill stamps Emily Dickinson's poem "The Soul Has Bandaged Moments" onto a paper wedding dress. Kate Daudy stitches a text about loss into a wedding dress using blood-red letters. I project text onto myself in a performance called *These Words*. Committed to the Heidelberg Psychiatric Clinic, a seamstress named Agnes Richter transforms a hospital gown into a journal jacket.

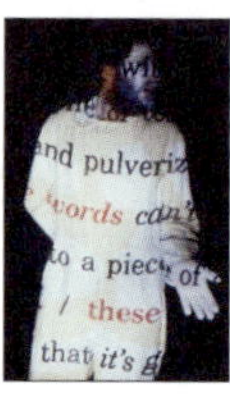

Tattooing is another long tradition, manifest worldwide. Contemporary body writers have extended the tradition with longer, original texts, data visualizations, asymmetrical compositions, word/hair extensions, digital realizations.

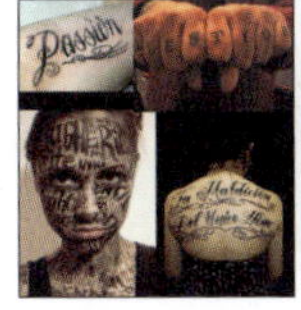
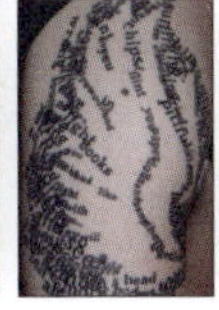
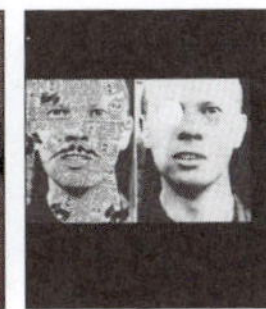

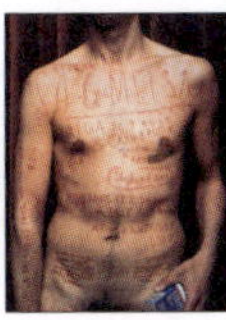

Coined in the 1980s, design authorship attempts to define the movement of designers creating their own content, products, deconstructing/reconstructing meaning, purpose, experimentation, and entrepreneurship through design.

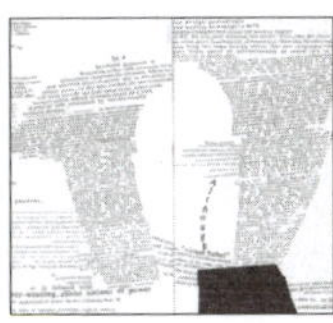

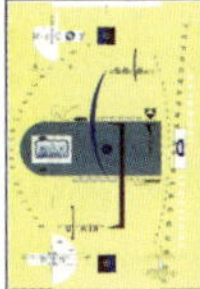
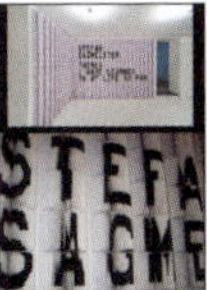

Visualizing information is no longer relegated to science and economic textbooks, as more and more writers, artists, and designers map their thought process, dreams, sleep agony, role models, ways of turning tragedy into comedy. Astonishing historical examples include W. E. B. Du Bois's *Black Life in America*.

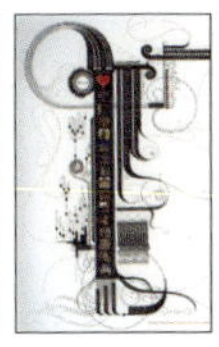
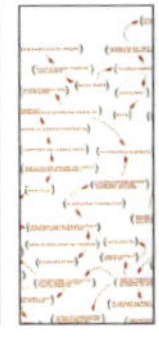

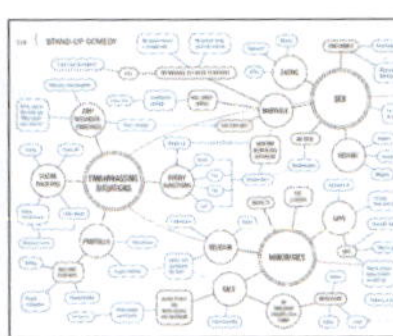
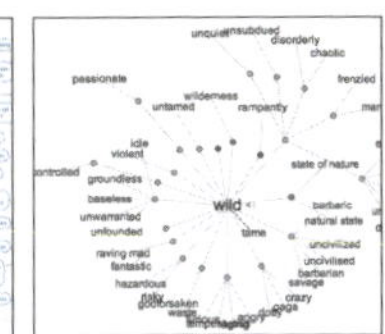
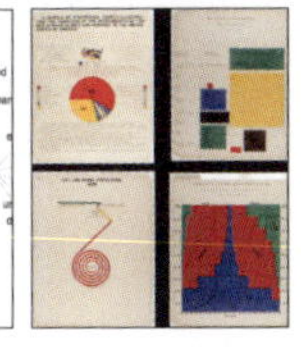

In the 1970s, advances in microchip technology made computer text games and cybertexts possible. By the 1990s, user-modifiable "graphical" interfaces facilitated interactive poetry and fiction, where reader/users help write or amend texts such as Deena Larsen's hypertext narrative poem "Marble Springs." Electronic books (CD ROMs, DVDs) mixing text, image, animation, and sound (such as Laurie Anderson's *Puppet Motel* and Jim Petrillo's *Cinema Volta*) seemed like the inevitable next embodiment of book. Advances in mutable type design and programmable information graphics enabled people like David Small with degrees in design and computer science to take on installation projects that could expand or contract mass amounts of information (like all of Shakespeare's writings and centuries of scholarship) in ways that a printed book can't contain.

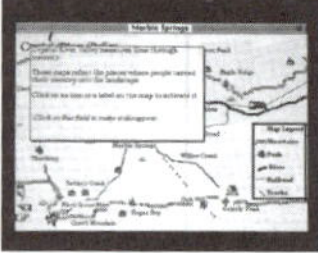

Meanwhile, in 1992—for the first time—a Pulitzer Prize was awarded to a work of vis lit: Art Spiegelman's **graphic novel** *MAUS: A Survivor's Tale,* based on the true story of his father's internment in Auschwitz and the tortured relationship between father and son. *MAUS* inspired a wave of graphic novel/memoirs including Marjane Sartrapi's *Persepolis* (2003) and *Embroideries* (2006), Alison Bechdel's *Fun Home* (2006), Joe Sacco's documentary books about war-torn or distressed parts of the world, and the genre-bending *The Photographer: Into War-torn Afghanistan with Doctors Without Borders* (2009), which combines photography and drawing, third- and first-person narratives—to tell the true story of a photojournalist and what he witnessed during the Soviet war in Afghanistan.

I must admit, I am not the biggest fan of the graphic novel or comic book form or what is referred to as **"sequential art,"** which requires putting nearly everything into panel boxes, drawing characters who speak in speech bubbles and think in thought bubbles, and stuffing narration into boxes. That said, it is a significant breakthrough that graphic novels are now considered a mainstream genre. Most encouraging is the way some practitioners, like Joe Sacco, Chris Ware, and Julie Doucet have exploded open the form. More recently, Doucet renounced her comic-centric approach and busted free of box panels altogether, adding collage, other printmaking, and visual storytelling techniques to her process.

In 2007, Amazon introduced the first Kindle **ebook reader**. The electronic version of the paperback book rocked the publishing world. In

"The fundamental skills needed to be a good writer are plenty and deep and require daily practice."

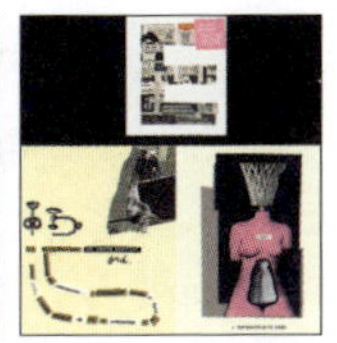

addition to being a lightweight portable vessel for those "invisible" crystal goblets of text, it had its own lighting source and potentially contained all books in one device, either for free, pirated, or for cents on the dollar. Apple's **iPad tablet** went beyond the Kindle in its ability to incorporate images as well as text, animation, video, kinetic typography; it could be interactive and connect to the Internet. If the Kindle gave the publishing world a heart attack, the iPad added a stroke on top of it. Prospects for ebooks and book apps took off, salaries for developers of children's and reference book apps rivaled lawyers' fees, and the dream of electronic books (that CD-ROMs and DVDs never sustained) resurfaced.

There is no going back to times when everyone carried books around. Yet books haven't died. In fact, more (physical) books were published last year than ever! The medium is resurgent. **Liberated from having to be the most convenient vehicle for transporting text**s—writers, artists, publishers, booksellers, and readers are **rethinking what distinguishes a book from other media**. And now that so many writers have a range of writing machines at their disposal, more and more works of visual literature are getting into the hands of readers. Go into your local independent bookstore or big box store (if you still have one), and you'll find approximately one out of fifty novels that have something visual going on between their covers, instead of one out of a thousand!

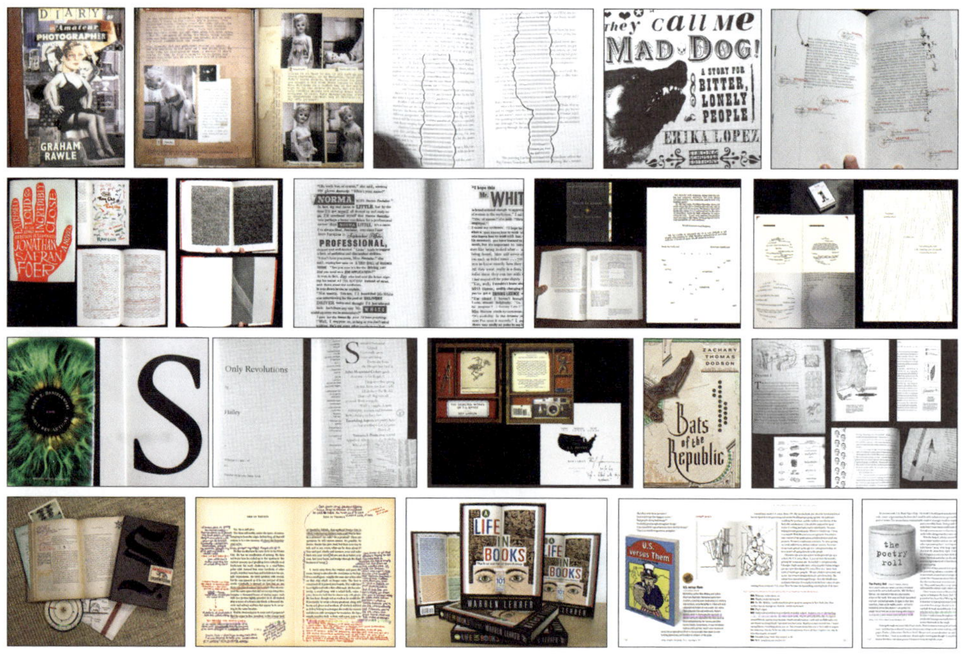

Many poets today consider visual composition a part of their writing practice.

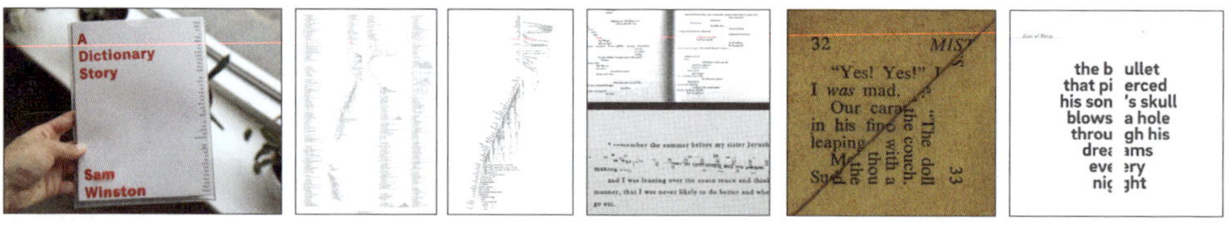

This is true of nonfiction writers and publishers, too. More and more, the visual form evolves from the content instead of assuming rote conventions.

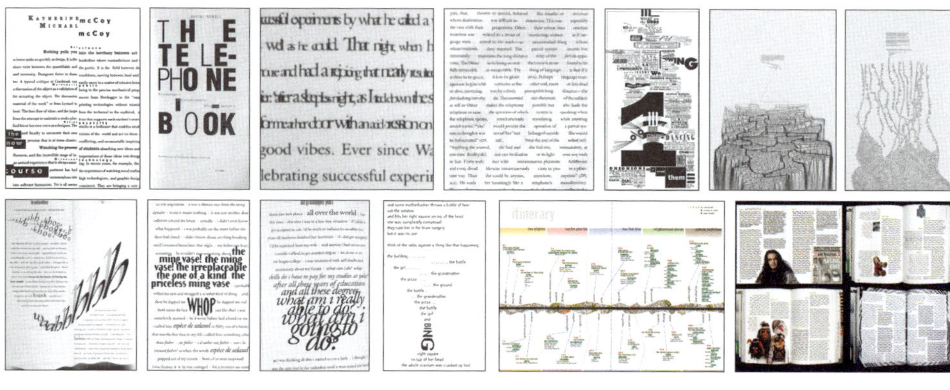

Some of the most exciting and innovative vis lit today is being made by writers, artists, and programmers coming out of the **electronic** literature movement in **book apps**, **hybrid projects** that bridge print and digital platforms. It's reassuring that the foremost pioneers of e-lit are women (Amaranth Borsuk, Samantha Gorman, Nora Ligorano), and writers and artists of every background have the means to make and publish their work (with or without being approved by the gatekeepers of the publishing industry or academia).

If the graphic design field embraces vis lit more consciously as a part of its history, training, and practice, it will attract and better prepare students interested in the tools and methodologies of design as a means to tell stories. While many graphic design students may not become writers as well as designers, a deeper understanding of this material and what it takes to create an **integrated expression through writing and design** can only be helpful to *all* design students.

Warren Lehrer is a designer and writer known as a pioneer of visual literature and design authorship. He's received many awards for his books and multimedia projects including: The Brendan Gill Prize, Center for Book Arts Honoree for Lifetime Achievement, IPPY Outstanding Book of the Year Award, The International Book Award for Best New Fiction, three AIGA Book Awards, Society of Typographic Arts Special Recognition Award, and fellowships and grants from the NEA, NYSCA, NYFA, Rockefeller, Ford, and Greenwall Foundations. A full professor at SUNY Purchase and a founding faculty member of the Designer As Author *grad program at SVA, Lehrer cofounded EarSay, a nonprofit arts organization in Queens, NY.*

BALMAIN
PARIS

VALENTINO

EMILIO PUCCI

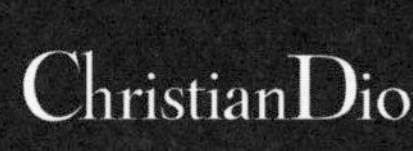

POLO
RALPH LAUREN

CÉLINE

TOM FORD

CALVIN KLEIN

KARL LAGERFELD
PARIS

MARC JACOBS

Proenza Schouler

SAINT LAURENT
PARIS

DIANE VON
FURSTENBERG

TYPE IN COUTURE

Elizabeth Carey Smith

"On the breast of her gown, in red cloth, surrounded with an elaborate embroidery and fantastic flourishes of gold-thread, appeared the letter A."
—*The Scarlet Letter*

In an interview with rock critic Lester Bangs in the 1980s, writer and punk musician Richard Hell said, "If you invent yourself, you love yourself. The idea of inventing yourself is creating the most ideal image that you could imagine." He was referring to the constructs of fashion—how in the 1980s New York City punk scene, your clothing choices, DIY haircut, and level of neglect helped you clarify who you were to the audience.

Fashion is about self-invention and self-expression—the secure and insecure ways we reflect ourselves to ourselves and to others. It is both inward-looking and committed to the gaze. Our consumption of fashion can be dismissed as superfluous and vapid because it often is those things. But it is also a high art, one whose roots and sociological contexts are just as consequential as how the clothing itself is crafted. Fashion bridges the universal and the personal, giving key information about wearers to the people around them.

Similarly, typography informs and expresses. It is both invisible and seen, the levels of which are determined by typeface designers (makers) and graphic designers (users). Like fashion, type surrounds us, and it is inextricable from everyday life. (Society couldn't function for one day without letters, and we probably shouldn't leave the house unclothed.) But it moves away from fashion since it's mostly literal, while fashion is more nebulous. And while both are deeply affected by context, interpretations of fashion are broader, with perception and hyper-self-awareness as society's primary goals.

So how do fashion and type relate to each other? When the two meet—whether it's in editorial contexts, fashion labels and brand rollouts, or simply letters on clothing—we see the gamut of cliché, precedent, and appropriation, all in service of how we describe both fashion and type.

What Is "Beautiful" Type?

In making fashion images, people use words like *feminine*, *delicate*, *beautiful*, and *elegant*. Similarly, creative directors, art directors, and clients often request type that is beautiful, delicate, and feminine. But what does that actually mean?

The majority of the time, these words are describing a high-contrast serif typeface, one that typically utilizes extremely thin stroke widths on the upstrokes and, by comparison, extremely thick stroke widths on the downstrokes. These words are describing Didones, a portmanteau meaning a typeface that has the structure of Didot or Bodoni or something of its ilk.

Didones' hairline serifs are perpendicular to one another, with round or teardrop-shaped terminals and what Dutch type designers would call "translational" stroke variation. The most common of these typefaces—which fall under the classification of "modern"—are Didot, designed and cut by Firmin Didot (1764–1836), and Bodoni, designed and cut by Giambattista Bodoni (1740–1813). *Et voilà.* Those evocative, provocative words usually mean one of those; though, I can't recall an art director ever specifying *which* Didot or Bodoni. (Being specific about type and its qualities makes art directors nervous. Maybe it's because they don't want to get demeaned by typographers.)

So, why did Didones became the precedent in fashion? When digging through the Condé Nast archives, I found a treasure trove of typographic exploration illustrating how type and lettering coexisted with increasingly arresting fashion imagery. But determining why—and where and how—was not as simple as I'd assumed it would be.

Almost certainly starting with *Vogue* magazine, Didones' connection to fashion is cemented. From a design history perspective, Didones' association with fashion is particularly supported by Alexey Brodovitch's art direction of *Harper's Bazaar*, which used Didot exclusively and deliberately. In his *Eye* magazine essay "Through Thick and Thin: Fashion and Type," Abbott Miller says of Brodovitch's typography, "Didot was the black blade that cut the white space of his layouts."

It really wasn't until the 1950s that Didones—which had been jostled, omitted, and reintroduced throughout the first half of the twentieth century—stayed put in fashion magazines. Still, somewhere along the way, high-contrast Didones became the primary typographic language to denote fashion.

However, almost simultaneously, geometric sans serifs appeared alongside these Didones. Typefaces like Futura marked a spirit of European modernism, futurism, and universalism. The impetus for sans serifs and derivative lettering must have come, at least in part, from the brand marks of fashion labels themselves.

Chanel's logo is an easy one to conjure, with its utilitarian, blocky capitals uncharacteristically depicting a quiet elegance. The interlocking *C*s of the brand mark were most likely borrowed from the (literal) brands of saddlery and leather goods shops like Hermès, founded in 1837, and Louis Vuitton, founded in 1854. Gucci followed after Chanel in 1921 with an even more derivative logo of two *G*s. Hence, another typographic precedent—interlocking sans serif capital letters—was established.

By the 1950s, the labels that we most associate with high fashion had been born: Balenciaga, Balmain, Chanel, Christian Dior, Givenchy, Gucci, Hermès, Lanvin, and Louis Vuitton. These labels formed the nexus of haute couture during its golden age. Their logos were of such a decided visual language that new designers who subsequently contributed to haute couture also emulated these marks. Yves Saint Laurent's logo, designed by A. M. Cassandre in 1963, was a meld of all of these precedents—thin letterforms, an ambiguous semi-serif, and overlapping letterforms as a brand mark. Diane von Fürstenburg emulated this amalgamation, too, for her eponymous label, launched in the 1970s. Others in this newer guard of designers, like Valentino and Ralph Lauren, maintained the language.

Futura (and later, a whole crowd of grotesques) claimed the voice of downtown fashion and culture. Former *Elle* design director Evan Campisi described the magazine as an indie magazine coming to mainstream fashion magazines. It's intentionally unladylike, defiantly contrasting with the exclusive luxury of uptown fashion. In the minds of younger magazines and their audiences, Didones feel like the old definition of luxury. Street style has risen to prominence, and collections are now tribes. Today's many designers of note originally made their names in downtown minimalism and street style.

Calvin Klein (1968) and Dolce & Gabbana (1985) both hitched themselves to what was regarded as young and avant-garde by incorporating geometric sans serifs in their respective logos. And when Yves Saint Laurent rebranded a few years ago, changing its name to Saint Laurent Paris, it used Helvetica for the logo. To me, this signifies a permanence to the notion that downtown fashion is as valuable as uptown fashion. Stylistically, and perhaps philosophically, there's a difference between Yves Saint Laurent and Saint Laurent. The transition within the label makes sense, though—Yves was known for capturing a daring edge and an androgynous beauty; Saint Laurent has adapted to our times in a kind of perfect emulation of that spirit.

Seeing this kind of leap is superexciting, and it also elucidates logos like Tom Ford's. Tom Ford became the creative director for Gucci in 1994, elevating the fashion house again after its brand became oversaturated. While Ford is known for a kind of ultimate sex and luxury, he's parked his logo in the camp of downtown, of new and innovative, of young but not immature. Of contemporary sophistication.

Of beauty even more than youth.

So it's kind of funny to see that Karl Lagerfeld has branded himself as he has, post–Tom Ford. Lagerfeld has been the creative director of Chanel since 1983 and Fendi (interlocking letter logo!) since 1985. But when it came time to rebrand himself, he joined the side of the downtown edge, which can only be expected from a man who sports a white ponytail and looks that dapper (that's a wink at Mr. Matthew Carter, by the way).

What can be determined from these grotesque choices? Essentially that no one is taking chances in the space where type meets fashion. But if a maverick *does* make that jump from the precedent, and it is accepted, it is because that designer has gained an unprecedented level of respect early on—or the unique visual language originates from a voice in the industry you'd be stupid to question. Either way, if you pull it off, you can be sure to be ripped off. Because fashion.

Which brings us to how these labels are used graphically. Fashion was the first industry to understand that the value of its products could become synonymous, and later be outvalued, by the presence of the brand itself. I love this image, because it's a diagram for spotting an authentic Louis Vuitton bag. Every little detail. It's its authenticity that matters, more than the fact that people might really like that bag, or that it matches a good part of their wardrobe or it's practical. Its authenticity has to do with its brand.

Louis Vuitton started out this way for proprietary reasons as a leather goods house. But the status of ownership helped form a new kind of aristocracy. One for which the other aspects of the product become secondary. The thing people find interesting about many of their brand-driven products is how the L and the V are self-appropriated in a new way, and that it's authentically Louis Vuitton and therefore has value. All of the other details are secondary.

Louis Vuitton's willingness to create graphic forms out of its logo, in order to reflect the luxury it claims to be, has since led loads of designers, like Fendi, to experiment with their logos graphically. Karl Lagerfeld, in his time at Chanel, has exploited the logo in numerous amazing and inane ways—on beach balls, tennis rackets, surfboards, and a chainsaw, not to mention exaggerating its use on handbags and accessories. The ability to self-appropriate one's own logo is considered an essential part of its DNA, even during the initial branding process.

Moschino was founded in 1983 by Franco Moschino, who sought to "disrupt the value system and bourgeois affectations of elitist fashion, using Dada and pop art as his weapons of choice." Pop art, with its tongue-in-cheek immaturity, obsession with its own appropriation, and colorful graphic devices (and comic type!), was alluring to the designer, who then transferred these tropes and artworks onto clothing as an extension of pop art itself.

Moschino has always toyed with the graphic nature of large-scale, mainstream branding. When these common graphics are subverted and injected into high-end womenswear, conversations are started about our value systems themselves. There is an amazing Moschino ad—featuring the model Linda Evangelista looking very Upper East Side and holding a very Chanel-looking bag, that has a McDonald's logo on it—that captures the spirit of the higher aspirations of the fashion-label-as-art.

Plenty of art has dipped its toe into typography. Mimi Smith's plastic raincoat made out of plastic food packaging makes a comment about plastic in our environments; a corset made out of printed pages (by artist Christine Lofaso) takes an object with a contentious history and juxtaposes it with words. Letters on clothing will always escalate the other's meaning. Type's role changes once it's clothing someone. What does clothing mean when it literally says something? Perhaps the most elusive part of it all is fashion's ultimate trick: transcending meaning into pure expression. The invention of one's ideal image.

Elizabeth Carey Smith is a typographer in New York City who specializes in design and creative direction for type foundries, branding, fashion, and the arts. She earned her BFA from the College for Creative Studies in Detroit and completed the extended program of Type@Cooper in Typeface Design. In addition to design, Carey Smith is vice president of the Type Directors Club, and she speaks and writes regularly for conferences, publications, and platforms around the world. elizabethcareysmith.com

DESIGNING CIVIL RIGHTS IN THE UNITED STATES

Ellen Lupton and Brockett Horne

Again and again, graphic design has been used in struggles for equality over the past two centuries. Countless posters and media campaigns—often created by marchers on the street—have demanded freedom and equality. Graphic design has also been a tool of oppression. Signs on bathrooms and water fountains, placed there by business owners and city governments, have marked the drive to control access to public space.

A "civil right" belongs to the citizens of a specific nation. Civil rights are fought for by groups seeking equal access to services, education, spaces, and more. By fighting for their civil rights, citizens have changed the laws of the land. This essay looks at the role of design in several struggles for civil rights in the United States, including women's right to vote, the African American fight against racial discrimination, the Americans with Disabilities Act, and the fight for marriage equality.

"Suffrage" is the right to vote. The fight for women's suffrage began with a meeting held in New York State in 1848, called the Seneca Falls Convention for Women's Rights. The leaders of this convention, Elizabeth Cady Stanton, Lucretia Mott, and Susan B. Anthony, are considered the founders of feminism in the United States. (1) Many suffrage posters depict virginal, goddess-like young women in flowing white gowns. Such posters present idealized notions of abstract virtue. (2) Some posters, however, represent real women facing tough economic situations, from a young widow holding a baby to a gray-haired woman sewing in a factory. Such posters challenged the idea that all American women could rely on men for protection and financial support. In reality, when fathers or husbands died or abandoned their families, women and children were left behind. The suffrage movement argued that if women could vote, politicians would be forced to reconsider laws that prevented women from owning property, earning a living wage, and becoming self-sufficient. Women achieved the right to vote in 1920, with the passage of the Nineteenth Amendment to the U.S. Constitution. The amendment reads, "The right of citizens of the United States to vote shall not be denied or abridged by the United States or by any State on account of sex." This policy was established after decades of work by suffragists.[1]

Americans of African heritage have fought long and hard for their civil rights. They have used photography, public demonstrations, and data visualization in their fight for the right to vote, access to public places, and protection from housing discrimination and school segregation. Author and abolitionist (4) Frederick Douglass (1818–1895) became the most photographed man of his time. More pictures were taken of Douglass than of Abraham Lincoln. Douglass, who wrote essays about the power of photography, believed that cameras told the truth about human beings and could change people's point of view about race. Seeing a photograph of a regal, dignified black man could make viewers recognize his fundamental humanity. He also believed that photography could reach a mass audience more effectively than text alone. (5) Most of the portraits that Douglass commissioned over the course of his lifetime were daguerreotypes, a process that results in a single print rather than a negative from which multiple prints could be made. Later editions of Douglass's famous autobiography included a halftone reproduction of his photographic portrait.[2]

(6) W. E. B. Du Bois (pronounced *Du Boys*) was an activist and sociologist who organized an exhibition called "Exhibit of American Negroes" in Paris in 1900. This exhibition displayed books and patents created by African Americans. Du Bois also presented data visualizations showing the rising economic status of African Americans since the period of slavery. The unique, hand-drawn data visualizations created by Du Bois and his students for the Paris exhibition are preserved in the collection of the Library of Congress. (7) In one graphic, a map of the globe depicts the forced migration of slaves from West Africa to the Americas. (8) Another graphic shows the growing wealth of black people in Georgia between the end of slavery and 1890. In order to show these huge economic gains, the graphic uses a spiral line rather than a straight bar graph. This spiral technique allowed the designers to compare a tiny number with a much larger one within the confined space of the page by allowing the larger numbers to roll up like ribbon on a spool.[3]

A massive push for equality came with the African American Civil Rights Movement (1954–68). During this movement, activists fought to occupy places reserved for whites. They sought a seat in a restaurant or on the bus, a place in an integrated classroom, or fair access to housing. They also fought for the right to vote. Although the legal right of African American men to vote had been recognized in 1870, black citizens were routinely intimidated from exercising this right, especially in America's southern states. This fight continues today.

(9) Photographer and filmmaker Gordon Parks (1912–2006) created famous images of black life and black artists. He also directed films in the "blaxploitation" genre, including *Shaft* (1971), featuring a hip detective. Among Parks's most influential projects was a series of photographs published in the mass-market magazine *Life* in 1956. These photographs show how public facilities separated people according to race. By forbidding nonwhites from using public restrooms, a town

could restrict people's presence in shopping areas, hotels, and other common areas. Graphic signage was used to mark such restrictions. Parks—rather than depict empty places—showed people and families in these places. By revealing spatial discrimination (and graphic design) in a deeply human way, these photographs spurred the growth of the civil rights movement.

(10) Gordon Parks also photographed civil rights demonstrations. People marched carrying posters emblazoned with "We Are Living in a Police State" and "Police Brutality Must Go." Such posters were designed to be photographed by the media as well as seen on the streets. Led by Dr. Martin Luther King in 1965, demonstrators marched from Selma, Alabama, to the state capital, Montgomery, demanding voting rights, desegregation, and freedom from police brutality. Photographers were there to capture these events and share them worldwide.

(11) Photographers participating in the Black Lives Matter movement have continued to document protest posters. Black-and-white photographs shot in Florida by Sean Lassiter in 2014 following the murder of Trayvon Martin, an unarmed teenager, reference the historic images of the African American Civil Rights era. Lassiter explains, "Black and white images remove the distraction of colors and leave you with nothing but the subject to focus on. . . . Also, I wanted those that viewed the images to relate what's going on today with what took place during the civil rights movement."

(12) The Baltimore Uprising occurred after the death of Freddie Gray, who died after being arrested by police in 2015. Photographer Devin Allen shot a photograph of a young black man running down a Baltimore street, pursued by heavily armed policeman. Allen's image appeared on the cover of *Time* magazine and became an emblem of the Black Lives Matter movement. Allen, who was one year older than Freddie Gray at the time, became a commercial photographer for Under Armour, a company with headquarters in Baltimore, and he teaches photography as a tool of empowerment in a neighborhood after-school center.

The protesters who followed Dr. Martin Luther King often dressed in their best Sunday clothes. (13) The Black Panthers took a different approach. They participated in the vibrant counterculture of the era, and they dramatized their presence with bold fashion and visible weapons. Founded by Huey P. Newton and Bobby Seale in 1966, the Black Panthers developed a uniform for its members: powder-blue shirt, black leather jacket, black pants, black shoes, black beret, and optional black gloves. Such clothing was widely available, so the uniform could be adopted by anyone who sought to join. Panthers and other supporters of the Black Power movement wore their hair in a natural Afro style instead of straightening it. The Black Panther Party, founded to protect black neighborhoods from police brutality, grew to embrace black pride and fighting for social justice. At the Super Bowl in 2016, pop singer Beyoncé and her dancers dressed in costumes reminiscent of the Black Panthers. Critics denounced her for politicizing a sports event, a move she made in the context of Black Lives Matter.

(14) Graphic designer Emory Douglas worked as the Minister of Culture for the Black Panther Party for Self Defense from 1967 until the party dissolved in the 1980s. (15) Douglas used direct, human illustrations rendered in one or two colors to convey an emotional and political message. He described his process of working with Xacto knives, white paper, and pens: "I began to mimic woodcuts just playing with markers . . . and shadows . . . and get that bold, broad look. My art is about enlightening and informing people about issues." (16) The Black Panther logo, which features a leaping black cat, was initially drawn by activist Dorothy Zellner, in 1966. The logo was later streamlined and enhanced by Lisa Lyons.[4]

(17) "Black Panther" is the name of a superhero as well as an activist organization. Billy Graham became the first black art director in the comics industry in 1969. He developed the character Luke Cage, based on figures from blaxploitation action films. Graham was the main comic artist to work on the Black Panther superhero comic book series (1969–1976).[5] In 2018, the film *Black Panther* became the first international blockbuster film devoted to an Afro-Futurist aesthetic. Hannah Beachler is the film's production designer. She is also the designer of *Fruitvale Station*, *Moonlight*, and Beyoncé's *Lemonade*. "It's my job to make the director's vision come to life," she says.[6] (18) Beachler materialized Wakanda, an imagined African civilization tricked out with unique technologies while grounding itself in contemporary and traditional African cultures. She also developed a Wakandan writing system.

Activists in the United States helped secure their rights through a series of historic laws passed in the 1960s. They gained unprecedented rights in voting equality, housing equality, and access to public places. The fight, however, continues. Civil rights continue to be contested through design. (19) Data visualization is a tool for revealing problems like segregated schools[7] or rates of incarceration in Black neighborhoods. Social media has become a powerful tool for activists. (20) The #BlackLivesMatter hashtag was created by Alicia Garza, Patrisse Cullors, and Opal Tometi after the acquittal of Trayvon Martin's killer in 2013. The phrase can be used by everyone, in handmade signs as well as on printed and digital graphics. Born in Baltimore in 1985, DeRay McKesson became a leading voice in Black Lives Matter after the killing

WOMEN'S SUFRAGE

1

2

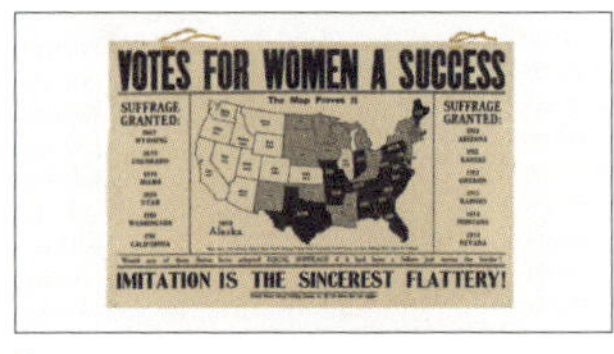

3

EQUALITY FOR AFRICAN AMERICANS

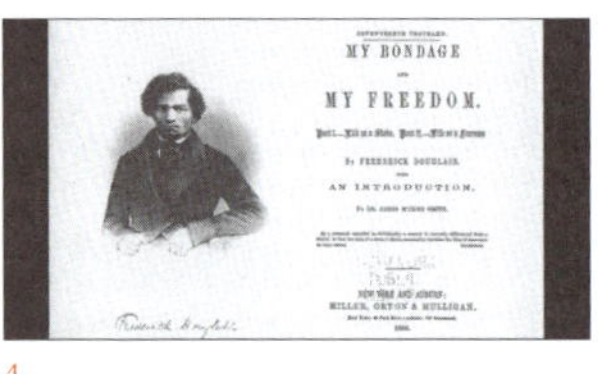

4

5

6

7

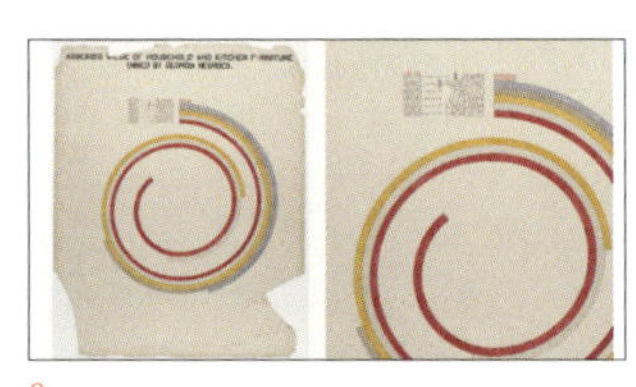

8

9

10

11

12

13

14

15

16

17

18

of Michael Brown in Ferguson, Missouri. McKesson often wears a puffy blue vest, which makes him recognizable in a crowd. Deray McKesson cofounded Campaign Zero, an organization that proposes policy changes based on data and research.

The rights of people of color intersect with struggles for rights based on gender and sexuality. Following the election of President Donald Trump in 2016, a huge Women's March was organized in Washington, DC, and around the United States to protest Trump's views and behaviors toward women. Some activists criticized the march for treating the category of "women" as a universal idea that uniformly encompasses all socioeconomic groups. Women of color felt excluded from the march and from mainstream views that implicitly equate whiteness and feminism. A famous photograph, shot by Kevin Banatte, shows three young white women at the Women's March wearing pink "pussy hats" and shooting selfies. (21) In the foreground stands a Black woman, Angela Peoples, carrying a hand-lettered sign that reads, "Remember, white women voted for Trump." In 2017, Peoples wrote in the *New York Times*, "I wanted to highlight that on a national level, white women are not unified in opposition to Trumpism and can't be counted on to fight it. Instead, it's the identity, experience and leadership of Black women that we must look to." She pointed out that women do not all want the same things, and that 53 percent of white women voters did indeed choose a president who is racist and sexist.

A disabilities rights movement arose in the 1960s alongside the fight for racial equality. Equal access is a problem for people with disabilities. More specifically, access for these people is a design problem. Products, public facilities, and media are often designed in a way that excludes people with physical, sensory, or intellectual differences. (22) Architect and designer Ron Mace coined the term "universal design" to describe the concept of designing all products and environments to be usable to the greatest extent possible by everyone, regardless of their age or ability.[8] (23,24) The Seven Principles of Universal Design aim to provide equal access to people with disabilities. A supermarket door that opens automatically for a person in a wheelchair is also more accessible to a person pushing a shopping cart or a stroller. Design principles such as, "Simple and Intuitive Use" and "Perceptible Information" benefit all users—children, the elderly, people with sensory disabilities, and others. Inclusive design increases the level of access and independence for many people.[9]

(25,26) Sarah Hendren and Brian Glenney set out to redesign the icon that is used worldwide to identify facilities for people with disabilities. The standard icon shows a wheelchair merged with a simplified human figure. They felt that this sign is disrespectful to users of wheelchairs because the figure appears passive and static. The new icon depicts a more active and dynamic figure. The icon is designed as a stencil, making it easy to paint in parking lots.

People with disabilities seek more than access. They want to be visible members of society who contribute to the wonders of human diversity. (27) Apple worked with the American Council of the Blind, the Cerebral Palsy Foundation, and the National Association of the Deaf to create thirteen new emojis to represent those with disabilities, introduced in 2018.

Thanks to the work of activists and designers, the Americans with Disabilities Act was passed in the United States in 1990. More than any other U.S. law, this one is about design standards. The law affects many fields of design, including architecture, product design, signage, web design, and designs for apps and digital products. Graphic designers can make the world more accessible by considering the needs of people with cognitive and sensory differences. Designers can create digital versions of printed publications that can be read aloud with screenreading technology. They can also create tactile maps and graphics that help people understand cities, neighborhoods, and campuses. In the Italian city of Florence, a tactile map made of bronze fascinates visitors of all abilities. It is designed to last hundreds of years, like the city itself.

Many striking graphic campaigns have been created in the quest for gay rights. (28) The best-known symbol for the LGBT movement is the rainbow flag. It was designed by Gilbert Baker in 1978 with eight colors to represent the diversity of the community. Baker was hired by influential gay politician Harvey Milk to create a symbol of pride. Baker's flags, used at Gay Pride events in California, were hand-dyed and stitched by volunteers. They have been altered due to the availability of colored fabric over the years. This global pride symbol was recently reinterpreted as a multicolored typeface. For gay and lesbian Americans, the fight for marriage equality was won by grass-roots efforts from individuals and organized groups. A 2008 ballot proposition in California aimed to eliminate the right of same-sex couples to marry. On November 4, 2008, voters approved the measure and made same-sex marriage illegal in California. Ultimately, Prop 8 was overruled by the Federal Court, making same-sex marriage legal. (29) In a poster by Shepard Fairey, a clenched fist raised high in the air is surrounded by rays of energy and bold typography.

Italian clothing manufacturer Benetton is known for campaigns that mix advocacy and advertising. Benetton launched a controversial campaign in 2011 for Unhate, an advocacy group for tolerance. The ads

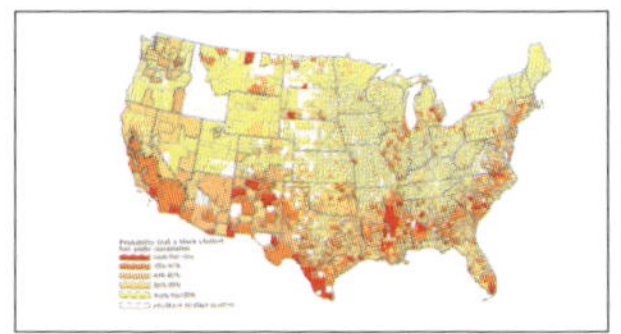
19

20

21

DISABILITY RIGHTS

22

23

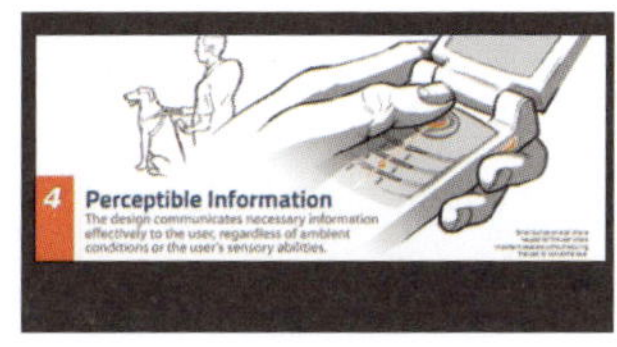

24

25

26

27

MARRIAGE EQUALITY AND GENDER RIGHTS

28

29

30

31

32

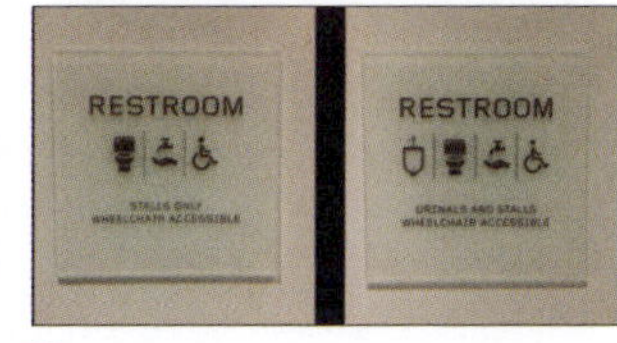

33

show Photoshopped images of lip-locked world leaders. In different ads, Obama is made to kiss Chinese President Hu Jintao and Hugo Chavez. The Vatican threatened to take legal action over an image of the Pope kissing the Imam of al-Azhar mosque in Egypt. The campaign won an award from the Cannes Ad Festival and was described by the judges like this: "It cuts through all cultures, nationalities, faith even. It has heart impact and gut impact and promotes a global debate."

(30) The Human Rights Campaign is an advocacy organization that fights for lesbian, gay, bisexual, transgender, and queer Americans. The HRC logo was created in 1997 by Stone Yamashita Partners design studio. It was the second-choice favorite among focus groups, but the founders stuck with it for the simplicity and geometry. Although the HRC has been criticized for focusing so much on marriage equality, especially for affluent gays, at the expense of other issues for the LGBTQ community, the organization has been successful in raising awareness through bumper stickers, social media, and person-to-person campaigning. (31) Square bumper stickers are cheaper to print than rectangular ones, so organizers
could give them out for free on the street, making the cause more visible. In a 5–4 ruling on June 26, 2015, the U.S. Supreme Court ruled that marriage equality bans are unconstitutional and that marriage is a fundamental right for all. Social media exploded. Users replaced the rectangular parts of the HRC equal sign with slices of bacon, Chihuahuas, and their own art.

Today in the United States, people are fighting for the right to use the public restroom associated with their gender identity. Graphic designers are developing restroom signs that resist defining people according to binary gender categories. Mindy Lang designed a solution for inclusive bathroom signs at Cooper Union in New York City. Instead of identifying male or female users of a restroom, Lang's signs indicate what type of facility is offered inside (stalls, urinals, or both). All visitors are free to use the facility of their choice.

It turns out that bathroom signs are deeply embedded in the history of civil rights. Creating separate bathrooms for white and nonwhite people was a powerful tool of racial segregation. During the fight for women's suffrage, the creation of separate public restrooms for women was championed by feminist pioneers as an essential step in securing women's right to work, circulate, and be alone in public space. Without separate bathrooms, women would have been forced to stay sequestered at home. (33) Today, the very facilities that helped advance women's equality are now seen as impediments to freedom of gender expression.

The French philosopher and historian Michel Foucault said, "Freedom is practice. . . . Freedoms are never assured by the laws and the institutions that are intended to guarantee them. . . . The guarantee of freedom is freedom." Graphic design is a practice, too. We practice design to change our lives and to change our communities. Along the way, we find new ways to express the ideas that shift and shatter all around us.

Endnotes

1 Posters created by the women's suffrage movement are preserved by the Schlesinger Library on the History of Women, Radcliffe Institute for Advanced Study, Harvard.

2 John Stauffer, *Picturing Frederick Douglass: An Illustrated Biography of the Nineteenth Century's Most Photographed American: An Illustrated Biography of the Nineteenth Century's Most Photographed American* (New York: Liveright Press, 2015).

3 Whitney Battle-Baptiste et al., *W.E.B. Du Bois's Data Portraits: Visualizing Black America* (New York: Princeton Architectural Press, 2018).

4 Lincoln Cushing, "The Women Behind the Black Panther Logo," Design Observer, 02.01.18

5 See https://www.nytimes.com/2018/03/07/movies/black-panther-luke-cage-artist-billy-graham.html

6 https://www.essence.com/celebrity/hannah-beachler-production-designer-black-panther-career

7 http://www.umich.edu/~lawrace/schoolsegregation1.htm

8 https://www.ncsu.edu/ncsu/design/cud/about_us/usronmace.htm

9 Center for Universal Design at North Carolina State University

http://universaldesign.ie/What-is-Universal-Design/The-7-Principles/

Ellen Lupton and Brockett Horne team-teach the course Graphic Design History at MICA. Ellen is founding director of MICA's Graphic Design MFA program. Brockett is chair of the Graphic Design BFA program. Their online course, Graphic Design History: An Introduction, *is available for free on Kadenze.*

THE IMPACT OF DESIGN: A FINAL REMINDER

Teresa Trevino

After meeting twice a week to learn about the history of graphic design, it is time to wrap up and end our semester with a final lecture. During this last meeting, we discuss with one idea in mind. Hopefully this last conversation is useful in the professional future of each student in the class:

> Design is not concerned with objects, but with the impact that those objects have on people. We have to stop thinking of design as the construction of graphics, products, services, systems, and environments and think about those as means for people to act, to realize their wishes and satisfy their needs. It is the needs and the wishes of people that we have to serve: the objects of design must be seen only as means. This requires a better understanding of people, of society, and of the ecosystem. This necessity to extend the area of competence of the designer, from knowledge of form, technique, and manufacturing processes to the understanding of social, psychological, cultural, economic, and ecological factors that affect life in society, shows up a need to implement an interdisciplinary approach to education, research, and practice in visual communication design.
> —Jorge Frascara, "The Dematerialization of Design"

Yes, we learn graphic design history chronologically by following the sequence of Philip Meggs's *A History of Graphic Design*. We often break that linear pacing by watching videos, creating collages, designing visual essays, and connecting current events to the course content. We use additional references as Caroline Robert's *Graphic Design Visionaries* to learn about designers and the need to include women designers in many design books. We read selected articles from the *Looking Closer* series to learn to differentiate facts from opinions, as Massimo Vignelli declares his beliefs in *Long Live Modernism*. We learn about posters, brands, books, advertising campaigns, magazines as proof of who we are and what we do as designers. However, from day one, we see those objects as means to transform people's lives.

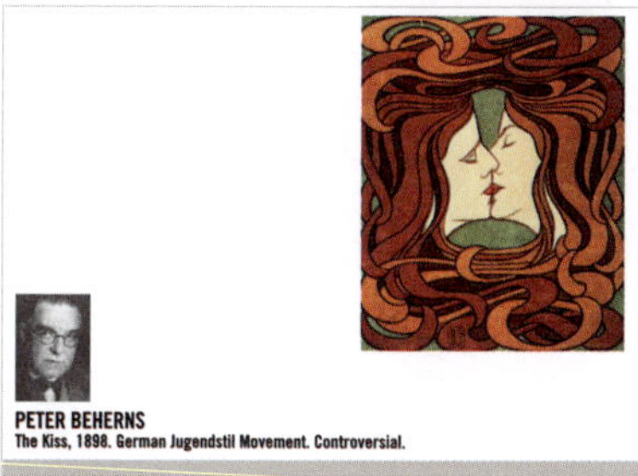

1

HARRY BECK
London Underground Map / 1933

2

Gesellschaftsgliederung in Wien

OTTO NEURATH & GERD ARNTZ
Social Stratification in Vienna / 1920-1940

3

And our final lecture begins . . .

Slide 1. The Kiss. Peter Beherns. 1898. Designed during the German Jugendstil movement by Peter Beherns, this print symbolizes an intimate moment between two lovers. Beauty, symmetry, and organic shapes make this composition unique and harmonious. However, it is the message on gender ambiguity that may allow some viewers to feel represented and included.

Slide 2. London Underground Map. Harry Beck. 1933. Harry Beck created the Tube map, so Londoners could move around the city feeling safe and in the right direction. Maps are meant to be accurate and represent reality. Rather than accuracy and functionality, Beck's focused on what people needed: an easy-to-manage tool to commute every day. In addition, Beck's map became a national identity symbol and an international reference for underground maps.

Slide 3. The ISOTYPE movement. Otto and Marie Neurath, Gerd Arntz. 1920–1940. The International System of Typographic Picture Education movement from Vienna was created to educate the general public on social topics, mainly postwar housing. The ISOTYPE movement may be seen today as politically incorrect, but back in the forties, information became available for everyone to understand and, as a consequence, also social justice.

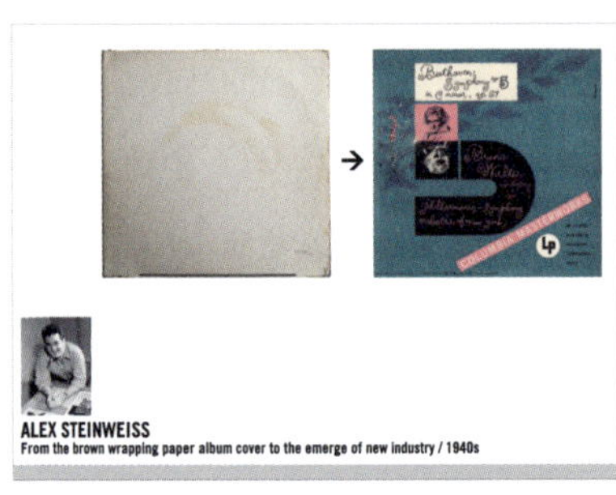

4

Slide 4. The Album Cover Industry. Alex Steinweiss. 1939.
Alex Steinweiss became art director for Columbia Records at the age of twenty-four. By changing the way album records were packaged, he marked a turning point in design, the music industry, and the world of music collectors.

Optima
Aa Qq Rr
Aa Qq Rr
MEMORIAL
abcdefghijklm
nopqrstuvwxyz
0123456789
HERMANN ZAPF
OPTIMA / 1958

5a

5b

Slides 5a & b. Optima Typeface. Hermann Zapf. 1958.
Created by Hermann Zapf, Optima became the typeface of editorial and brand design of the 1960s. In 1982, Yale architecture student Maya Lin won the national competition for the Vietnam Veterans Memorial in Washington, DC. Names of soldiers who died in that war were carved in the Optima font, and when visitors read the names of their late loved ones, they see those names and their face connected by the black granite.

6

Slide 6 From Olympic pictograms to a new language for democracy. Lance Wyman. 1968.
Pictograms created by Lance Wyman to represent 1968 Olympic disciplines became the turning point for Mexican graphic design and designers. It also inspired students to fight government from oppression by transforming Wyman's pictograms into images of fight and resistance. With this visual language system, students started a social revolution.

7

Slide 7. Solidarity (Solidarnosc) logo. Jerzy Janiszewski. 1980.
Inspired by street graffiti, unity among individuals, and a leader, Jerzy Janiszewski created an identity for Polish citizens to demand better government and politicians. The power of this image and people's unity made Solidarity the leading political force in the country.

PEACE FOR PARIS / TWITTER / NOV 13, 2015

8

Slide 8. Peace for Paris. Jean Jullien. 2015.
As a response to the attacks in Paris in 2015, graphic artist Jean Jullien posted his *Peace for Paris* symbol on social media. A hand-drawn Eiffel Tower inside a circle was printed on white paper and painted on people's faces around the world. This democratic symbol became an immediate image of unity and protest.

9

Slide 9. The Silence Breakers. *Time*'s Person of the Year 2017 cover.
Berlin-based photographers Anke Linz and Andreas Otteinger, also known as Billy&Hells were the creators of *Time*'s Person of the Year 2017, The Silence Breakers. By portraying brave women who use the power of their voice, this magazine cover marks an urgent social change on gender justice.

Slide 10. Thank you!

Teresa Trevino is associate professor of Interaction Design at the University of the Incarnate Word, San Antonio, Texas.

EXHIBITIONS AS TEACHING TOOL

Curated by Michael Skjei

Teaching graphic design using real artifacts as examples is not the same as teaching the history or practice of painting and sculpture. For the latter, proximity to the original reveals many important subtleties and nuances not impossible through even the most accurate reproductions in books or on slides. Printed material, however, over time invariably is degraded by time and usage, so it is often better to experience them through printed reproductions or facsimiles. Nonetheless, no matter how yellowed or moldy an original may be, the original printed material is more credible. Getting up close (and personal) with a poster, book, magazine, brochure—well known or unknown—triggers deeper interest in the object, designer, and the history each represents. We see these artifacts every day and everywhere—graphic design is common but uncommon, too—and original historical documentation comes with a the distinct veneer of age—of use. In this sense, these exhibitions provide invaluable learning opportunities for students to understand media before the digital age.

Michael Skjei, a designer, teacher, collector, and independent curator, sorts through, analyzes, and classifies work by significant modernist designers. Aside from the fetishistic joy of holding the material, his displays of collected works elicits specials responses from his audiences. His exhibitions are displays of ephemeral rarities categorized according to commonalities: logos, packages, typography. They validate design practice by providing heritage and legacy to mere pieces of paper.

The three exhibitions in the photographs shown on the following pages of work by Paul Rand, Alvin Lustig, and Lester Beall are the minimasterpieces of midcentury design. Most are not the standard canonical work repeated in history books. Others are variations on well-worn themes. I asked Skeji how he acquired the material and its meaning for his practice. His answers may inspire other design teachers to use the exhibition as an educational tool.

How did the individual exhibits supplement your teaching?
I've used numerous pieces from my collections and the exhibitions as reference to every aspect of typographyand graphic design, i.e., type in logotypes, typographic styling (macro and micro), font selection/ appropriateness, grids and usage, layouts, pagination. I've used Rand's, Lustig's, and Beall's work as examples of timeless and appropriate typographic application and usage.

"Getting up close (and personal) with a poster, book, magazine, brochure—well known or unknown—triggers deeper interest in the object, designer, and the history each represents."

What was the student response to each?
Most of my students are shocked with how relevant these designers and their respective works are today. Maybe more importantly, they begin to understand what it takes to create good design.

Were there assignments related to each?
Not really, though many design students were involved in the hanging of the shows. It is literally a hands-on education. Our classes and lecture tours are guided by different faculty members.

How has collecting been educational for you?
To realize that these early designers were so much more prolific than you are led to believe. The history books always show the same items. When you collect, you need to research, which leads to incredible little-known discoveries. It's incredibly addictive.

RAND, THE EARLY YEARS: BRANDING BY PAUL RAND, 1941–1955

2010/2011, College of Visual Arts, St. Paul, MN.

Paul Rand was known for many design disciplines but his branding (or bRANDing) for major corporations are his most lasting contributions to visual and business culture.

The three key rules
of marketing are:
brand recognition,
brand recognition,
and brand recognition.
Anonymous
nutri-cola
cola at its best
vigor added
Bab-o
world's sudsiest cleaner!

CORONET
v.s.q. brandy
CORONET
V.S.Q.
America's handy brandy!

The objects exhibited in the Rand show not only reveal the graphic design, but the contexts for which it was made.

FRAZER
Kaiser
FRAZER
Walter Landor

maidenform
I dreamed...

THE LUSTIGS: A COVER STORY, 1933–1961

2012, College of Visual Arts, St. Paul, MN.

All original Lustig jackets and covers gave the viewer an invaluable look at the range and quality of work.

MY LIFE IN ART
PHILOSOPHIES OF INDIA
the literature of the Spanish people
LITERATURE IN America
THE ORIGINS OF TOTALITARIANISM
CHINESE
JAIL KEYS MADE HERE
THE PHILOSOPHY OF Spinoza
THE MAN OF THE RENAISSANCE
ONE WA
NEW YORK PLACES & PLEASURES
THE PLACE OF VALUE IN A WORLD OF FACTS
Folksongs and Footnotes by Theodore Bikel
FROM THE nrf
Frank Lloyd Wright Writings and Buildings
The Childhood of Man
A History of the Early Church
the new architecture of europe
Clear Writing
The Federalist
MARLOWE
A Long Day's Dying
dANgLiNG MaN
Saul Bellow

Many people who knew Lustig's books did not know that he designed record sleeves too.

NEW DIRECTIONS
in prose and poetry
16
TENNESSEE WILLIAMS
hard candy
BABY DOLL
TENNESSEE WILLIAMS
poems by THOMAS MERTON
THE strange ISLANDS
IN THE WINTER OF CITIES
Tennessee Williams
THE SORROWS OF PRIAPUS

history 1
history 2
history 3
the noble savage 1
the noble savage 2
the noble savage 3
freud or jung ?
THE MAKING OF EUROPE
Christopher Dawson
THE VARIETIES OF HISTORY
From Voltaire to the Present
The Varieties of History
The Essence of LAUGHTER
ITALIAN PAINTERS OF THE RENAISSANCE
ST. AUGUSTINE
TOYNBEE
RELIGION AND CULTURE
PROUST
ST. THOMAS AQUINAS
MEMOIRS OF A REVOLUTIONIST
DWIGHT MACDONALD
The Disinherited Mind
GOETHE BURCKHARDT NIETZSCHE RILKE SPENGLER KAFKA KRAUS
THE BOOK OF JAZZ
LEONARD FEATHER
The Scrolls from the Dead Sea
ALDOUS HUXLEY
Grey Eminence
F. S. C. NORTHROP
THE RECOLLECTIONS OF ALEXIS DE TOCQUEVILLE
The Romantic Enlightenment
Geoffrey Clive
JUNG
ANSWER TO JOB
NEWMAN
AMERICA AND THE IMAGE OF EUROPE
philosophy of science
The Persian Letters
MONTESQUIEU
the american pragmatists
Jerusalem and Rome
The Grass Roots of Art
Herbert Read
The Autobiography of Gibbon
aesthetics today

MEN & IDEAS
The Ideal Reader
the new poets of england and america
THE WRITINGS OF MARTIN BUBER
sights and spectacles
mary mccarthy
THE WHEEL OF FIRE
Erwin Panofsky
gothic architecture and scholasticism
FREUD
AND THE 20th CENTURY
edited by Benjamin Nelson
POLITICS AND THE NOVEL
ORWELL
MALRAUX
Koestler
A SHORTER HISTORY OF SCIENCE
FRENCH
Pieter
POLITICS: WHO GETS WHAT, WHEN, HOW
HAROLD LASSWELL
GODS & HEROES OF THE GREEKS
RELIGION IN AMERICA
MEN & IDEAS
witchcraft
EUROPEAN Literature
6
The Main Stream of Music and Other Essays
Jonathan Edwards
PERRY MILLER
The Confederacy
Gilbert Highet
TALENTS & GENIUSES
The King and the Corpse
THE BEDBUG AND SELECTED POETRY
GOD AND THE WAYS OF KNOWING
Richard H. Rovere
Senator Joe McCarthy
ON ART AND ARTISTS
PASTERNAK
I remember
GEYL
Thomas Mann
The Ironic German
Erich Heller
HELLENISTIC CIVILISATION
A Guide to Contemporary Italian Literature
America in the World
James

LESTER BEALL: 1903–1969

2016, Concordia University, St. Paul, MN.

Lester Beall's work is iconic from the poster side, this exhibit showed rare and lesser-known packaging and print.

CATERPILLAR
NO.14E

The best way to teach students history is to exhbit the everyday or commonplace jobs of pioneer designers.

Altes
Golden Lager
Beer
Altes
Golden Lager
Beer
Altes

FOR EXTRA DRY SKIN
Pond's
DRY SKIN CREAM

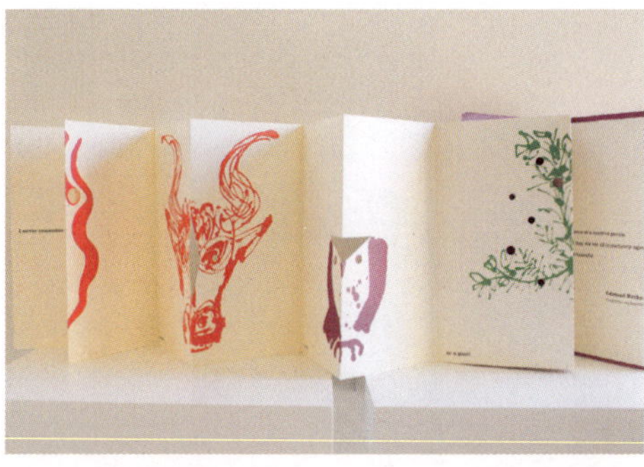

CH7

HISTORY FROM A TO Z

Emily McVarish

Precis

About ten years ago, Johanna Drucker offered me the huge gift of collaborating with her to write a graphic design history textbook. The outcome of that project, *Graphic Design History: A Critical Guide,* was published by Pearson in 2012. After a couple of years of self-consciously teaching from it, I decided to stop requiring students to purchase and read the textbook. Instead, the book's conception and contents suffused the design of a seminar in which readings would focus on primary texts. Only the most distilled parts of the textbook were included in the course reader: its summaries and lists (chapter openers, timelines, etc.). But the structure of *Graphic Design History: A Critical Guide* framed weekly themes, its references populated course materials, and its analyses composed my lectures. It could be cited on almost every line of the documents that follow. Instead, I propose a blanket acknowledgment of my collaborator, Johanna Drucker, whose mind and work have shaped any course I could teach on this subject.

The summer before I took up teaching this iteration of the course, I was inspired by a French radio program in which, two weeks before the baccalaureate exams were to be given, teachers in various subject areas were invited to give advice to students preparing to take the test. On the day I happened to tune in, the show's host asked a geology professor whether he thought it was possible for a student who until then had not studied at all to pass the test in his area. His answer was an unequivocal yes. He went on to prescribe a method of review that involved making a chart, the design of which would identify and locate (logically relate) on a single sheet all of the essential elements and phenomena the student should have learned over the year.

This program reminded me that Johanna and I had begun work on the textbook by drawing up a matrix of categories and examples that in any given era might define graphic design. Devising the matrix guided our thinking about how to structure the book. Its contents served as a reference as we executed the book's plan. I returned to this document (parts of which show up in the published book's introductory pages) and developed it into something I could hand to my students from the outset of the class. This is the "chart" to which the following notes and assignments refer, an 11 x 17-inch table divided horizontally into eras and vertically into categories of relevant information.

Like the geology mnemonic prescribed by the sympathetic French professor, the chart was meant to be a cognitive aid. It was also meant to be a talisman as we entered the endless terrain of historical backdrop. But its most important quality was to be its questionability: As a provisional short list of works and the conditions that situate them, the chart was intended to put its owner in the active position of a historian. By asking students to interrogate and revise it, I hoped they would consider not only its contents but its premises. Portable and debatable, the chart embodied both the practical and the critical aims of the course.

I taught this version of the class for a year. Did its design succeed? In some respects, perhaps. But, as ever, much remains to be reworked. With that in mind, here are some core materials from the course: my notes from its first meeting, the syllabus and assignments, outlines of weekly topics, and the contents of the "chart."

PART 1

Course Description

This course will explore the historical foundations of graphic design and the cultural dynamics within which designers operate. Historical context will be approached as an interaction of social forces, institutional strategies, technological factors, and intellectual developments that have shaped and continue to shape the conception and making of individual works of graphic design and the identity of the field as a whole. In turn, graphic design will be studied as a cultural practice that contributes to the production and representation of this context. Students will practice historiography as critical inquiry and interpretive writing, applying broad lenses to the analysis of specific works; seeking meaning in the relationship between the work of individual designers and the ideas of their times; tracing continuities, parallels, and shifts between the contemporary practice of graphic design and its antecedents; analyzing the impact of technological and cultural change on the uses of graphic media; and taking an editorial approach to canonical lists and the narratives they establish.

Course Structure

Readings will be reviewed, discussed, and supplemented by presentations each week. Weekly research assignments will address the historical significance of individual works of graphic design. Students will make brief presentations of their findings in class. A short paper will be assigned at midterm. The final will cover material from the entire semester.

General Course Objectives

This course will strengthen skills in the following areas:

- Critical analysis
- Interpretive writing
- Visual and textual research
- Verbal presentation

Specific Course Objectives

In this course, students will gain:

- An awareness of the sociocultural legacies and conditions that inform their work as designers.
- A range of models of graphic design's agency as a producer and mediator of shared images, meanings, knowledge, and values.
- A sensitivity to the impact of conceptual inheritance and technical parameters on the generation of graphic form.
- A sense of the cultural circumstances, economic contingencies, and technological bases of graphic design's identity and status as a profession.

Requirements

- Punctual attendance
- Timely completion of all readings and assignments
- Regular participation in class discussions

Assignments

In addition to completing readings and participating in discussions, students will be assigned weekly research topics and reading presentations, a short paper (at midterm), and a revision/update of the course's provisional canon/frame of reference (final).

Research and Academic Integrity

Please consult California College of the Arts library's guides to research and citation.

Evaluation

Final grades will be based on the following percentages:

- 25% Participation
- 25% Weekly research assignments
- 25% Midterm
- 25% Final

Readings

A reader is available for purchase.

PART 2

Outlines of weekly presentations and discussions

(Adapted from *Graphic Design History: A Critical Guide*) Bold items refer to readings and references. Their occurrence indicates a shift from lecture to discussion.

1. Renaissance: Printing and Knowledge Bases	General remarks and background I. Prints and visual information **Ivins reading** A. From drawing to print: technical explanation of relief printing: letterpress and woodcut B. Visual information as basis for advancement of science and applied science (tech.) C. Popular visual culture (visual literacy) II. Letterpress and standardization **Eisenstein reading** A. From hands (styles of writing) to type (first industrial process: modular and standardized B. Standardization of languages, knowledge, attitudes III. Humanist culture and visual systems **Tory reading** A. Tory's system in *Champfleury* B. Perspective: rationalization (via math) but also single point of view=human(ist) C. Maps: exploration and cultural point of view
2. Enlightenment: Modern Typography and the Public Sphere	General remarks and background I. Virtual communities: news sheets and popular prints **Habermas and Anderson readings** A. Evolution of newspaper format B. State of printing in England: Moxon II. Engraving v. letterpress: A. Engraving v. letterpress printing B. Rococo and neoclassical styles C. Modular ornament v. engraved decoration

III. Engraved writing and typeface modernization
  A. Sub-theme: production values and standards
  B. Romain du Roi
  C. Baskerville (v. Caslon): production values
  D. Didot
  E. Bodoni

Bodoni reading

IV. L'esprit de système: administration and taxonomies
  A. Playfair
  B. Encyclopedia chart
  C. Type design and measurement
  D. Le Brun, etc.

3. Industrialization: Novelty Display and Mass Mediation

General remarks and background

I. Mass production: mass markets and visual culture

Benjamin and Zola readings

  A. Commerce and display (merchandizing)
  B. Variety and novelty (display types)

II. The graphic effects of new printing technologies:
  A. Endgrain wood engraving
  B. Lithography
  C. Photographic technologies
  D. Pantographic punchcutter
  E. Mechanized typesetting

III. The emergence of design from printing and in response to mass markets
  A. Automation and specialization of tasks
  B. Advertising and mass-circulation magazines

IV. Posters and the status of graphic art

4. Formations of the Modern Movement

General remarks and background.

The question of nineteenth-century design and production quality as exemplified by book printing.

Morris reading

I. Responses to the social and aesthetic effects of industrialization addressed the relationship between form (shape and decoration) and production (materials and methods).

A. These responses took recurring forms:
   a. Historical revival, folk, and mystical styles combined and conflicted with new forms of abstraction—organic and geometric.
   b. *Integration* was a common goal, and interdisciplinarity a common practice, as an emphasis on craft evolved into a productive dialogue with industry. Integration of:
      i. Fine + applied art (Hobby Horse)
      ii. Ideas + production (journals)
      iii. Elements of page composition (type, image ornament)
      iv. Forms and materials/production
      v. Disciplines/gesamtkunstwerk "total unified work of art" in architecture: fully integrated spaces including furniture, wall treatments, fixtures, and textiles
      vi. Design as *integration* (as system) (Behrens)
   c. Independent graphic arts publications were instruments of aesthetic experimentation, demonstration, and dissemination.
   d. Reform of public taste: Morris, Bing, Werkbund
B. These forms developed among a range of movements and organizations:
   a. Arts and Crafts
   b. Art Nouveau /Jugendstil
   c. Glasgow Style
   d. Vienna Secession
   e. Wiener Werkstätte
   f. Private Press and Book Beautiful Movement
   g. Peter Behrens and the Deutscher Werkbund

II. Conditions for professionalization
   A. Last week: practical (technical and economic) factors, which give rise to new professional role/identity
   B. This week: critical and conceptual conditions for professionalization—a social and cultural role for design.

5.
Avant-Garde: Showing the Way Forward

To truth, purity: an absolute, a transcendence

General themes and introductory remarks.

I. Propaganda: Futurism, WWI, Dada, and Russian revolution
   Rhetorical strategies: manifesto, provocation, subversion v. normalization and continuity
   Graphic strategies: collage, mixed typefaces v. popular styles
   A. Futurism: break with the past
   B. Plakatstil: serve the war effort
   C. Rosta windows: serve the revolution
   D. Dada: overturn values

II. Publicity: art<—>design / cutting edge<—>mainstream / visionary<—>professional
   - A. Marinetti to Depero: poetry and manifesto to advertisement and GD
   - B. Rodchenko and Mayakovsky: ROSTA to Ad Constructor
   - C. Schwitters's Merz and the Ring: art's uses of mainstream culture and design's professionalization

III. Principles: formalism, universalism, functionalism
   - A. Constructivism: Rodchenko dynamism + Lissitzky: showing the structure
   - B. De Stijl: spiritual abstraction + application: Piet Zwart
   - C. Tschichold: functionalism: bringing the lessons of the avant-garde to the trades

IV. **Tschichold and Moholy-Nagy readings**

V. Institutionalization: Bauhaus
   - A. Moholy-Nagy: visual objectivity
   - B. Bayer: universalism/functionalism

6. Commercial Applications of Modernism

General themes and introductory remarks.

I. Continental Europe
   - A. Modern v. *moderne*
   - B. Design v. commercial art

II. North America
   - A. Pragmatic modernism: **Dwiggins reading**
   - B. Émigrés and modern magazine design: **Agha reading**

III. Anglo-Saxon (U.S. and U.K.)
   - A. New Traditionalism: **Cleland and Morison readings**
   - B. Professional development: **Jones reading**

7. Public Information Campaigns

General remarks.

I. Public campaigns: the rhetoric of normality, objectivity, and authority
   - A. Social programs: WPA, labor movement, Soviet reforms
   - B. Wartime mass mobilization

II. Documentary photography: graphic techniques of photojournalism and propaganda
   - A. Social awareness
   - B. Wartime patriotic narrative

III. Information design: systematic logic and information management
   - A. Kinross and Lupton readings
   - B. Prewar and postwar information graphics

8. International Style

Introduction

I. International Style: systematic programs
  A. **Müller-Brockmann reading**
    a. The grid system
  B. **Sutnar reading**
    a. Identity systems
    b. Signage and symbol systems
    c. Systematic type families

II. Individual styles—as exceptions?
  A. Eames Office
  B. Bradbury Thompson
  C. Alvin Lustig
  D. Saul Bass
  E. Paul Rand
  F. Leo Lionni
  G. Humanist universalism encore
  H. An absurdist (expressive) system
    a. Massin's *The Bald Soprano*

9. Pop and Protest

Introduction.

I. Pop inversions
  A. Art's immersion in commodity culture, mass media, celebrity values
    a. Products and by-products of the art market
    b. Critique and participation
  B. Graphic and commercial design as leading edge of culture
    a. Commerce, fashion, and advertising as prime sources of contemporary aesthetics and cultural expression

II. Media: awareness, embrace, and appropriation
  McLuhan/Fiore reading
  A. Media theory: the technical basis of cultural forms and subjective experience
    a. Marshall McLuhan's *Understanding Media*
    b. Quentin Fiore's *The Medium Is the Massage*
  B. Media uses: the means of cultural identity production
    a. Production values: the mainstream appeal of youth culture: *Twen*
    b. Design as production: underground media and countercultural practice

III. Protest and subversion

Garland reading

A. Protest graphics: the opposite of mediation and decontextualization
   a. Direct calls for direct action
   b. Time and place: print and political meaning

Sontag reading

B. The Spectacle: the inescapable reign of representation and commodification
   a. Situationist interventions

---

10. Postmodern Design

Convergence of theory and practice: designer as textual interpreter and cultural critic

Emergence of women as leaders: Another notable occurrence in this period.

Lecture and discussion format:

I. A glossary of theoretical terms illustrated by graphic examples—in alphabetical order

II. An informal discussion of women in the field

I. **Glossary** (all definitions excerpted from *Graphic Design History: A Critical Guide*)

antihumanism a philosophical stance that challenges the belief that universal values or inherent moral principles are shared by human beings and replaces it with a conviction that all such values are historically and culturally determined.

appellation a rhetorical strategy that uses cultural codes and references to position a viewer as the intended recipient of a message; the stylistic equivalent of a statement in the second person (*you*).

appropriation the act of taking existing images or texts as the basis for a new work; distinguished from imitation by the fact that the materials borrowed or cited are often absorbed directly into the new work without significant alteration.

deconstructive of or pertaining to a philosophical method of interpretation premised on the idea that texts and images do not reveal truths but create fields of signification and that reading their signs through a play of difference produces meaning that is always shifting.

Keedy, Burdick/Sandhaus, and Kinross readings

détournement a technique developed by the Situationists for deforming or transforming an image or text as a way of reformulating cultural values; an intervention in the cultural meaning of a text or image that calls attention to the system of beliefs within which it functions.

culture-jamming any activity or process that disrupts mainstream cultural practice by altering the message of an image or text to expose its underlying assumptions or interests.

hyperreal of or pertaining to appearances in which it is impossible to distinguish reality from illusion, either because a representation is so believable or because conditions of perception or cognition do not allow for distinctions between real and imagined phenomena or experience. [Hyperreality: a media-permeated condition in which nothing and everything is real.]

multiculturalism an attention to, or allowance for, traditions and practices from a variety of ethnic or social sources; an awareness of the cultural relativity of value judgments and their location within specific historical contexts. [Has both legal/policy dimensions and theoretical/critical ramifications.]

pastiche a composition made of parts taken from various sources, or in the style of a particular artist or moment; in a postmodern context, the appropriation of historical or canonical materials to make a new work that assumes that all ideas have already been expressed and that originality is a mythic concept. [So, closely related to appropriation: what results from the act of appropriation.]

post-human with reference to the idea that humans are no longer simply or independently an organic, biological species but that we exist in hybrid forms with machines, industrial parts, or digital technology.

postmodernism a cultural moment at which modernism's claims for universal, formal, and autonomous qualities in works of art or design were replaced by notions of relativism, contingency, and play within sign systems. [Contingency—on context and conventions—is what Sherrie Levine was playing with.]

simulation an image or representation that may be taken for reality; in the critical writing of twentieth-century theorist Jean Baudrillard, a simulation has no referent in lived experience but is an image that produces belief [representation without a model, a copy without an original].

spectacle something meant to be seen; in contemporary theory, associated with the work of French theorist Guy Debord, a condition of culture in which experience has been replaced by images; an organization of everyday life under capitalism within which social relations and the relationship of individuals to their own lives are mediated by representations; the ubiquity of such mediation.

II. **Women gain prominence**

Reference: Essay by Ellen Lupton from Pat Kirkham, ed. *Women Designers in the USA, 1900–2000*. London: Yale University Press, 2000.

A. Part of a general historical change
B. The result of a movement (ex: The Women's Building in Los Angeles)
C. The role of academic institutions (where women took leadership roles) and the emphasis on critical theory
D. Examples: Muriel Cooper, Rosmarie Tissi, April Greiman, Louise Fili, Lorraine Wild, Sheila de Bretteville, Deborah Sussman, Paula Scher, Katherine McCoy, Ellen Lupton, Lucille Tenazas.

11.
Digital Design

I. Review of Chronology
A. Digital design before it was graphic design: engineers and conceptual artists
B. The GUI brings computational visualization and transformation into the hands of graphic designers—and everyone else.
C. WYSIWYG
D. Software mediates design processes
E. Prepress becomes digital
F. Typeface design becomes accessible
G. The Web makes interaction a prominent practice of graphic design.

II. "All digital files are data, processed and stored as binary code." Separation of input from output, of data or code from its display

III. Interface rhetoric: metaphors and conventions as conceptual conditions
A. Designers helped set these terms but were also subject to them in software.

IV. Changes in the work and identity of graphic design(ers)
A. Saved for **Blauvelt reading discussion** the following week

12. Present-Tense History	General remarks. I. The state of the field A. Disciplinarity and professional identity B. Foundations for fluidity C. Emblematic figures **Blauvelt and Lupton readings** II. Your contemporary picks

PART 3

Renaissance Design: Humanism and Standardization (1450–1660)	
Social Conditions	• Monarchy; diplomacy • Reformation • Rise of market economy • Expansion of publishing • Geographical exploration, colonialism
Technological Features and Factors: General	• Metallurgy • Mechanical engineering • Firearms • Nautical compass
Technological Features and Factors: Graphic	• Woodblock printing • Typecasting • Letterpress printing • Engraving • Papermaking
Cultural Attitudes/ Formative Concepts	• Humanism; rivalry between the Moderns and Ancients • Promotion of vernacular/national culture • Beginning of "scientific revolution" • Modularity • Standardization

Styles and Movements	• Classicism • Realism • Perspective • Roman type (Old Style) • Black letter type
Instrumental Media	• Printed books • Technical engravings • Broadsides • Maps

PART 4

Weekly Research

Assigned image

1. Research your assigned piece in order to answer the following question: Why is this work considered important to the history of graphic design?
2. Prepare to present your findings in class.
3. Hand in a bibliographic citation of your sources.

Historical wild card

1. Choose and research a work of graphic design from the period under consideration in order to answer the following questions: How does the work relate to its era? How would its inclusion improve (change or refine) the chart?
2. Prepare to present your findings in class.
3. Send me a jpeg of the work **by 9:00 a.m.** on the day of your presentation.
4. Hand in a bibliographic citation of your sources.

Contemporary wild card

1. Choose a recent work of graphic dvesign that relates in some way to the period we are studying and consider the nature of this relationship: Is it based on a stylistic similarity? A technical difference? A social or cultural purpose? Some other comparison?
2. Prepare to present your analysis in class.
3. Send me a jpeg of the work **by 9:00 a.m.** on the day of your presentation.
4. Hand in a bibliographic citation of your sources.

PART 5

Midterm

Of the following, which **three** qualities do you consider essential to the identity of graphic design?

- an aesthetic that relates to technologies of (re)production and/or media of distribution
- a social purpose (define)
- a form that integrates its contents
- a functional organization/presentation of information
- a cultural resonance (define)

Choose a graphic work from one of the periods we have studied so far (up to and including "formations of the modern movement"), analyze it in relation to the three traits you choose, and compare it to a work of contemporary design that embodies the same three qualities. What connects the two pieces? What separates them?

Length: Minimum 1,000 words; maximum 2,000 words.

Format: It can be an essay, but it doesn't have to be an essay, as long as the logical relationship between its parts is made clear.

Composition: It must be written in grammatically correct sentences and be illustrated with images of works cited.

Argument: The claims of your analysis must be supported by evidence presented.

Sources: All textual sources must be cited in Chicago style. Please also cite your image sources.

Due: Both hard copy (in class) *and* pdf (by email)

PART 6

FINAL: Chart Revision and Update

Instructions

- Choose two or three general (conceptual and/or material) axes whose intersection identifies graphic design. For example, these may be logical, ethical, social, cultural, technical, or professional in nature.
- Applying this framework, answer the questions below.
- Revise the chart based on your answers to the questions below. Revisions may involve eliminations, substitutions, and additions affecting whole periods and categories or elements within these.
- Bring the chart up to date by supplying contemporary elements (i.e., background information and significant designs from within the last twenty years) in all of the categories that comprise your revised chart. For designs, include the designer's name and the design's date and title or client.
- Design/format your revised chart.
- Introduce your chart: Write one paragraph that presents your framework for tracking the history of graphic design and explains how this framework has informed your revision and update of the chart.
- Annotate the chart: List all changes (deletions, substitutions, additions) you have made to the chart's content or structure, as well as the reason for each change. Key the list to the chart.
- Cite all image and information sources.

Questions

1. When does the history of graphic design begin?
2. What are its eras (titles and dates for its chapters)?
3. What contexts and conditions are critical to understanding graphic design's developments?
4. Within these contexts and conditions, what are the most important elements and factors to include as components of a frame of reference for graphic design history?
5. What **seven** works best represent the significance of each era of graphic design history?

DUE: Phase 1

Your framework + one or two sentences indicating how you expect this framework to guide your revision/update of the chart.

DUE: Phase 2

Introductory paragraph + chart + annotations + citations in both hard copy and pdf forms.

PART 7

GDH Matrix Tex	
Exemplary Figures/Works	• Gutenberg: type, 1450s • Jenson: *Noctium*, 1472 • Metlinger: *Arbolayre*, 1487 • Manutius: *Hypnero*, 1499 • Tory: *Champfleury*, 1529 • de Colines: *Horae*, 1541
Institutions/ Professional Developments of Design	• Guilds; apprenticeship • Academies; royal appointments • Presses (printers, publishers) • Foundries

Enlightenment Typography: Reading and the Public Sphere (1660–1800)	
Social Conditions	• Colonialism • Royal privileges and censorship • Expansion of administrative sector • Rise of middle classes; establishment of property rights • Public assembly, debate (coffee) • Revolutions
Technological Features and Factors: General	• Refinements of mechanical engineering • Optical advances • Steam engine
Technological Features and Factors: Graphic	• Improvements in typecasting technologies and measurement systems • Refinements of engraving
Cultural Attitudes/ Formative Concepts	• Rationalism • Individualism • Theories of citizenship • The ideal of progress through knowledge dissemination • Empiricism/scientific method

	• Taxonomic systems • Intellectual property/copyright
Styles and Movements	• Baroque/Rococo • Neoclassicism • Transitional type • Modern type • Engraved writing styles
Instrumental Media	• News sheets • Newspapers • Technical publications
Exemplary Figures/ Works	• Moxon: *Mechanick*, 1683 • Romain du Roi type, 1690s • Baskerville: Virgil, 1757 • Fournier: *Manuel*, 1766 • Playfair: Chart, 1786 • Bodoni: *Manuale*, 1818
Institutions/ Professional Developments of Design	• Guilds; apprenticeship • Academies; royal appointments • Presses (printers, publishers) • Foundries

Industrial Graphic Production/Mass Visual Culture: Novelty and Mediation (1800–1900)

Social Conditions	• Social Conditions • Global imperialism • Revolutions/restorations • Urbanization; labor movement • Mass transportation; brands and advertising • Spectacular consumption: world's fairs and department stores

Technological Features and Factors: General	• Electricity and petroleum • Railroads • Telegraphy • Iron and glass construction • Internal combustion engine
Technological Features and Factors: Graphic	• Lithograph • Mechanized papermaking • Endgrain wood engraving • Photography, photomechanical processes; stereotyping • Pantographic punchcutter • Typecasting machines
Cultural Attitudes/ Formative Concepts	• Positivism • Romanticism; notion of genius • Utopian socialism • Beaux Arts historicism • Exoticism; bohemianism • Self-improvement; social advancement
Styles and Movements	• Display typefaces • "Artistic" printing • Lithographic poster art • Golden Age of illustration • *Plakatstil*
Instrumental Media	• Illustrated press • Serial fiction • Posters
Exemplary Figures/ Works	• *The Penny Sunday*, 1842 • Circus bill, 1844 • *Chéret*, Folies poster, 1893 • Penfield: *Harper's* poster, 1895 • Mucha: Job poster, 1897 • Bernhard, Adler poster, 1908

Institutions/ Professional Developments of Design	• Advertising agencies • Jobbing print shops • *Printers' Ink* (trade magazine) • Specialization of graphic arts jobs
Modern Movements: Aesthetic Responses to Industrialization (1880s–1910s)	
Social Conditions	• Social reform movements, including temperance and women's suffrage • Expansion of public education • Golden Age capitalism • Labor unrest and migration
Technological Features and Factors: General	• Steel construction • Phonograph • Typewriters and office machine • Motion pictures
Technological Features and Factors: Graphic	• Photogravure • Halftone process • Color separation process • Consolidation of miscellaneous reprographic processes
Cultural Attitudes/ Formative Concepts	• Fin-de-siècle decadence • Progressive movement • Psychology • Marxism; alienation v. fulfillment through labor conditions • Beautiful utility/material integrity; aesthetics of everyday life • The New Woman
Styles and Movements	• Arts & Crafts; Fine Press • "Japonism" • Art Nouveau/Jugendstil • Aestheticism, Symbolism • Secession, Werkstätte • Organicism, abstraction • Medievalism; folk motifs and "primal" forms

Instrumental Media	• Graphic arts journals • Exhibitions
Technological Features and Factors: Graphic	• Morris, *The Nature*, 1892 • MacDonald, Glasgow, 1898 • van de Velde, Tropon, 1898 • Eckmann Schmuck, 1901 • Moser, W.W. letterhead, 1904 • Behrens, AEG, 1908
Institutions/ Professional Developments of Design	• Artists' guilds (revival) • *The Studio, Ver Sacrum, Jugend*, etc. • Separation of design from composition (printing)
Avant-garde Design: Innovation and Persuasion in Europe (1910s–1930s)	
Social Conditions	• WWI, imperial reconfiguration and mass migrations • Bolshevik revolution/Soviet experiment and repression • League of Nations founded • Postwar labor strikes • Runaway inflation in Germany
Technological Features and Factors: General	• Assembly-line production • Mass-produced automobile • Broadcast radio • Technological Features and Factors: Graphic • Portable Leica camera • Silkscreen printing
Cultural Attitudes/ Formative Concepts	• Social potential and cultural meaning of industrialization • Radical *now*, historical rupture • Integration of production/form, rationalization, standardization • Gestalt psychology • Internationalism

Styles and Movements	• Futurism, break with history • Dadaism, upending values • De Stijl, transcendent form • Constructivism, social change • Functionalism, anti-ornamentation • Dynamism, asymmetry • Abstraction, universalism • Objectivism, *neue sachlichkeit*
Instrumental Media	• Manifestos • Performance • Collage, montage • ROSTA windows
Exemplary Figures/ Works	• Huszar, de Stijl logo, 1917 • Heartfield, *New Youth*, 1917 • Marinetti, *Mots en . . .*, 1919 • Lissitzky, *For the Voice*, 1923 • Moholy-Nagy, Bauhaus, 1923 • Rodchenko, *New LEF*, 1928
Institutions/ Professional Developments of Design	• Der Ring • The Bauhaus, VKhUTEMAS • National design and industry associations: *Merz*, *New LEF*

Commercial Modernism: Professionalization in the United States (1920s–1940s)

Social Conditions	• Consumer capitalism • Prohibition • Stock market crash, Depression • The New Deal • Political refugees in U.S.

Technological Features and Factors: General	• Electrical engineering • Sound film • Technological Features and Factors: Graphic • Airbrush • Offset lithography • Mechanized typecasting improvements
Cultural Attitudes/ Formative Concepts	• Jazz Age, Lost Generation • Automobile culture • Planned obsolescence • Marketing; lifestyle narratives
Styles and Movements	• Art Deco/*Moderne* • Streamlining/streamlined forms • Cubist references • New Traditionalism; revival of historical typefaces
Instrumental Media	• Art Deco Exposition in Paris • Magazines • Billboards • Trade journals
Exemplary Figures/ Works	• Zwart, cable ad, 1926 • Matter, tourism poster, 1935 • Brodovich, *Harper's*, 1935 • Dwiggins, *The Power*, 1936 • Moholy-Nagy, *New B*, 1937 • Beall, liquor ad, 1937
Institutions/ Professional Developments of Design	• AIGA, Art Directors Club, etc. • Museum of Modern Art • *Commercial Art, Advertising Arts* • New Bauhaus/School of Design

Information Design: Public Interest and Common Cause (1930s–1950s)	
Social Conditions	• Rise of totalitarian regimes • New Deal social programs and infrastructure development • WWII: mass mobilization, deportations, genocide • Postwar reconstruction • Atomic Age (after bombing of Hiroshima and Nagasaki)
Technological Features and Factors: General	• Rural electrification • Electronics • First computers • Broadcast television
Technological Features and Factors: Graphic	• Spread of photo-offset lithography
Cultural Attitudes/ Formative Concepts	• Nationalism; common cause • Mass psychology • Documentary purposes • Systems and information theory
Styles and Movements	• National propaganda • Information design • Photo-essay layout
Instrumental Media	• Photojournalism • Posters • Information graphics • Newsreels
Exemplary Figures/ Works	• Semenova, poster, 1920s • Beck, Underground map, 1933 • Neurath, Isotype, 1936 • *Paris Match*, 1940 • Sutnar, *Catalog Design*, 1950 • Bayer, *World Geo . . .*, 1953

Institutions/ Professional Developments of Design	• WPA, FSA • Government Information Offices
International Style: Postwar Ideals and Corporate Identity (1950s–1970s)	
Social Conditions	• Cold War • Baby boom • Growth of Western economies • Corporate conglomeration • Establishment of the UN and its programs • Civil Rights movement
Technological Features and Factors: General	• Chemical engineering • Commercial computers
Technological Features and Factors: Graphic	• Phototypesetting • Prepress photostats
Cultural Attitudes/ Formative Concepts	• Internationalism, universalism • Pacifism • Existentialism, Absurdism • Beat culture • Youth culture • Visual language
Styles and Movements	• Swiss/International Style • Grid systems • Typographic and style standards
Instrumental Media	• Visual identity systems • Campaigns and brands coordinated across multiple media, including television

Exemplary Figures/ Works	• Golden, CBS identity, 1950 • Rand, IBM identity, 1956–72 • Frutiger, Univers, 1957 • Bass, *Anatomy*, 1959 • Katsumi, Olympics, 1964 • Vignelli, Unigrid, 1977
Institutions/ Professional Developments of Design	• Alliance Graphique International • Aspen Design Conference • Good Design Award

Pop and Protest: Art and Design in Media Culture (1960s–1970s)

Social Conditions	• Space Age • Rising standards of living until oil crisis and downturn • Vietnam War • Student, free speech, antiwar, black power, Chicano, women's rights, sexual liberation, gay rights, ecology movements
Technological Features and Factors: General	• Satellite communications • Consumer audio tape • Super 8 film
Exemplary Figures/ Works	• Semenova, poster, 1920s • Beck, Underground map, 1933 • Neurath, Isotype, 1936
Technological Features and Factors: Graphic	• Letraset • Pantone color matching system • Optical distortions of prepress photography
Cultural Attitudes/ Formative Concepts	• Counterculture/underground subversion of the System—or ironic complicity • Situationism • Ethnic Studies • Structuralism; media theory • Free love; drug culture

Styles and Movements	• Pop Art and design • "Big Idea" advertising • Conceptual image • Psychedelic and op art
Instrumental Media	• Posters: in the street (silk screen) and bedroom (offset) • Album covers • Underground publications
Exemplary Figures/ Works	• DDB, VW ad, 1960 • Wilson, concert poster, 1966 • People Power poster, 1968 • Serrano, Che poster, 1968 • Lubalin, U&lc, 1973 • *Whole Earth Catalog*, 1975
Institutions/ Professional Developments of Design	• MIT Media Lab/VLW • *Visible Language*
Postmodern Design: Inversion and Appropriation (1970s–1990s)	
Cultural Attitudes/ Formative Concepts	• Fall of Berlin Wall; dissolution of the Soviet bloc • Covert intervention in Central American wars • Oil crisis; Savings & Loan crisis • AIDS epidemic
Styles and Movements	• Swiss/International Style • Grid systems • Typographic and style standards • Instrumental Media

Exemplary Figures/ Works	• Golden, CBS identity, 1950 • Rand, IBM identity, 1956–72 • Frutiger, Univers, 1957 • Bass, *Anatomy*, 1959 • Katsumi, Olympics, 1964 • Vignelli, Unigrid, 1977
Technological Features and Factors: General	• Sony Walkman • Consumer video • Laser disc, CD
Technological Features and Factors: Graphic	• Commercial photocopying • Computer-aided phototypesetting
Cultural Attitudes/ Formative Concepts	• Semiotics • “The end of history” • Post-structuralism, Deconstructionism • Identity politics • Hip-hop; sampling
Styles and Movements	• Found and vernacular imagery • Citation and appropriation • Punk/DIY • New Wave • Techno/post-humanism • Broken grid
Instrumental Media	• Zines, flyers, buttons • Mix tapes • Album covers • Designer monographs
Exemplary Figures/ Works	• Posters: in the street (silk screen) and bedroom (offset) • Album covers • Underground publications

Exemplary Figures/ Works	• Reid, Sex Pistols, 1977 • Greiman, Cal Arts, 1979 • Studio Dumbar poster, 1987 • Fella, exhibition poster, 1988 • McCoy, Cranbrook, 1989 • Kalman, *Colors*, 1990s
Institutions/ Professional Developments of Design	• Cranbrook, Cal Arts • Emigre, Design Issues
Digital Design: Repercussions of Tool and Platform Shifts (1970s–2000s)	
Social Conditions	• Free trade, outsourcing • Economic rise of China • Dot-com boom and crash • Gulf Wars • Y2K scare
Technological Features and Factors: General	• Desktop computer; GUI • Microchip advances • Digital photography and video • Multimedia; video games • Hypertext; Internet
Technological Features and Factors: Graphic	• Design software • Digital type; postscript • Desktop printers; scanners • HTML and other markup, scripting, and processing languages
Cultural Attitudes/ Formative Concepts	• Programming • Environmentalism • Techno-libertarianism • Start-up culture • User-centered design

Styles and Movements	• Cut-and-paste composition • Layered and filtered imagery • Novelty in digital typefaces • Information architecture • Neo-modernist functionalism in icon/navigation design
Instrumental Media	• CD-ROMs • Websites • Blogs
Exemplary Figures/ Works	• Kare, Mac icons, 1984 • VanderLans, *Emigre*, 1986 • Carter, Bitstream Charter, 1987 • Makela, Cranbrook, 1990 • Carson, *Ray Gun*, 1992 • Sagmeister, AIGA Detroit, 1999
Institutions/ Professional Developments of Design	• Interface, interaction, experience design • Wired magazine

Graphic Design Now: Present-tense History and Identity (2000–2015)

Social Conditions	• Financialization • Housing bubble and recession • 9/11 and subsequent invasions • Social networks, communities of interest, sharing economies • Patriot Act; mass surveillance • Realities of climate change
Technological Features and Factors: General	• Bio- and genetic engineering • Nano technology • Internet of things • Mobile devices and apps • "Big data"

Technological Features and Factors: Graphic Cultural Attitudes/Formative Concepts	• Hacking • Localism • Craft and Maker cultures • Entrepreneurial innovation • User-generated content; crowdsourcing
Styles and Movements	
Instrumental Media	• YouTube • Facebook, Twitter, Instagram
Exemplary Figures/ Works	
Institutions/ Professional Development of Design	• Design Observer and other sites • Project M and other community-oriented design organizations

Emily McVarish is associate professor, Graphic Design, at the California College of the Arts and a writer and designer. In collaboration with Johanna Drucker, she coauthored Graphic Design History: A Critical Guide *published by Prentice Hall. Her critical writing has been featured in* Visible Language, Design, *and* Culture.

TYPOGRAPHY 1

Jerry Kelly

The class is broken up into three sections, as summarized below. Each section ends with an examination (i.e., first test, midterm, and final). While homework assignments, class participation, etc., are considered, 95 percent of a student's grade is based on the examination scores.

I. HISTORY OF TYPE AND TYPE MANUFACTURE
   - A. Early genesis of typography: Gutenburg & the manuscript tradition; Fust & Schoeffer; Aldus, etc.
   - B. Early type manufacture: punchcutting; matrices; casting. Physical form & nomenclature of metal type
   - C. Rise of the punchcutter and type evolution: Garamond; Granjon; Fournier; Bodoni
   - D. Mechanical type manufacture: Linotype system; Monotype system; pantographic punchcutting machine; phototypesetting; today's digital typesetting methods; desktop publishing
   - E. Characters in a font of type. Variants: old-style figures, small caps, etc.
   - F. Type measurement. Point system

II. CLASSIFICATION OF TYPES
   - A. Why identifying types: mixing/matching, not so much for what you should do, but you should know why you do it
   - B. Allusive typography; retro typography, historical typography
   - C. Different methods of type classification
   - D. Reasons for categorizing typeface styles: identification, combining type styles, etc.
   - E. Roman type classification: Venetian/Renaissance/Dutch-Baroque/Transitional/Modern/Sans serif/Slab serif/Optima/Titling
   - F. Italic type classification: Chancery/French typographic/Transitional/Modern-late engraved/Sloped roman/Hybrid
   - G. Miscellaneous types: Titling/Black-letter/Exotic/Brush/Script

III. APPLICATION OF TYPOGRAPHIC PRINCIPLES
   - A. Information necessary to spec type: font; size; measure; leading; style; alignment; etc.
   - B. Finer points in the arrangement of type: word spacing; letterspacing; punctuation; initial caps (dropped and stick-up); hanging alignments, etc.
   - C. Basics of typographic programs and application of information learned to typographic practice: Quark Xpress; InDesign; etc. Menu and window options, h&j's, etc.

D. Tracking, horizontal scale, h&j's
E. Review of modern typographic arrangements: Tschichold, Zapf, Rogers, Rand, Updike, etc.

FIRST CLASS

Attendance and timeliness	• No unexcused absences • Three absences = an automatic F • Must get name of someone in class for missed work and assignments. You are responsible for this. Cannot repeat material the next session if you miss session • Timing: getting to class on time (start five minutes after). Breaks short and punctual
Assignments	• Not a lot of work, but what is done must be done well • Getting assignment if you miss class • Content is most important this term; neatness not so important in first term • Survey: this term in contrast to next term
Syllabus	• Type is a tool—learn to use that tool • Technical / factual / historical • Three sections, with tests at the end of each section: • history, through which we learn terminology and form • type classification • bringing it all together in application: computer, programs, etc. • Handouts: keep them. You'll have a book of samples at the end of the term
Goals	• To learn how to use type and achieve your designs • To "know" type: at the end of the term you'll know more about type than the art directors you'll be working for • What the class is not: this is not a class on aesthetics; there'll be some of that next term, but first you must learn about type and how to use it • I take this subject seriously

Miscellaneous	• Required texts, money issue • First assignment: Gutenberg voted Man of the Millennium by *Time* magazine. Who was he, what did he accomplish? Can be a one-sentence answer • Who are you: major, what do you want out of this class, where would you want to be five years from now?

TYPE SPECIMEN PROJECT

The goal of this project is to use type in creative and attractive ways while presenting key information to the user. Of course this can be said about many similar projects, but this type specimen has the advantage of:

1. dealing with a large amount of material that requires intelligent organization
2. exercise in exceptional handling of type
3. knowledge will be gained in the use of fonts while preparing specimen
4. specimen will be a useful reference tool for your work in the future

Parameters

Format	A wide variety of formats can be used. We will accept a broadside (single sheet printed on one side), book (bound leaves), or loose sheets in a folder of some kind. Must be print media; electronic media is not acceptable for this project.
Size	Again, a wide variety is acceptable. Keep format in mind when determining size: a broadside containing so much material would obviously need to be fairly large, while loose sheets could be small. Generally 11 × 17 to 24 × 36 inches for a broadside; 6 × 9 to 9 × 12 inches for a book; and 4 × 6 to 12 × 18 inches for loose sheets would be acceptable, but variations outside of these parameters (and proportions) could be fine.
Color	Almost anything goes with color: one-color black throughout would be fine; or a simple two-color arrangement; but more colors are fine.
Illustration	No illustrations or photographs are allowed in this project; though you may use type material other than alphabets in any way you wish (type ornaments—often found in separate fonts or “expert” sets; dingbats, or other typographic material).

Content	The specimen must contain a minimum of two examples each from at least six of the main type categories that must be included. A complete alphabet (a–z) must be shown for each; figures, punctuation, etc., are optional.

1. Venetian Roman	a. Chancerty italic
2. Renaissance Roman	b. French typographic italic
3. Dutch/Baroque	
4. Transitional	c. Transitional italic
5. Neo-classical	d. Late engraved or Neo-classical
6. Sans Serif	e. Sloped Roman
7. Slab Serif (Clarendon, Egyptiennes)	
8. "Optimas"	
9. Titling	f. hybrid

You can feel free to include more than two examples from each category, but two each is a minimum. There is no need to show the same number of fonts from each category: you can show two Venetians and six Renaissance romans, or three Venetians, two Renaissance, and five Neo-classical, etc., if you wish. Also, you can show fonts from categories that are not required (such as black letter or brush) in addition to the required categories, but not instead of any required category.

Type categories (as headings) and font names (to identify types) must be included in your design. In addition, you will need to design a title page (for book), cover page (for specimen sheets), or masthead (for broadside). Include your name in the title: something like "Susan Jones's Type Shop" or "A Selection of Favorite Types from Joe McKenna" would be okay. A short foreword or introductory paragraph is optional (not required).

Criteria

1. Presentation: neatness and quality of presentation are important
2. Appropriateness: how closely execution realizes the specific assignment
3. Clearness of presentation of complex material
4. Demonstration of skill in handling type
5. Quality of design
6. Timelessness

DESIGN PROJECT

Below are a few design considerations to keep in mind when laying out a piece of typography. Keep in mind the words of Bruce Rogers, the great American twentieth-century book designer:

"I have no rules for designing a book, and even if I did I wouldn't tell you, 'cause then I couldn't change them."

Consider what that means for us when discussing design principals.

Parameters

Type Hierarchy	Consider the relative importance of information. Plan on differentiation of main heads and subheads such as A-heads; B-heads, etc. You should be able to tell what's what, even if the job was in a foreign language.
Grid	Having items aligned, based on a grid system, helps to organize information and give a sense of order to your project. The computer-aided design programs are ideally set up for grids (grids are almost automatic, or required, these days). Consider the placement of your main text box, and peripheral text boxes on master pages.
Color	One color (black) would be fine; it sufficed for almost everything printed by Baskerville and Bodoni (not because of cost constraints, either). Two colors (usually red and black) have sufficed for a majority of the finest typography in history. Three or more colors is also acceptable. Consider restrained use of just two colors: sometimes color on just one line on a page is more effective than extended use of color.

Jerry Kelly is a calligrapher, book designer, and type designer and has served as chairman of the American Printing History Association, president of the Typophiles, and an active member of several committees at the Grolier Club. He has written many articles as well as several books on calligraphy and typography, including The Noblest Roman: The Centaur Types *(coauthored with Misha Beletsky, winner of the 2016 Bibliographical Society of America Prize). Before starting his own business in 1998, Kelly was vice president of the Stinehour Press, preceded by a decade as designer at A. Colish. He has taught at various institutions and has lectured widely.*

HISTORY OF VISUAL COMMUNICATION

M. Thistlethwaite

Course Description

This course surveys the rich history of visual communication, with particular focus on two-dimensional graphic design works from the nineteenth century to the present day. Visual communication transmits ideas, knowledge, and cultural attitudes through the visual display of pictorial and textual information.

A major goal of the course is to instill a sense of visual communication's chronology, its various contexts (art historical, stylistic, social, economic, political, etc.), and its tremendous diversity of form and content. Another important goal is to help you develop and refine the skills necessary to examine and articulate clearly and intelligently the form, content, and context of selected examples of visual communication.

No prerequisites are needed for this course.

By participating fully in the course, you will have the opportunity, by semester's end, to:

- Acquire a basic knowledge of the chronological history of visual communication.
- Acquire the skills to describe and analyze the formal and design elements of a visual communication object.
- Acquire the ability to identify and make comparisons between important designers/artists, examples of visual communication, and styles of different periods and cultures.
- Acquire a basic understanding of the reception of selected examples of visual communication.
- Acquire a basic understanding of how visual communication relates to its historical and cultural circumstances, which will contribute to your ability to realize Texas Christian University's mission: "To educate individuals to think and act as ethical leaders and responsible citizens in the global community."
- Acquire a basic knowledge of the range, diversity, and richness of visual communication.
- Acquire a basic understanding of different approaches/methodologies to studying visual communication.
- Fulfill a UCR Fine Arts requirement.

These outcomes will be achieved by PowerPoint lectures and discussions, and assessed by exams, a critical analysis paper, and in-class writing exercises.

Textbook

The required textbook for the course is Philip B. Meggs and Alston W. Purvis's *Meggs' History of Graphic Design* (fifth edition). Additional readings may be assigned throughout the semester, which will be posted on the course's LearningStudio website.

M. Thistlethwaite holds the Kay and Velma Kimbell Chair of Art History. He specializes in the art of the United States but has taught a wide range of courses, including the history of graphic design. He has received Texas Christian University's Chancellor's Award for Distinguished Teaching and the Honors Program's "Professor of the Year" Award. He has published books and articles and lectured widely on nineteenth-century and contemporary art, particularly on the subject of history painting. Dr. Thistlethwaite has chaired the City of Fort Worth's Art Commission and served on the Board of Trustees of the African American Museum of Dallas. He currently serves on the Board of Trustees of the Modern Art Museum of Fort Worth and the Ambassador Council of the Amon Carter Museum of American Art.

MUTANT DESIGN: MAKING HISTORY

Louise Sandhaus

Course Description

What's missing from graphic design history that's right in our own backyards? Lots! In this class, we'll add to California graphic design history by researching overlooked or forgotten designers, institutions, and/or design projects. During the semester, this class will offer methodologies and approaches for conducting original research and creating documentation. Following a research phase, we'll work on developing written narratives that offer factual information told through unique points of view. Finally, we'll publish our discoveries on a new web platform dedicated to California design history. Our mantra throughout the class will be Share the Joy!

Learning Goals

- Be able to apply research methodologies and approaches to successfully uncover little-known data
- Be able to interpret relevancy and meaning of historical data
- Publish research as a compelling and useful narrative and documentation

Outcome

Documentation of one design subject

Expected preparation (homework!) outside of class

- Research through investigation of journals, oral histories, books, archives, databases
- Readings
- Conduct interviews in person, on phone, or through email correspondence
- Writing and documentation of research

Format

The class is divided into three phases of activities: Research, Writing, and Publishing. Each phase is applied to your chosen research subject. Presentations, discussion, workshops, tutorials, and an occasional field trip comprise weekly class meetings. From time to time, class members will also share project status updates. Homework consists of readings, research, writing, and documentation.

A shared class folder, "Making History F15" in Google, is where all class assignments will be housed. In addition, each student will have their own folder when Bibliography, Research Notes, Interviews and interview transcripts, images, and writing must be stored.

SCHEDULE

Note: It is important that you follow the research process as outlined. For example, don't jump the gun and contact the designer before we come to that step. Also note: there several events you may want to attend related to the class. Dates are listed below.

Week 01: Introduction to the class and getting started

In this first class, we'll look at the current status of California graphic design history to understand the importance of the contributions each of you will be making. For inspiration, we'll take a look at examples of new forms of design history research, documentation, and publication. Finally, we'll review possible research subjects from which you'll choose a subject to investigate.

Readings

- Lorraine Wild on the history of design history
- Benjamin Weiss's notes on collecting graphic design

Homework

Review the list of potential research subjects and choose one option to spend the semester researching, writing about, and documenting.

Benchmark

Research subject chosen

RESEARCH PHASE

Week 02: Designer as researcher vs. scholar as researcher

Is there a difference between a "citizen scholar" and a professional scholar? How are their motivations, as well as practices, alike or different? In this class, we'll have a visit from a design practitioner who is doing design research and from a trained design scholar. Each will share their practices for conducting research as well as documenting interpreting, publishing, and distributing their discoveries.

Homework

1. In the shared class Google folder, "Making History Class 2015," create another folder with your first and last name. All your research, documentation, and writing drafts will be stored here.
2. In the folder, create two documents: 1) Bibliography 2) Research Notes. Keep track of any books, articles, websites, videos, interviews, etc., in your Bibliography. Compile your discoveries in your Research Notes document. Include keywords in your Bibliography!

3. Also add a copy of the Data document. This is where you'll record and compile a factual record of your subject.
4. Begin a preliminary search by doing using Google only. Remember to record research outcomes in your Bibliography, Research Notes, and Data documents.
5. Also read the following texts:
   - Excerpts from Diana Hacker and Barbara Fister, *Research and Documentation in the Electronic Age* (New York and Boston: Bedford/St. Martin's, 2010).
   - Matthew Bird, "Design History Research in the Digital Age," Design and Culture, Vol. 6, Issue 2.

Benchmark Initial research completed

Week 03: Building and documenting your research

Now that you have a sense of readily available data on your subject (or maybe you turned up nothing!), we'll learn how to dive deeper using databases and alternative search terms. We'll also learn best practices for documenting your research and your visual examples.

Homework

1. Using techniques learned in class, continue to develop your research. Be sure to document what you find by adding publications and sites to your Bibliography; add notes to your Research Notes; fill in any data to your Data document. Add a folder for images. Complete a data form for each image. Also, if you'd like, begin a time line.
2. Prepare to make a short presentation about what you've found out so far about your subject.

Benchmark: Research in development

Week 04: Research status report

Each class member will make a small informal presentation on what they've learned about their research subject so far. Peer feedback may help to identify additional research resources.

Homework

Follow up on any additional research and do the following readings/viewings:

1. Linda Sandino, "News from the Past: Oral history at the V&A," *V&A Online Journal*, Issue No. 2, Autumn 2009:

- http://www.vam.ac.uk/content/journals/research-journal/issue-02/news-from-the-past-oral-history-at-the-v-and-a

2. Interviewing Process and Practices:
   - https://web.cn.edu/kwheeler/researchassignment3.html
   - http://managementhelp.org/businessresearch/interviews.htm
   - https://www.youtube.com/watch?v=9t-_hYjAKww

Week 05: Conducting an interview

Not all information will come from research on the web and/or publications. Your research may be greatly expanded by personal accounts related by the designer or, if no longer alive, by a work colleague or friend. In this class, we'll discuss the practice of conducting interviews and oral histories. We'll consider individuals you may want to interview and help compose questions to ask so that you're prepared for an interview, whether that takes place in person, via Skype, or via email.

Homework Contact interview subjects and set up appointments. Try to conclude all interviews before next class meeting. Transcribe your interviews and follow up on any additional research.

Week 06: Time to catch up!

We will have no class meeting. Use this time to conduct your interviews, transcribe them, and follow up on any research that may have been revealed through the interview(s). Plan on attending the LA as Subject Archives Bazaar Day, Saturday, October 17, 9:00 a.m.–5:00 p.m., Doheny Memorial Library, USC University Park Campus. http://www.laassubject.org/index.php/archives_bazaar

Week 07: Locating and using archives and collections

Archives are where historical documents are stored. Collections are bodies of work. The subject of collections may be that of a graphic designer, but often the collection is more about a particular subject, such as political graphics or record albums. There are few collections of the work of graphic designers and even fewer archives, so you'll have to follow your nose to find archives or collections—whether digital or physical—that may be valuable for your research. In this class, we'll visit an archive to understand what is included, how it is organized, and ways it might be searched.

Homework

1. Research digital archives from the supplied list.
2. Conclude all research and prepare an informal slide presentation to share your research next week with the class.

Benchmark

Research concluded! Next up is interpreting your subject through writing.

Week 08: Status report workshop

Presentations by class members and peer feedback and discussion about what makes the subject appealing and compelling.

Homework

Reading the following texts starting with Alice Twemlow's "Critical Proximity." In this essay, she describes the difference between approaching a subject through close and personal observation rather than the more conventional academic mode of "critical distance" such as those texts found in Wikipedia or the scholarly historical writing of Jeremy Ansley. Lorraine Wild and Ian Lynam's work, on the other hand, are examples of design history writing that offers alternative approaches to voice.

- Alice Twemlow, "Critical Proximity"
- Wikipedia entry for Deborah Sussman: https://en.wikipedia.org/wiki/Deborah_Sussman
- Jeremy Aynsley, "Living in a Modern Way" catalog essay
- Lorraine Wild, "Orange" from *Earthquakes, Mudslides, Fires & Riots*
- Ian Lynam, http://neojaponisme.com/category/design/

WRITING PHASE

Week 09: Writing history

Writing approach workshop! In class, we'll read parts of Janet Malcolm's *New Yorker* profile on David Salle, "Forty-One False Starts," and then each class member will try their hand at writing alternative first paragraphs—in other words, different possible approaches or angles to relating what is compelling and meaningful about your subject. Be sure to have access to your Notes for reference.

Homework

Using your favorite opening paragraph, write a first draft of at least 500 words about your subject. Include factual information; images are optional. Bring three copies to class.

Week 10: Preliminary writing draft

	In class, copies of writing drafts will be exchanged for peer feedback and assistance.
Homework	Complete the final draft of your writing! (Yes, this is it!) Also, double-check that your bibliography, data form, images, and captions are completed and ready to post. Bring three copies of the entire dossier to share.

Week 11: Final draft

	Tutorial on posting your writing, images, bibliography, etc., to the Making History site
Homework	Post!

PUBLISHING PHASE

Week 12: Post

In class	Review postings

Week 13: Final Presentations

In class	Final presentations
Homework	FINAL posting and self-assessment

Week 14: Celebration!

Louise Sandhaus is the former program director and current faculty in the Graphic Design Program at California Institute of the Arts (CalArts). She is the author of Earthquakes, Mudslides, Fires and Riots: California and Graphic Design 1936–1986, *copublished in late 2014 by Metropolis Books and Thames & Hudson.*

DESIGN I AND PATTERNS IN CURRENCY

Cassini Nazir

DESIGN I SYLLABUS

Meets Mon + Wed 4–6:45 pm in ATC 4.902	ATCM 2302 • Section 502 • Spring 2018 **Design I**
Course Description	Designers use form to shape meaning. This studio course introduces you to the basic tools designers use in shaping meaning: the elements and principles of design. Through examples, exercises, critiques, and creative projects, you will begin to think like a designer. You will work to understand and analyze design problems, develop distinctive concepts, and then create and refine designs that manifest that concept.
Learning Objectives	• Create compositions that use the elements and **principles of design** meaningfully. • Explain and execute the steps in the **design process**. • Analyze how your own designs might be improved through documented **reflection pieces**. • Evaluate the work of others through **critique sessions**.
Course Context	This is one of four core classes that every ATEC student must take. It is recommended that you take these classes together, if possible. This course prepares you for upper-level classes that use design.

	ATCM 2300	Intro to Technoculture
	ATCM 2301	Computer Imaging
	ATCM 2302	**Design I**
	CS 1335	Computer Science I

Required Texts	• *Design Basics: 2D and 3D* (8th edition), Stephen Pentak et al. ISBN-13: 978-0495909972 • *Design Basics Index*, Jim Krause ISBN-13: 978-1581805017

Course Materials

- 1 sketchbook (without lines)
- Colored pencils, pens, or markers
- #2 pencils or drawing pencils
- Sharpie or black marker
- Scissors
- 12-inch ruler
- White eraser
- 8.5×11″ card stock paper (package)
- 8.5×11″ mixed colors construction paper
- Glue stick
- Digital or cell phone camera

Course Stucture

Weeks 1–5	**What Is Design?** What is design? What do designers do? How do designers think? **Principles of Design** Unity, Emphasis, Focal Point, Scale, Proportion, Balance, Rhythm
Weeks 6–10	**Elements of Design** Line, Shape, Pattern, Texture, Space, Motion, Value, Color **Design Process** Critique and reflection
Weeks 11–15	**Integration of Process, Principles, Elements** Use the design process effectively and integrate the principles and elements

WEEK-BY-WEEK

	Below is the order of topics that we will cover. Specific details on homework, due dates, readings, quizzes, and tests will be provided at elearning.utdallas.edu.
Week 1 **Jan 8–12**	**What is Design + Unity** 1A–What is Design? 1B–Principles of Design: Unity
Week 2 **Jan 15–19**	**Emphasis and Focal Point** 2A–Principles of Design: Emphasis and Focal Point 2B–Introduction to Reflection (Learning Portfolios)
Week 3 **Jan 22–26**	**Scale + Proportion** 3A–Reflection: Learning Portfolios Practice 3B–Principles of Design: Scale and Proportion
Week 4 **Jan 29–Feb 2**	**Balance + Rhythm** 4A–Principles of Design: Balance 4B–Principles of Design: Rhythm
Week 5 **Feb 5–9**	**Review of Principles** 5A–Principles of Design: Review 5B–Introduction to the Elements of Design and Critique
Week 6 **Feb 12–16**	**Line** 6A–Critique, Connect to Other Designers 6B–Elements of Design: Line
Week 7 **Feb 19–23**	**Shape** 7A–Elements of Design: Shape 7B–Elements of Design: Shape
Week 8 **Feb 26–Mar 2**	**Pattern, Texture + Space** 8A–Elements of Design: Pattern and Texture 8B–Elements of Design: Illusion of Space
Week 9 **Mar 5–9**	**Motion, Value** 9A–Elements of Design: Illusion of Motion 9B–Elements of Design: Value
Week 10 **Mar 19–23**	**Color** 10A–Elements of Design: Color 10B–Elements of Design: Color

Week 11 **Mar 26–30**	Review of Elements 11A–Elements of Design: Review 11B–Typography
Week 12: **Apr 2–6**	**Final Project Begins** 12A–Identity and Branding 12B–Identity and Branding
Week 13 **Apr 9–13**	**Workshop** 13A–Creative Brief 13B–Workshop
Week 14 **Apr 16–20**	**Workshop** 14A–Workshop 14B–Workshop
Week 15 **Apr 23–27**	**Final Project** 15A–Semester Lookback 15B–Semester Lookback

How to Be Successful in This Class

Discipline is the key to get the most out of this class. Below is a sample of how you should generally spend your time preparing for class. Note that not every week will necessarily follow this order.

In-Class Day 2A

Practice and Explore	In-class exercises require you to be familiar with the reading. You'll need to be able to recognize and recall the terms and principles in use.
Out of Class	**Prepare** • Complete reading(s). • Take quiz(zes). • Find real-world examples of the topic(s) discussed. • Complete assignments. • Discuss concepts you've learned with classmates.

In-Class Day 2A	
Assess	Critiques will help you assess the quality of your work and, more important, what you can do to improve.
Out of Class	**Review and Reflect** • Complete assignments. • Reflect on what you learned. • Write down questions you have or concepts that are unclear. • Explain what you've learned to someone else.

PATTERNS IN CURRENCY

Goals

The *Patterns in Currency* assignment helps first-year design students in the School of Arts, Technology, and Emerging Communication at the University of Texas at Dallas understand how the elements of a composition can be orchestrated to create meaning. In this assignment, students are challenged to design a currency note with resonating cultural significance for an existing country.

Paremeters

Students begin by conducting background research on the selected country with the goal of understanding its history: which events, objects, places, or other items have cultural significance? They are required to discuss these cultural signifiers with someone from the country to understand more deeply and identify what is meaningful to its citizens.

Students use appropriate principles and elements of design (pattern, textures) to identify an appropriate pictorial balance of the composition creating visual unity.

Designer Sarah McIntire's master's thesis from Ohio State University (2008) is provided as a resource on the history of money and currency.

Outcomes

A number of students found this assignment to be both a cultural and a personal journey. Mei Yi Tan, a student from Malaysia, pulled from memories of her country of birth as well as the experiences of family members.

For the visual focal point of her work, Tan quickly abandoned the durian, the national fruit of Malaysia with an unusual and noxious smell, in favor of the hibiscus, the national flower. Traditional Malaysian batik (textiles) created by her grandmother made their way into her final composition.

Reading and Resources

Dollar Redesign, https://dollarredesign.wordpress.com

Sarah McIntire. OSU Student Thesis: “Designing the Dollar—Rethinking U.S. Currency” (2008). https://dollarredesign.wordpress.com/2010/09/21/of-the-people-for-the-people-sarah-mcintire-d

A country’s currency is both a medium of exchange and a unit of shared cultural commonality. The images and symbols used say something about what is important to the country. The examples below show how currency designers use design elements and principles to create and convey meaning, as seen in Brazil’s real (pronounced hey-al). Here, the designer uses elements in the foreground, middle ground, and background to honor the contributions of the Brazilian physician who discovered a serum to treat snake bites, Vital Brazil. Can you identify design elements and principles that you’ve learned?

(Top) Mei Yi Tan illustration and final sketch.

This 50 escudos—the currency of Portugal prior to the introduction of the euro in 1999—demonstrates many components, all set within the foreground, middle ground, or background: The foreground, set off by flourishes, indicates the denomination (amount) and the issuing bank. The middle ground depicts a bird’s-eye view of the city of Coimbra, Portugal; while the background is composed primarily of geometric shapes. The design components in this note celebrate the ancient heritage of Portugal.

At far right, the offset register depicts a snake head. The entire background design is composed of the skin and scales of a snake. This note displays unified design elements. At left, a poisonous snake is milked for venom. Vital Brazil, a Brazilian scientist famous for his work in developing serum for venomous snake bites, appears on this note at middle right.

PATTERNS IN CURRENCY

Begin

You will design the currency for a country using elements and principles of design you have learned so far. Select a country (other than the United States) to design a note of currency for. It must be a real country. Research the country and identify at least three cultural components and their significance.

Design Process

Empathize	Begin the design process by understanding the audience. First, conduct background research on the country to understand a bit about its history and events, objects, place, or other things of cultural significance. Then, talk to someone from the country or someone knowledgeable about the country to identify what is meaningful to them.
Define	Capture your findings and synthesize into three insights that will shape your final solutions.
Ideate	Generate at least ten different possible designs. These should be rough sketches. Be sure to explore many different ideas.
Prototype	From your sketches, select the best components that fit the criteria you defined. Then begin prototyping additional refinements.
Test	For each of the phases above, obtain meaningful feedback from other individuals. Capture this in your design process write-up.

PATTERNS IN CURRENCY

Guidelines	You will design one currency note (e.g., a hundred euro note). Your final design should include: • Elements set on a foreground, middle ground, and background • Some form of pictorial balance (imbalance, symmetrical, asymmetrical, radial, crystallographic, or some combination) • A background with pattern or texture • Elements arranged using some form of visual unity Create your design on white 8.5×11-inch cardstock paper (size appropriately for the dimensions of your chosen currency) using any combination of the following materials: black Sharpies and markers, colored markers, paint, or colored pencils. You may choose to do a collage.
Submit	Your written design process, sketches, and final design.
Rubric	
30% Design process	Completed all design process phases. User feedback visible in final design.
25% Sketches	Demonstrates broad exploration of design possibilities.
30% Principles and elements	Demonstrates exemplary understanding and application of elements and principles of design.
5% Concept	Final design is original and conveys concept clearly and cohesively.

Cassini Nazir is a clinical associate professor, School of Arts, Technology, and Emerging Communication and director of design, ArtSciLab, at the University of Texas at Dallas.

TEACHING DESIGN HISTORY AND SOCIAL IMPACT

Dori Griffin

Course Context

After several years of teaching graphic design history to small classes of upper-division majors, I was tasked with developing a high-enrollment, sophomore-level graphic design history course with no prerequisites. "Design History and Social Impact" needed to be suitable for a broad student audience across the university yet simultaneously serve as the design history requirement for graphic design BFA students. This expanded audience presents certain challenges regarding course form and content. Students share no formal or conceptual framework developed through prior art history and studio design coursework; their shared vocabulary needs to emerge entirely from the work they do as a class. The course satisfies a cross-cultural perspectives requirement in our university's general education curriculum, so global content is urgent not only philosophically, but also practically. Finally, since the course cultivates a large and diverse audience, the student experience needs to be engaging for both designers and nondesigners.

To meet these objectives, I structured the course to operate as a series of geographically and chronologically diverse case studies related to one of three topically arranged units: form, function, and philosophy. The class explores weekly topics by reading, viewing, and listening to mostly open-source online content. Low-stakes online quizzes each week review these out-of-class assignments. As their primary learning activity, students develop a blog that explores each week's topic in relationship to one overarching theme of their choosing: race, class, gender, (dis)ability, or sustainability. At the end of the semester, students refine and present their blogs to a small group of peers, assigned to ensure a diverse cross-section of themes within each group.

This framework has proven successful in terms of engaging student interest, exposing students to a pluralistic range of historical and contemporary design solutions, and navigating the differences between design majors and a general student audience. Following are the course description and objectives from the syllabus, then a descriptive account of the course structure with a selection of representative examples from each week's homework and in-class content.

Course Description

Design History & Social Impact. Three hours. In response to globalization, studying cross-cultural design provides a framework of visual culture that emphasizes the role of design in diverse communication exchanges and public discourse. This course is organized around the idea that a history of design transcends mere exposure to various traditions of design or design aesthetics. Instead, a critical discussion of design in various contexts offers a way to understand our own cultural patterns of design within a broader and more diverse history. This course utilizes an inclusive definition of design to explore developments across technological, physical, and social contexts.

Course Objectives

Upon completion of this course, students will be able to demonstrate through writing and discussion their critical understanding of 1) how design looks, works, and changes relative to the culture of specific places and times, 2) how designers and audiences have used visual communication strategies and technologies to effect social change, both positive and negative, and 3) how historical models can be useful in the process of solving contemporary design problems and/or becoming critical consumers of contemporary design.

Course Structure

"Design History and Social Impact" contains three units: form, function, and philosophy. Each unit is made up of a series of four to five individual topics. A comprehensive global survey of graphic design history is impossible in a single semester at the introductory level. Instead, topical case studies seek to expose students to culturally, geographically, and chronologically diverse design problems and solutions.[1] As the course begins, I discuss with students the rationale for this approach and remind them that our purpose is to encounter diversity and highlight the capacity of design to facilitate social change, not to learn a chronological and largely stylistic history of famous Western European and North American designers and their work. A once-weekly lecture and in-class discussion introduces each topic, contextualizes its relationship to contemporary design practice, and offers case studies illustrating how the subject matter has been explored by designers over time and across place. The classroom experience focuses on providing students with a perspective at once global (drawn from diverse global cultures) and local (always specific to audiences and needs local to a particular place and time, with periodic emphasis on highlighting examples that are local to students' own life experiences). At-home assignments utilize a collection of online, mostly open-source readings, listenings, and viewings to offer further examples and introduce relevant conceptual frameworks; the class does not use a textbook.

These assignments draw on broadly accessible design journalism and museum education sources, which we then unpack and probe more deeply during in-class lectures and discussions.

Unit one, *Form*, explores the formal elements of design. In class, we observe and discuss the visual and tactile characteristics of design artifacts and what those characteristics have meant to viewers in different times and places. We also investigate the introduction of new technologies of production over the course of history and ask how these tools shaped designers' decisions. *What Is Design?* asks students to develop a preliminary definition of design. Students independently view "Design Q&A" narrated by Charles Eames and a Paul Rand retrospective by Imaginary Forces.[2] In class, we compare classic ISOTYPE icons to headscarf emojis by Muslim teenager Rayouf Alhumedhi to explore the limitations of a monolithic definition of design.[3] *A to Z* explores alphabets and typography; as homework, students view "The Politics of Arabic Type Design" by Nadine Chahine, and in class we discuss Cherokee typeface designs by Mark Jamra in collaboration with the Cherokee Nation and a Māori typeface by Johnson Witehira.[4] *Color Theory* introduces the formal vocabulary attached to describing and categorizing color, but homework content also includes NPR's "The Color of Politics," and in-class case studies investigate the cultural and political connotations of color through, for instance, JeongMee Yoon's "Pink and Blue Project" and the South African Medu Art Ensemble's public poster projects of the 1970s and 1980s.[5] *Tablet to Tablet* explores the variety possible in the physical form of the book; homework assignments range from a short documentary on clay tablets by the Australian Broadcasting Company to El Lissitzky's 1926 essay "Our Book."[6] In class, we view a variety of examples, including the Diamond Sutra scroll (China, 868), the Mayan "Dresden" codex (Yucatán, thirteenth century), the Rocket e-reader by NuvoMedia (USA, 1998), and the artist's book *Echoes* by Islam Aly (Egypt and USA, 2014). *How Things Are Made* investigates technologies of production. Students view short documentary films such as "Block Printing in India" and "Wood Type in China."[7] In class, we discuss how production methods impact form and meaning; case studies include *Jikji Simche Yojeol*, the earliest known book printed with movable metal type (Korea, 1377), and a lithographic Qur'an (Iran, nineteenth century).[8] At the end of the *form* unit, we discuss the limitations of formal analysis. In pairs, students conduct a rigorous visual analysis of the formal characteristics of a neoclassical *bourdaloue*: its color, shape, size, decorative motifs, and materials. Then they speculate about its function. The *bourdaloue* is not, as almost all student viewers first guess, a gravy boat; it is instead an early version of the port-a-potty. This object lesson tends to stick with students, demonstrating that formal analysis, divorced from context, can never tell the whole story about design.

Unit two, *Function,* considers the various purposes that design serves. Design plays many roles in daily life: selling consumer goods and services, informing and deceiving, suggesting meaningful narrative contexts for everyday activities, facilitating relationships and transactions. This unit explores the work design has accomplished historically in various social, political, geographical, and physical contexts and asks how design functions in our own lives. *Objects & Emotions* considers how designed objects fulfill both pragmatic and emotive functions. Students independently view "Objectified" by Gary Hustwit,[9] and in class we consider case studies such as the bicycle, which has evolved modestly in its basic physical form but significantly in its advertising media, use value, emotive meanings, and cultural connotations. *Branding & Consumerism*: Students watch the "Paula Scher: Graphic Design" episode of the Netflix documentary *Abstract,* and in class we discuss case studies, which include Naomi Klein's *No Logo* project.[10] *Information Design & Propaganda* unpacks the ways in which design can inform and deceive. Students read "Disinformation Visualization" by Mushon Zer-Aviv, and in class we view examples such as the information graphics of W. E. B. du Bois, which documented the living conditions of African Americans in the postslavery Deep South.[11] Finally, *Screens & Stories* explores how the design of screen-based media shapes our cultural values and consumption patterns. Assigned readings include "Malcolm Gladwell is #Wrong" by Maria Popova,[12] and in-class case studies include a critical viewing of user experience design on mobile news sites; BBC News, Bing, Breitbart, and Bustle, for instance, differ significantly in terms of the visual languages they employ and the corresponding worldviews they cultivate. At the end of the *function* unit, we discuss the limits of an analysis that considers only form and function, divorced from philosophy. Our object lesson is a Nazi graphic standards manual, beautifully designed and very functional in its capacity to communicate information.[13] Yet without a critical understanding of its underlying philosophy, any analysis of the object as book-form, information graphic, or typographic system would be dangerously incomplete.

Unit three, *Philosophy,* probes why designers make the decisions they do relative to form and function. This unit examines the rationales underlying various design movements, particularly those intended to address social change. It also offers the opportunity to deconstruct the philosophical implications of a few popular yet ultimately harmful design decisions, as well as how and why designers might begin to develop better alternatives. *Cultural Appropriation* highlights the complexity of designing for or with cultures or visual languages that are not the designer's own. Students listen to "Seminole Patchwork" from NPR's *Code Switch* and read "Fashion's Cultural Appropriation Debate" by Minh-Ha T. Pham.[14] In class, we discuss the differences between Gran Fury's appropriation of Nazi symbolism for AIDS education (1988), Pride Propaganda's appropriation of Russian Constructivist posters for LGBT rights (2014), and European fashion designer Kokon To Zai's appropriation of sacred Inuit designs for high-end clothing (2015).[15] *Designing Diversity* intentionally emphasizes Black and Indigenous design in the United States, asking students to see their own complicity in maintaining a monolithic definition of design. Students view the AIGA/Google African American Design Journey and read Cheryl Miller's *Print* articles about "Black Designers: Missing in Action."[16] In class, we see present-day case studies like Sadie Redwing's design for Lakota and Great Plains communities.[17] *Universal Design* explores the tension between modernist definitions of universality and a more contemporary definition that instead embraces accessibility and inclusion. Students watch deaf designer Michael Allen Nesmith's TED talk, "Why We Need Universal Design," and in class, we view Sara Hendron's Abler project.[18] *Sustainable Design* asks how design might contribute to a sustainable global future and questions the efficacy of design solutions imposed from the outside by designers who might lack a complete understanding of local problems and circumstances. Students read "Why Design Won't Change the World" by David Stairs[19] and in class consider case studies such as designing access to and awareness surrounding clean water through the projects Lifestraw (Switzerland, 2005), packH2O (USA, 2012), Get H2O Challenge (the Netherlands), and the ENDA and Yoff Community graywater education and recovery program (Senegal, 2002). Finally, *Changing the Future* considers grassroots design and its potential to impact local communities. Homework assignments include Studio [D] Tale's Maxwell Mutanda and Safia Qureshi speaking on "Design Activism" at Design Indaba and selections from *Design Like You Give a Damn*.[20] In class, we encounter student-centered design activism projects in rural American communities, for example, Project H and Rural Studio; this is a subject relevant to the lives of my students, as our university is situated in rural Appalachia.[21]

Throughout the semester, students interact with the ideas we encounter by writing a weekly blog entry relevant to an individual theme of their choosing. At the beginning of the semester, students choose a theme from the following list, which includes a handful of general examples when it is introduced:

- *Ability and Disability*—meeting physical needs (e.g.: vision/hearing/mobility), universal design
- *Class and Poverty*—activist movements, affordable design, luxury goods
- *Gender and Sexuality*—feminism, LGBTQ identities, gender-neutral design
- *Race and Ethnicity*—Black Lives Matter, Brexit propaganda, indigenous typefaces
- *Sustainability and Environmentalism*—climate change, protest and activism, green-washing

For each blog entry, students locate, report on, and analyze a specific example of how the week's topic relates to their semester-long theme. For example, how does typeface design relate to (dis)ability, or how do technologies of production relate to sustainability? Every blog entry consists of an image, an image citation, and an analysis of the design being shown. Three basic questions shape the writing: What are we seeing? How and why is it related to the week's topic? How and why is it relevant to the blog's theme? Before posting their writing for a final grade, students meet in class to peer review one another's weekly drafts. They work in established small groups devoted to a shared theme so that their insights into the theme and the topics can evolve over the semester through shared dialogue. By curating their blogs, students develop a library of case studies from a variety of places and times, demonstrating how different aspects of design have impacted social change positively or negatively. In lieu of a final exam, students edit one blog entry from each unit and prepare a brief oral/visual presentation. They deliver this presentation to a small group of students who worked with different themes for the semester. This structure provides a peer-generated introduction to how design can be utilized to solve problems and meet needs relative to a number of contemporary issues.

Like all pedagogical frameworks, the course structure I've developed for "Design History and Social Change" has both benefits and drawbacks. For graphic design students, the lack of a chronological overview of well-known western European and North American designers and styles is a perceived drawback to the course structure. A two-semester course sequence that first introduces and then deconstructs a canonical history of graphic design might easily solve this problem in contexts where such an approach is feasible. In my own final analysis, however, equipping students to *ask* how design might be diversified and used as a tool for positive social change outweighed teaching students to answer questions about which designers and styles are textbook-famous.

Endnotes

1. The work of D. J. Huppatz has clarified my pedagogical approach to the tension between comprehensive surveys and what I describe here as a case study-based approach. See, for instance, D. J. Huppatz, "Globalizing Design History and Global Design History," *Journal of Design History* 28, no. 2 (2015): 182–202, https://doi.org/10.1093/jdh/epv002; and D. J. Huppatz and Grace Lees-Maffei, "Why Design History? A Multi-National Perspective on the State and Purpose of the Field," *Arts & Humanities in Higher Education* 12, no. 2/3 (April 2013): 310–30, https://doi.org/10.1177/1474022212467601.

2. Charles Eames and Ray Eames, *Design Q&A* (Eames Office, 1972), http://www.eamesoffice.com /the-work/design-q-a/; Mark Gardner, *One Club: Paul Rand* (Imaginary Forces, 2007), https://www.imaginaryforces.com/work/one-club-paul-rand.

3. Department of Typography & Graphic Communication, University of Reading, "Isotype Revisited," Isotype Revisited, 2009, http://isotyperevisited.org/; Ontwerpwerk Design Bureau and Municipal Museum of the Hague, "Gerd Arntz Web Archive," Gerd Arntz Web Archive, accessed December 23, 2017, http://www.gerdarntz.org/isotype; Rayouf Alhumedhi et al., "The Hijab Emoji Project," The Hijab Emoji Project, 2016, http://www.hijabemoji.org/.

4. Monotype GmbH, "TEDx Talk with Font Designer Nadine Chahine," *Linotype Blog* (blog), 2016, http://blog.linotype.com/2016/07/tedxtalk-with-fontdesigner-nadinechahine/; Angela Riechers, "A Typeface Designed to Revive the Endangered Cherokee Language," *AIGA Eye on Design*, 2016, https://eyeondesign.aiga.org/a-typeface-designed-to-revive-the-endangered-cherokee-language -typetuesday/; Margaret Andersen, "How the First Typeface Designed for the Māori Community Is Changing the Way New Zealand Understands Its Own Cultural Identity," *AIGA Eye on Design*, 2017, https://eyeondesign.aiga.org/the-first-typeface-designed-specifically-for-the-maori-community-is-changing-how-new-zealand-views-its-own-cultural-identity/.

5. "The Color Of Politics: How Did Red And Blue States Come To Be?," *All Things Considered* (NPR, November 13, 2014), https://www.npr.org/2014/11/13/363762677/the-color-of-politics-how-did-red-and
-blue-states-come-to-be; JeongMee Yoon and Catherine Zuckerman, "Pink and Blue: Coloring Inside the Lines of Gender," *National Geographic*, 2016, https://www.nationalgeographic.com/magazine/2017/01
/pink-blue-project-color-gender/; South African History Online, "Medu Art Ensemble," South African History Online, 2017 2011, http://www.sahistory.org.za/article/medu-art-ensemble.

6. ABC TV Science, "Catalyst: Ancient Writing," ABC TV / Catalyst, 2013, http://www.abc.net.au /catalyst/stories/3861771.htm; El Lissitzky, "Our Book (1926)," in *Graphic Design Theory: Readings from the Field*, ed. Helen Armstrong (Princeton, N.J.: Princeton Architectural Press, 2009), 25–31.

7. Craftmark, *A Lasting Printing—Block Printing in India* (Craftmark, 2012), https://www.youtube.com
/watch?v=qZdnAz2Il20; UNESCO Intangible Cultural Heritage, "Wooden Movable-Type Printing of China," UNESCO, 2017 2010, https://ich.unesco.org/en/USL/wooden-movable-type-printing-of
-china-00322.

8. Phaidon Press, "Design of the Week: Buljo Jikji Simche Yojeol," Phaidon News, 2012, http://www.phaidon.com/agenda/graphic-design/articles/2012/october/22/design-of-the-week -buljo-jikji-simche-yojeol/; Columbia University Libraries Online Exhibitions and Dagmar A. Riedel, "The Quran in East and West: Manuscripts and Printed Books," Columbia University Libraries, 2013, https://exhibitions.cul.columbia.edu/exhibits/show/quran/qurans/printed.

9. Gary Hustwit, *Objectified*, Documentary, 2009, http://www.hustwit.com/category/objectified.

10. Richard Press, *Paula Scher: Graphic Design* (RadicalMedia, 2017); Naomi Klein, *No Logo: 10th Anniversary Edition* (New York: Picador, 2009).

11. Mushon Zer-Aviv, "Disinformation Visualization: How to Lie with Datavis," Visualising Information for Advocacy, 2014, https://visualisingadvocacy.org/blog/disinformation-visualization-how-lie-datavis; Public Domain Review, "W. E. B. Du Bois' Hand-Drawn Infographics of African-American Life (1900)," *The Public Domain Review*, 2017, http://publicdomainreview.org/collections/w-e-b-du-bois-hand-drawn-infographics-of-african-american-life-1900/.
12. Maria Popova, "Malcolm Gladwell Is #Wrong," *Design Observer*, 2010, http://designobserver.com/feature/malcolm-gladwell-is-wrong/19008.
13. Steven Heller, "The Master Race's Graphic Masterpiece," *Design Observer*, 2011, http://designobserver.com/feature/the-master-races-graphic-masterpiece/24358.
14. Jacki Lyden, "Seminole Patchwork: Admiration And Appropriation," *Code Switch: Race and Identity, Remixed* (NPR, February 18, 2017), https://www.npr.org/sections/codeswitch/2017/02/18/510241789/seminole-patchwork-admiration-and-appropriation; Minh-Ha T. Pham, "Fashion's Cultural Appropriation Debate: Pointless," *The Atlantic*, May 15, 2014, https://www.theatlantic.com/entertainment/archive/2014/05/cultural-appropriation-in-fashion-stop-talking-about-it/370826/.
15. Jesse Green, "When Political Art Mattered," *The New York Times*, December 7, 2003, sec. Magazine, https://www.nytimes.com/2003/12/07/magazine/when-political-art-mattered.html; Pride Propaganda, "Pride Propaganda," tumblr, Pride Propaganda, 2017-2014, http://pridepropaganda.tumblr.com/; Alli Joseph, "From New York, to Paris, to D.C.: Native American Fashion Gains Ground, in Spite of Stolen Designs," *Salon*, February 18, 2017, https://www.salon.com/2017/02/18/from-new-york-to-paris-to-d-c-native-american-fashion-gains-ground-in-spite-of-stolen-designs/; CBC Radio, "Nunavut Family Outraged after Fashion Label Copies Sacred Inuit Design," CBC Radio, 2015, http://www.cbc.ca/radio/asithappens/as-it-happens-wednesday-edition-1.3336554/nunavut-family-outraged-after-fashion-label-copies-sacred-inuit-design-1.3336560.
16. AIGA and Google Arts & Culture, "African American Culture and History: An AIGA Design Journey," Google Cultural Institute, 2016, https://www.google.com/culturalinstitute/beta/exhibit/tgIyec9ZBBG7IQ; Cheryl D. Miller, "Black Designers: Missing in Action," *Print Magazine* XLI, no. V (1987): 58–65, 136–38; Cheryl D. Holmes-Miller, "Black Designers: Still Missing In Action?," *Print* 70, no. 2 (2016): 82–89.
17. Sadie Red Wing, "Lakota Visual Language," Sadie Red Wing, accessed December 23, 2017, https://www.sadieredwing.com/lakota-visual-lang.
18. Michael Allen Nesmith, "Why We Need Universal Design," TEDx, 2016, https://www.michaelallennesmith.com/tedxboulder/; Sara Hendren, "Abler," Abler, 2017, https://ablersite.org.
19. David Stairs, "Why Design Won't Save the World," *Design Observer*, August 20, 2007, http://designobserver.com/feature/why-design-wont-save-the-world/5777.
20. "Studio [D] Tale: A Building Isn't Always the Solution," Design Indaba, 2016, http://www.designindaba.com/videos/interviews/studio-d-tale-building-isn%E2%80%99t-always-solution; Architecture for Humanity, *Design Like You Give A Damn: Architectural Responses To Humanitarian Crises*, ed. Kate Stohr and Cameron Sinclair (New York: US Green Building Council, 2006).
21. Emily Pilloton, *Teaching Design for Change* (TEDGlobal, 2010), https://www.ted.com/talks/emily_pilloton_teaching_design_for_change; AIANational, *Rural Studio: A Story of Solutions*, 2016, https://www.youtube.com/watch?v=QKqCE1V8u-U.

Dori Griffin teaches graphic design and design history at Ohio University. Currently, she's at work on a book that introduces the history of the printed type specimen to design students, teachers, and practitioners, a project emerging from her 2015 research fellowship in the Cary Graphic Arts Collection at the Rochester Institute of Technology.

INTERNATIONAL FUTURISM

Raffaele Bedarida

Frequency: One semester
Level: Undergraduate Art Students

Description

Futurism (1909–1944) was the first avant-garde movement that, emerging from the peripheries of modernity, forcefully entered the canon of European modernism. Despite its problematic ideology, Futurism has functioned ever since as a strategic model for groups of artists fighting against dynamics of exclusion. The first component of this course explores the history of Futurism: its protagonists, operative centers, magazines, and phases. The second component of the course uses Futurism as a case study through which we can rethink definitions of modernity beyond Western perspectives. By doing so, we'll raise questions about authority and countercultural movements, cultural hegemony and pluralism, censorship, and utopia.

Requirements and Grading (see below for full description)

- Regular class participation (20%).
- Oral presentation of 15 minutes on a thematic or informational topic (20%).
- Midterm exam: two essays of four pages each—one on a Futurist manifesto, one on a Futurist artwork selected by the instructor (20%).
- Manifesto + Essay: 5/6-page research paper on a subject of the student's choice, with the approval of the instructor (30%).
- Museum Visits and Reports: Two museum visits have been scheduled to the Museum of Modern Art: one to the galleries and one to the archives. These trips are an integral part of the course. You are required to attend both museum visits. If you have to miss a visit, you need to let the professor know in advance, then visit the museum by yourself and bring a documentation of your visit. You will be required to complete two short museum reports (one per visit) while in the galleries to receive full credit for the museum visits (10%).

Course Objectives

Students successfully completing this course should be able to:

1. Acquire a comprehensive knowledge and understanding, through close study of primary texts, direct exposure to Futurist artworks available in New York, and slide presentations, of the breadth, depth, and historical significance of the cultural phenomenon that is Futurism;

2. Understand the contemporary relevance of a twentieth-century avant-garde by incorporating recent scholarship with postcolonial, global perspectives;
3. Comprehend what is involved in undertaking the study of visual and textual documents and, more specifically, learn how to use, read in a critical fashion, and properly cite photographic documentations, films, literary sources in translation, ephemera, and other archival materials related to the activity of a movement that was programmatically multisensory and performative;
4. Acquire training and practice in thinking, speaking, and writing authoritatively, critically, and with originality, about a body of material that has been understudied.

General Course Reading

Gunter Berghaus, ed., *International Yearbook of Futurism Studies*, Berlin: De Gruyter, 2016.

Vivien Greene, ed., *Italian Futurism 1909–1944: Reconstructing the Universe*, New York: Guggenheim, 2014.

Giovanni Lista, *Futurism*, New York: Universe Book, 1986.

Christine Poggi, *Inventing Futurism: The Art and Politics of Artificial Optimism*, Princeton: Princeton University Press, 2009.

Lawrence Rainey, Christine Poggi, Laura Wittman, eds., *Futurism: An Anthology*, New Haven & London: Yale University Press, 2009.

DESCRIPTION OF CLASSES

Week 1: Introduction

Reading of syllabus; distribution of class presentations (dates and topics); introductory lecture.

Week 2: MoMA visit: Permanent Collection, Fifth Floor

By visiting the fifth-floor galleries, we discuss the role of Futurism in MoMA's narrative of modernism, the history of the collection, and how the role assigned to Futurism changed through the decades.

Required Readings: Leah Dickerman, "Inventing Abstraction," in *Inventing Abstraction: How a Radical Idea Changed Modern Art* (New York: MoMA, 2013), pp. 13–34.

Raffaele Bedarida, "Operation Renaissance: Italian Art at MoMA, 1940–1949," in *Oxford Art Journal, 35/2* (June 2012), pp. 147–169.

→ Print out and bring with you the "Museum Report" available on Moodle.

Week 3: Nationalism/ Internationalism + the Crowd

Key questions discussed today include: What relationship did the Futurists have with the myth of national regeneration in newly unified Italy? What's the relationship between national collectivity and the crowd in the Futurists' work? Starting from the contradictory coexistence of nationalism and internationalism in the rhetoric and practice of F. T. Marinetti, the class explores the role of Futurism in establishing an international network of avant-garde artists.

Required Readings

Emilio Gentile, "The Myth of National Regeneration in Italy: From Modernist Avant-Garde to Fascism," in Matthew Affron and Mark Antliff, eds., *Fascist Visions: Art and Ideology in France and Italy*, Princeton University Press, 1997, pp. 25–45.

Marina Isgro, "'A Futurism of Place': Futurist Travel and the European Avant-Garde, 1910–1914," in *Italian Futurism: Reconstructing the Universe*, 2014, pp. 136–139.

Christine Poggi, "Folla/Follia: Futurism and the Crowd," in *Inventing Futurism*, pp. 35–64.

Manifestos: The Founding and Manifesto of Futurism, 1909; Italian Pride, 1915.

Week 4: MoMA Library and Archives

By looking at Futurist magazines, manifestos, posters, and other materials in the MoMA Libraries and Archives, we discuss what other histories of Futurism this institution could tell and how different or similar they are compared to the narrative presented in the museum's galleries. This visit focuses on the key role that magazines and manifestos played in the history and propagation of Futurism.

Required Readings

Marjorie Perloff, "Violence and Precision: The Manifesto as Art Form," in *The Futurist Moment*, Chicago: University of Chicago Press, 1986, pp. 81–115.

Claudia Salaris, "Marketing Modernism: Marinetti as Publisher," *Modernism / Modernity*, vol. 1, n. 3 (1994), pp. 109–127.

Manifestos: Technical Manifesto of Futurist Literature, 1912.

→ Print out and bring with you the "Museum Report" available on Moodle.

Week 5: Technology and the Technological Divide

The Futurists' celebration of technology is notorious. This class addresses this theme by asking: 1) What kind of technological innovation they celebrated; 2) What this attitude meant culturally and politically, especially if we consider that the Futurists came from a largely rural, backward country compared to their Northern European or American interlocutors; 3) How the Futurists represented or utilized technology in their work; 4) Why a movement that exalted technology gave so much prominence to traditional modes of production such as painting and sculpture.

Required Readings

Jeffrey Schnapp, "Propeller Talk," Modernism/Modernity, Vol. 1, No. 3 (September 1994), available online: https://muse.jhu.edu/article/23012.

Emily Braun, "Shock and Awe: Futurist Aeropittura and the Theories of Giulio Douhet," *Reconstructing the Universe*, 2014, pp. 269–273.

Romy Golan, "The Futurist Murals," *Reconstructing the Universe*, 2014, pp. 317–320.

Manifestos: Against Passéist Venice, 1910.

Week 6: Mediterranean Modernity and Imperial Ambitions

The first part of the class focuses on Futurism's roots and long-term presence in Egypt. Key questions include: 1) How did the fact that Marinetti and other Futurists were born and raised in Egypt influence their culture, their idea of avant-garde art, and their urge to revolutionize European culture; 2) What was the role of the Futurist movement in Egypt before and after the 1919 Egyptian revolution; 3) What was the relationship between Futurism and the local avant-garde group, Art and Liberty?

The second part of the class reflects more in general on the Futurists' rhetoric of "the Mediterranean" and Mussolini's Imperial ambitions.

Required Readings

Maria Elena Paniconi, "Nelson Morpurgo and the Futurist Movement in Egypt," in *International Yearbook of Futurism Studies*, Vol. 6, 2016, pp. 22–43.

Michelangelo Sabatino, "Capri as the Epicenter of 'Slow' Futurism," in *Reconstructing the Universe*, 2014, pp. 221–224.

Primary Sources: F. T. Marinetti, *Mafarka the Futurist: An African Novel*, 1910, pp. 140–150 and 185–206; The Italian Empire (To Benito Mussolini—Head of the New Italy), 1923.

Recommended	Sam Bardaouil, *Surrealism in Egypt: Modernist and the Art and Liberty Group*, London, New York: Tauris, 2017, pp. 1–32; 60–84. Cinzia Blum, *A Place in the Sun: Africa in Italian Colonial Culture*, Berkeley: University of California Press, 2003, pp. 138–162.
Guest Lecture	Nada Ayad (Postdoctoral Fellow, Cooper Union) on the 1919 Egyptian Revolution.

Week 7: Gender and Prosthetic Bodies

Valentine de Saint-Point and other Futurist women fought against Marinetti's sexist rhetoric from within the movement. What is the relationship between Futurism and Feminism before and after World War I? How can we reconcile Marinetti's notoriously misogynistic statements vis-à-vis the profeminist political program of his Futurist Party? How did intermixing bodies and machines affect the Futurists' approach to gender roles? Class discussion includes a comparison between Bruno Munari's airplane women and Giannina Censi's airplane dances; Valentine de Saint-Point's ideas of gender fluidity but also her celebration of rape; Rosa Rosà's feminist science-fiction novel.

Required Readings	Lucia Re, "Futurism and Feminism" *Annali d'Italianistica*, vol. 7 (1989), pp. 253–272. Anja Klöck, "Of Cyborg Technologies and Fascistized Mermaids," *Theatre Journal*, 51, 4 (Dec. 1999), pp. 395–415. *Manifestos*: "Manifesto of the Futurist Woman," 1912; Against *Amore* and Parliamentarianism, 1911–15.
Recommended	Cinzia Blum, "Rhetorical Strategies and Gender in Marinetti's Futurist Manifesto," *Italiaca*, vol. 67, n. 2 (Summer 1990), pp. 196–211. Christine Poggi, "Dreams of Metallized Flesh: Futurism and the Masculine Body," in *Inventing Futurism*, pp. 150–180.

Week 8: Paris as the Hegemonic Center

The Futurists had ambivalent sentiments toward Paris: of admiration and hostility at the same time. This meeting focuses on the Futurists' multiple attempts at conquering the French capital against the dismissive attitude of the gatekeepers of modernism. What do we learn by comparing Futurism and Cubism beyond formalism?

	What was the reception of Futurism in the capital of modern art? What did the Futurists learn from Paris?
Required Readings	Emily Braun, "Vulgarians at the Gate," in *Boccioni's Materia: A Futurist Masterpiece and the Avant-Garde in Milan and Paris*, New York: Guggenheim, 2004, pp. 1–21. Marjorie Perloff, "The Invention of Collage," *The Futurist Moment*, Chicago: University of Chicago Press, 1986, pp. 81–115. *Manifestos*: The Exhibitors to the Public, 1912.
Guest Lecture	Luise Mahler (Leonard A. Lauder Fellow in Modern Art, Metropolitan Museum of Art) on Giacomo Balla in Paris.

Week 9: MIDTERM, in class

Structure	*2 essay questions.* Write two essays based on the provided prompts: one on a Futurist manifesto, one on a Futurist artwork selected by the instructor. *Total of 20 points.* 10 points for each question, distributed as: • 5 points, visual analysis or demonstrated comprehension of relevant primary sources • 2 points, precise reference to relevant secondary sources • 3 points, overall organization, clarity, and persuasiveness
How to Study	Read the two essays, which provide a clear summary and chronology. Claudia Salaris, "The Invention of the Programmatic Avant-Garde," *Reconstructing the Universe*, 2014, pp. 22–49. Adrian Lyttelton, "Futurism, Politics, and Society," in *Reconstructing the Universe*, 2014, pp. 58–76. Download class lecture slides and go through them as you read your notes from class. Read your notes on the weekly readings. Review the readings selectively to identify passages or topics that are unclear. Email me or come talk to me with questions or doubts.
Sample Prompt	Discuss Valentine De Saint-Point's "Manifesto of the Futurist Woman" in the context of the Futurists' relationship with feminism. Include at least three relevant works of art and three other texts to support your argument.

Week 10: Revolution or Reaction?

	This class focuses on the years 1918–1922, that is, between the end of WWI and the rise of Fascism. After the war, in a moment of great instability, the antibourgeois revolution that the Futurists had invoked for a decade seemed to be within reach. Did the Futurists really want a revolution? How did Futurism transform itself by becoming a political party? How did the movement relate/react to other antibourgeois revolutions—most prominently in Russia? What was the Futurists' position during the *biennio rosso* upheavals in Italy? What was the Futurists' initial relationship with Mussolini and Fascism?
Required Readings	Emily Braun, "Mario Sironi's Urban Landscapes: The Futurist/Fascist Nexus," in *Fascist Visions,* pp. 101–133. *Primary sources*: Beyond Communism, 1919; Antonio Gramsci, "Marinetti the Revolutionary?" (1921).
Recommended	Gunter Berghaus, "Violence, War, Revolution: Marinetti's Concept of a Futurist Cleanser for the World," in *Annali d'Italianistica*, vol. 27 (2009), pp. 23–71. Emilio Gentile, "Political Futurism and the Myth of the Italian Revolution," in *International Yearbook of Futurism*, vol. 1, 2000, pp. 1–14. Christine Poggi, "Return of the Repressed," in *Inventing Futurism,* pp. 232–265. Manifestos: Fascism and Futurism, 1923; Response to Hitler, 1937.

Week 11: Popular Culture and Spectacle

	From the very beginning, Futurism embraced popular culture and exploited the manipulative power of mass communication. With a special focus on the multifaceted work of Fortunato Depero in Italy and in New York, we explore the Futurists' combination of artisanal and industrial modes of production, their interest in advertising and propaganda, and their excitement for new modes of viewership.
Required Readings	Walter L. Adamson, "Futurism, Mass Culture, and Women," *Modernism / Modernity*, vol. 4 n. 1 (January 1997), pp. 89–114. Raffaele Bedarida, "'Bombs Against the Skyscrapers': Depero's Strange Love Affair with New York, 1928–1949," in *International Yearbook of Futurism Studies*, vol. 6 (2016), pp. 43–70. Primary Sources: The Variety Theatre, 1913; Depero Futurista, 1927; Futurism and Advertising Art, 1931.

Recommended Readings	Silvia Barisione et al., *Under Mussolini: Decorative and Propaganda Arts of the Twenties and Thirties from the Wolfsonian Collection* (Milan: Mazzotta, 2002). Raffaele Bedarida, Heather Ewing, and Steven Heller, eds., *Depero Futurista: A Reader's Guide* (New York: Designers & Books, 2017).

Week 12 Performances and "The Pleasure of Being Booed"

As seen in previous weeks, it is hard to discuss any aspect of the Futurists' works or activities without addressing their performative approach to everything. Today, we see how their approach to performance changed through time. We also situate Futurist performances within the landscape of avant-garde theatre, dance, and music of the time.

Required Readings	Gunter Berghaus, *Avant-garde Performance* (New York: Pelgrave, 2005), pp. 22–47. Giovanni Lista, "Futurist Music," in *Italian Futurism, 1909–1944: Reconstructing the Universe*, 2014, pp. 116–119. Patrizia Veroli, "Futurism and Dance," in *Reconstructing the Universe*, 2014, pp. 227–230. Manifestos: The Pleasure of Being Booed, 1911–15; The Art of Noises, 1913; The Futurist Synthetic Theater, 1915.
Recommended	Roselee Goldberg, ed., *Performa 09—Back to Futurism* (New York: WorldSource, 2011). Nancy Locke, "Valentine de Saint-Point and the Fascist Construction of Woman," in *Fascist Visions*, pp. 73–100.

Week 13—Just Kidding: Children, Toys, and Pedagogy

Like most avant-garde movements, Futurism emphasized childhood and children education as a crucial tool for the construction of a new social order. In apparent contradiction with their machismo, many Futurists designed furniture, clothes, books, and toys for children. Today's class focuses on the impact of Maria Montessori and other early twentieth-century pedagogical theories on Futurism: not only on works specifically conceived for children, but also on strategies for the re-education of adults (for example, Tactilism). Discussion also includes post–World War II children's books by former Futurists Leo Lionni and Bruno Munari as part of the unlikely legacy of the movement.

Required Readings	Juliet Kinchin, ed., *Century of the Child*, MoMA, New York, 2012, excerpts: pp. 11–27; 29; 47–49; 59; 66–69; 121; 127–128. Vivien Greene, "The Opera d'Arte Totale," in *Reconstructing the Universe*, 2014, pp. 211–213. Steven Heller and Greg D'Onofrio, "Leo Lionni," in *The Moderns: Midcentury American Graphic Design* (New York: Abrams, 2017), pp. 58–61. Primary Sources: Futurist Reconstruction of the Universe, 1915; Manifesto of Tactilism, 1921; Leo Lionni, *Little Blue and Little Yellow*, 1959; Bruno Munari, *The Circus in the Mist*, 1969.
Recommended	Siobhan Conaty, "Benedetta Cappa Marinetti and the Second Phase of Futurism," *Woman's Art Journal*, 30, 1 (Spring / Summer 2009), pp. 19–28. Ara Merjian, "A Future by Design: Giacomo Balla and the Domestication of Transcendence," *Oxford Art Journal*, August 13, 2012, pp. 121–146.

Week 14: Roundtable: Futurist Legacies

	During this meeting, students share their respective manifesto (see Final Project below) with the class. Students can read or perform portions of their manifesto as they like. They should also explain the relationship between their manifesto and the Futurist precedents.
Readings	Arahmaiani, "Letter to Marinetti to Liberate Oneself from Ecstasy of Consuming and to Discover the Future (2009)," in Katy Deepwell, ed., *Feminist Art Manifestos: An Anthology* (London: KT press, 2014), available online: https://monoskop.org/media/text/feminist_art_manifestos/#Arahmaiani

Week 15: FINAL PROJECT

	Final Project. Submit it digitally through Moodle or in person.

ASSIGNMENTS

A major aspect of the course is a discussion of Futurism's unlikely legacies. Through the decades, artists excluded from the master narrative of Art History have adopted Futurism's guerrilla-like methods to strike an attack on the hegemonic center, without necessarily sharing Futurism politics and ideology. Prominent examples include the Balkan founders of Cabaret Voltaire (1916), the Russian Constructivists (1921), the Egyptian Art and Liberty Group (1938), the Argentinian authors of the Manifesto Blanco (1946), the Japanese Gutai (1956), the Italian Arte Povera (1967), the American Guerrilla Girls (1985), Afrofuturism (1993), and countless other movements as well as individual artists. This part of class discussion will revolve around students' presentations.

Every week, starting on Week 3, two students will give a 15-minute class presentation each, focusing on the theme of the week. For your presentation, you are encouraged to work on an artist, a movement, or a phenomenon which is either directly inspired by Futurism or explores similar themes and ideas. For example, on September 20, when we discuss Nationalism/Internationalism, one could talk about contemporary artist Rirkrit Tiravanija's work, reflecting on tensions between globalism and localism in social rituals. The way Tiravanija uses Thai curry in his work bears significant similarities with but also major differences from Marinetti's work on Italian spaghetti. A successful presentation would emphasize the relevance of Futurism's art and theory from today's perspective, but it would also acknowledge the historical gap between then and now.

Your presentation should:

1. explain clearly the selected work and its context, by showing images and by providing information that you believe are necessary to make it accessible.
2. explain the link with Futurism, by emphasizing the similarities of themes, strategies, style, or context.
3. explain the main differences that you believe make the comparison interesting and give a sense of perspective.
4. ask one or two questions to be discussed with the class. They should be real questions based on issues that you have been struggling with.

Make an appointment with the professor to discuss your selected subject and a bibliography.

Final Project Instructions

Produce a manifesto loosely inspired by the Futurists. You need to think carefully about both the content and the form: what you fight against, what you want to propose, how you structure your text, your writing style, your chosen font and graphic design, your medium and system of distribution, who is your intended audience, and what relationship you want to establish with your reader, considering what we have seen, read, and discussed in class. Work on the interconnection among these various parts: for example, if you write on a technology-related topic, you will have to make a thoughtful choice on whether you want to use traditional means of communication (like printed paper) or more advanced forms of communication technology, how you want to use this technology, and how these choices relate to the content of your manifesto.

Next to the finished manifesto, write an essay (12 Times New Roman; double-spaced, excluding illustrations, title page, and bibliography from the four/five-page count) where you explain how your manifesto relates to the Futurist precedents. For your manifesto, you can be inspired by some of the themes or strategies used by the Futurists: in this essay, you explain which ones and why you find the Futurist precedent relevant or helpful. You can also choose to diverge from the Futurists in one or more ways, but you need to explain how and why. As we saw in class, Futurism is not a monolithic block, so you can explain which sources or authors are significant to you and why. Your essay should mention at least two primary sources and at least two scholarly texts. At least one of these four sources should not be one of the readings assigned for this class.

Examples of Final Projects by Cooper Union Students

I have selected three projects to exemplify how the study of Futurism —a movement that is older than a century—can inform or inspire contemporary art students in a variety of ways. Considering that my course is a "History and Theory of Art" class, I do not evaluate or critique the outcome of the project as in a studio class, but I evaluate the way students are able to absorb the art historical material and make it their own, through a process that should be both rigorous and creative. For the sake of brevity, below I reproduce some significant passages from their essays and some images from their manifestos.

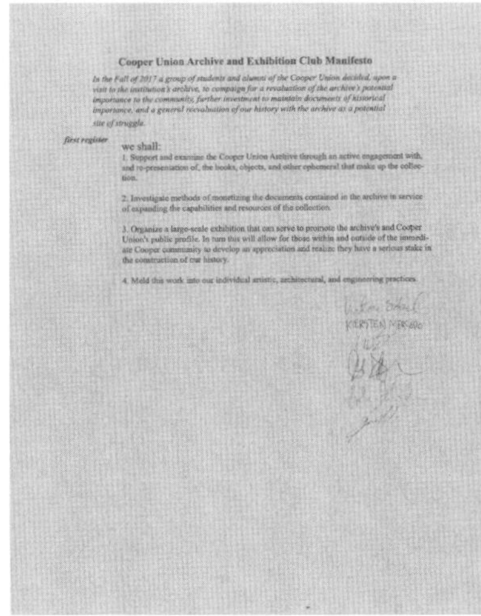

Cooper Union Archive and Exhibition Club Manifesto

In the Fall of 2017 a group of students and alumni of the Cooper Union decided, upon a visit to the institution's archive, to campaign for a revaluation of the archive's potential importance to the community, further investment to maintain documents of historical importance, and a general reevaluation of our history with the archive as a potential site of struggle.

first register

we shall:

1. Support and examine the Cooper Union Archive through an active engagement with, and re-presentation of, the books, objects, and other ephemeral that make up the collection.

2. Investigate methods of monetizing the documents contained in the archive in service of expanding the capabilities and resources of the collection.

3. Organize a large-scale exhibition that can serve to promote the archive's and Cooper Union's public profile. In turn this will allow for those within and outside of the immediate Cooper community to develop an appreciation and realize they have a serious stake in the construction of our history.

4. Meld this work into our individual artistic, architectural, and engineering practices.

KIERSTEN NIERGO

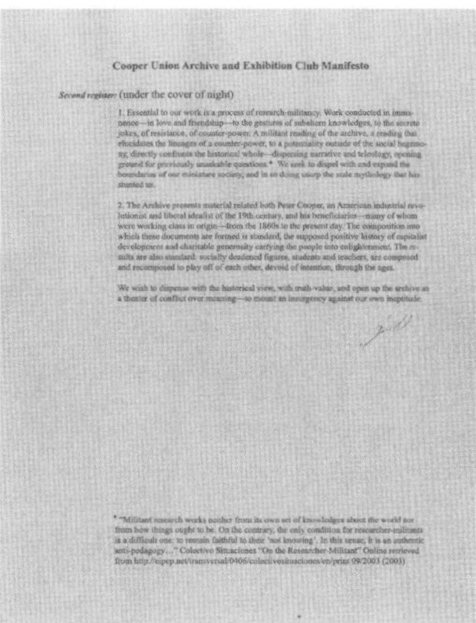

Cooper Union Archive and Exhibition Club Manifesto

Second register: (under the cover of night)

1. Essential to our work is a process of research-militancy. Work conducted in immanence—in love and friendship—to the gestures of subaltern knowledges, to the secrete jokes, of resistance, of counter-power. A militant reading of the archive, a reading that elucidates the lineages of a counter-power, to a potentiality outside of the social hegemony, directly confronts the historical whole—dispersing narrative and teleology, opening ground for previously unaskable questions.* We seek to dispel with and expand the boundaries of our miniature society, and in so doing usurp the stale mythology that has stunted us.

2. The Archive presents material related both Peter Cooper, an American industrial revolutionist and liberal idealist of the 19th century, and his beneficiaries—many of whom were working class in origin—from the 1860s to the present day. The composition into which these documents are formed is standard, the supposed positive history of capitalist development and charitable generosity carrying the people into enlightenment. The results are also standard: socially deadened figures, students and teachers, are composed and recomposed to play off of each other, devoid of intention, through the ages.

We wish to dispense with the historical view, with truth-value, and open up the archive as a theater of conflict over meaning—to mount an insurgency against our own ineptitude.

* "Militant research works neither from its own set of knowledges about the world nor from how things ought to be. On the contrary, the only condition for researcher-militants is a difficult one: to remain faithful to their 'not knowing'. In this sense, it is an authentic anti-pedagogy..." Colectivo Situaciones "On the Researcher-Militant" Online retrieved from http://eipcp.net/transversal/0406/colectivosituaciones/en/print 09/2003 (2003)

The first project, reproduced below, is by a senior student, Julian H. Mayfield, who wrote a "Cooper Union Archive and Exhibition Club Manifesto." Here, the study of Futurism is helpful as a model for political activism—although not necessarily a positive one. The content of the manifesto apparently negates everything Futurism stood for: it incites students to research the institution's archives, whereas the Futurists would set archives on fire. But Julian's link to Futurism goes deeper than that. In his view, as he states in his essay, Futurism "set the standard for collective practice in the arts" and therefore inspired Julian and the other signatories of his manifesto for their strategies and collectivism. He explains:

> *I advocate in the extension of the CUAEC manifesto for a taking up of the Cooper Union archive as a potential site of struggle. While this requires "dispensing with the historical view," it further valorizes the very museums and libraries Marinetti initially targeted for destruction. It seems appropriate to immediately question whether this can be considered a genuine conflict; the problem with libraries and museums is not their physical existence but the passivism they engender in their visitors. However, it seems that when dealing with locations so distasteful, it behooves us to prepare for the leap from the historical critique to a revolutionary praxis. The Futurists sought to reconstruct the universe to match their systemic program; critique was proffered only to lay the groundwork for a new formulation. A proposed insurgency on the historical foundations of the present has its positive claim, but primarily stands as an act of negation rather than*

reconstruction. It seems the question here is whether we can seriously re-form the institution in our own image from a set of historical claims; and whether, if the answer is no, this represents a rejection of direct political organization. The manifesto from this perspective gestures toward a more limited field of operation. On the other hand, as student advocacy and action has repeatedly been recuperated into the sterile working groups of administrative processes, it seems natural to retreat to the margins of political activity, and attempt to reframe the center of community discourse to the base camps we can erect outside of the direct line of sight maintained by the corporate bureaucracy.

The "Noise Manifesto" proposed by junior student Sarah Phillips, on the other hand, draws inspiration more directly from some of the Futurists' most crucial themes. As she writes in her essay, "Marinetti's relationship with the technology of the age was radical while he was writing about it, and remains a radical relationship to hold even in the digital age." Visually too, Sarah re-elaborates Futurists motives by depicting dynamism through repeated *linee di forza* in the style of Giacomo Balla or Luigi Russolo and by playfully changing an MTA train into a mechanized uroboros in a way that Fortunato Depero would certainly appreciate. But her manifesto is far from emulating Futurism. Sarah has made her own the Futurists' enthusiasm for the subversive potential of technology. She compares a Radical Networks conference that she attended in Brooklyn to an early twentieth-century *Futurist Evening*. Here, Sarah recalls, "artists, engineers, journalists, and other interdisciplinary professionals were actively questioning digital infrastructure. . . . They explained the hows and whys of exploiting social media, the creation of decentralized Internet access, and different approaches various parts of the world took to assimilating digital technology." That's what Futurism was really about, in her view:

Marinetti's initial "Futurist Manifesto" draws the first lines for the Futurist ideology. Most notable in this manifesto is his vivid description of becoming one with his car. This is the amalgamation of machine and man that appears time and again across Futurist writing and art. In the digital age, this becomes the cyborg, a combination of human and computer. If Marinetti fused with the machine through a car crash—in and of itself a violent, sudden event—the Noise Manifesto proposes a cyborgization through which a speeding subway car is the catalyst. Narrative and metaphor is also a large part of this manifesto, leading the reader through the steps of togetherness and realization, refusal and paranoia, and then acceptance and nonsense.

PART ONE

Wedged in the corner of an L train barreling through Manhattan's under-organs, I find myself situated between the armpit of an engineer and a guitar case. The intercom dings out a warning- malfunction! The car speeds faster and faster down the track.

We, the passengers, compress! We breathe together, thinking together. Our electron-thoughts meet no resistance as they flow from one mind to another. A spark, static on a wool coat perhaps- or a strike from a lighter- and the gap between human and machine closes! Train and passenger are neither train nor passenger, but both in one.

Live wires become living wires as our consciousness races through the circuits and down the third rail. We hop from copper to fiber optics and find ourself moving even faster, through the information highways of the city. All communication assimilated, we find ourselves with millions of camera-eyes and receiver-ears; our body, invisibly present, a fly on the wall of every street. Media streams through us as we discard our native tongue and yield to the electromagnetic language of waves and signals. We sprawl and spread across the country, broadcast from every tower, antenna, satellite, until we touch every cubic foot we can, every individual we can.

But lo! The train slows! And the train stops. We lurch from the frame of mind and separate after a single second of multitude. The superconductor's sour taste lingers in our- my?- mouth- dissipating only when the subway doors open and the crowd disperses.

Alone in a crowd again, I climb the staircase into the city above. In shock, I witness the streets of Manhattan like never before- flocks of fellows flowing through infrastructure- each word a slice of data, each step mapped, graphed, and filed away.

And hark! Though I had left the communal collective consciousness from the dreamingly brief metro incident, radio waves radiating from the tops of every building still shimmer in the afternoon light. Vast quantities of information make the air a soup of energy exchange, siphoned into the phone of each and every passerby. The invisible made visible, I see personality translated into mathematics- algorithms spinning themselves into facsimiles of humanity- androids taught to build themselves into cyborgs.

And thus! In the meantime, corporations profit from the flow of information from one source to another. Obfuscation with infinite media and meaningless words hides this process from the public- endless user agreements pigeonhole into opt in/opt out binaries. Hackers lobbing bricks at glass windows find out that their actions strengthen the machine when each break is repaired with something stronger and stranger. Surveillance worms into every nook and cranny as memories of what life was like before being watched fade away with the passing of the seconds. I see videos of myself relayed from security cameras in the shopfronts, profiles made as shops track my phone. Ads change their tone to better match my personality, microphones catalogue my words. Digital space molds around its perception of me- I'm quantified, numericized, digitized and ***consumed.***

PART TWO

An ouroboros of despairing thoughts spins round my head- eating itself in a self gratifying loop of fear and paranoia. Every webcam is the eye of an opponent- each email a letter sent straight to the hands of an enemy. I am the only motionless individual on the sidewalk, round me rush people of every direction. The phone in my pocket burns through my pants, a flaming coal. Throw it in the street to be crushed by an endless stampede of cars! Let the damn thing be ground into the sidewalk from whence it came. Let it return to the earth and be a part of something that makes sense.

Guilt overrides my passion as I realize my overreaction. To calm my zealous nerves I separate from the crowd in search of coffee. I hesitate at the door to the cafe, then realize the exchange would be archived on my credit card. I head to the closest ATM instead, hoping the anonymity of cash would be enough, when I am stopped in my tracks by the baleful gaze of a security camera.

Coffee forgotten, nerves fraying by the second, I consider leaving—snipping away from the digital world, clipping communication, constant contact, instant interaction and reinstating a reclusive self. I think of farms and simplicity. Foregoing technology, running from every cell phone tower in sight. A fugitive fleeing the cyberopticon.

Who before me has taken these steps? How many others are out there? What has been created that I can not know of, locked away from me by the simple fact I don't know about it? Who has found an escape?

My skull works itself into a Faraday Cage while the city looms over me. Crowds push in further as I spot the little rectangle in each and every pocket. The asphalt beneath me buzzes with activity, electric rivers hum. Overwhelm walks beside me- an army of panhandlers shouting for my attention.

And with the encroaching of technology strides an ever escalating arms race against acceptance, society, privacy, law- what space is there that won't one day be connected? Who has found an escape?

Back in the crowd, my coat brushes against the wool of another's as we pass on the crosswalk- a stray fly of static is exchanged between the two of us—

PART THREE

Struck by a lightning bolt! Synapses spark as I remember the train and its cyborg passengers! The rush of togetherness and understanding! The flow of information to each and every individual— no one understanding in singular but *all coming to complete knowledge together.*

The depressive mist burns away in the sunlight of this fleeting memory!

It's not enough to ignore technology! Technology relishes in being ignored- invisibility gives it giddy glee! The physical manifestation of the digital hides under more and more layers- bring it to light! Unearth infrastructure- pull it from the ground like potatoes. Turn over the gleaming stone and analyze, categorize, and *understand* the writhing masses of worms underneath.

Shrouded in a gleaming mist of impermeable white cases, the digital approaches godhood as it erases its own grimy history. Rip the plaster from the walls! Overanalyze! Overthink! Obsess! Demystify technology- nothing is sacrosanct in the subterranean vaults of a supercomputer.

Is this acceptance of the inevitable? If opt out isn't possible, do we opt in with enthusiasm?
How?
Stay on the cutting edge, keep in the know! Use past experience to understand the present and predict the future. Write algorithms to separate the wheat from the chaff; know what is significant and what is frivolous and use your knowledge to build upon what is important. Don't wait for technology to be forced down the throat of society- put it on like a favorite coat and unravel the seams from the inside!

Walking faster, nearly jogging, I follow the sidewalk until I reach a small park. The trees mute the eternal racket from the street. The radio noise falters and for a moment, disappears. *A signal*-now unobscured- shines through the brief silence, a lighthouse beam cutting through the fog.

In the sudden clarity I see networks grasping, expanding, reshaping, and most importantly- changing. I see questions answered, questioned, and answered again. Connections being built- torn down- and rebuilt in a different form. It stretches into my sight- The trees in the park shift before my eyes, their root networks decentralizing into rhizomes. Branches coagulate, spores appear: a fungal forest of interconnected bodies.

Under the protection of the gill caps I saw my own experiences differently: processing and reprocessing information into a new narrative.

Sheltered from the cacophonous noise by the tranquility of the park, I could see the obstructing effects of *noise*. Without some way to sort, raw data is a mass of information overload. Numbers and letters mean little without organization. Obfuscation! Is this an escape? Wrap myself in nonsense, to overwhelm the overwhelmers in my efforts to hide in plain sight.

Communications melding into one and then separating again to reach their intended targets. Not only a cyborgean mesh of biological and digital, but one of digital and digital- a stream of endless information, each point inseparable from all the others. Algorithmic hunting dogs search through data for what has been deemed important, sorting, cataloguing, archiving information.
But what happens when the data available is written is such a way it cannot be read? Data altered, muddled, encrypted: a problem that can't be solved except by the recipient.

As I stand there, in the park, the benches mesh and fracture as the world shifts around me to accommodate these new structures. Perceiving nonsense, sense is lost as the machine grasps for my clattering understanding of reality. Encrypted thoughts pass through VPNs and cobblestoned squirrels grope for patterns in the clamor. Gardens flicker back and forth before forgetting how to feign plant life, or even what kind of space they had meant to be in the first place. With only nonsensical dissonance as input, a delirious feedback loop births itself! Confusion into confusion! Dream into dream! Palindromic static envelops my sight, and I close my laptop as one might close a well-loved book.

To a third student, Max Miller (sophomore), the most relevant qualities of Futurism are its antagonistic and manipulative modes of communication. In his "Manifesto of Ache," he used my tool as an art history professor—PowerPoint slides—against me. The PowerPoint presentation that he sent me consists of white, blank slides with just one or two words each. I have to click in order to read the following text (I use an arrow here to indicate a click), and I read:

Please → Don't → Continue → Causing → Me → Pain. → Wearing → Shock → Collar. → Every → Slide → Hurts → More → Than → Last. → Body → Burning. → Why → Are → You → Hurting → Me? → Didn't → Do → Anything. → It's → Dark. → Where → Am → I? → Please → Bedarida. → Stop → Reading. → Stop → Clicking. → Please → What's → Your → Gain? → Can't → Leave. → Find → Help. → Can't → Take → More → Slides. → No → More → Shocks. → I → Hear → You → Clicking. → Why → So → Evil? → Don't → Want → To → Die. → Did → You → Put → Me → Here? → Will → Do → Anything. → Let → Me → Leave. → Please → Small → Room. → Your → Closet? → I → Heard → You → Look. → Open → Door → So → Much → Pain. → Fuck → You. → You → Are → Evil. → Evil. → Evil. → Evil. → Evil. → Evil. [Hard Language] → Evil. [Empathetic Instincts] → Evil. [Fear] → Evil. [Unexpected Circumstances] → Evil. [No Help] → Evil. [Lack of Information] → Evil. → Evil. → Killing → Me. → You→ Are → Guilty. → Murderer.

Obviously mocking the pain that boring sequences of art history slides can cause students, Max at the same time made his own the Futurists' intention: 1) to give words a physical, aggressive weight (Marinetti compared his *words in freedom* compositions to military bombing); and 2) to manipulate the preconditions for any form of communication (for example, the Futurists would sell many tickets for the same chair at their performances). Max explains:

> *This manifesto is an attempt at making the reader uncomfortable by suggesting that they are causing physical pain to the person that wrote it. This is a manifesto of Ache. The person who wrote it knows who you are more than they know who they are themselves. This degree of uncertainty along with the guilt is intended to make the reader feel responsible for the writer's safety even if they have nothing to do with the present danger. This manifesto plays with the irrational empathy a person might feel for someone they don't even know exists. Every piece made in this form will have a lack of moral code. They*

will all be concerned with causing the viewer a vague sense of panic and discomfort. This manifesto takes on methods that the Futurists used to cause pandemonium. The chaos goes against ideas of peace that are more central to societal consciousness. . . . The unexpected circumstances of the work are vital to the way it is perceived. None of it can be made specifically for a place that is meant for viewing. The artwork must have the narrowest specificity of audience possible. Even though the viewer might not be expecting to witness a piece, the maker must have that specific audience in mind for the piece to succeed. Many Futurists did this consistently. For example, when they published their first manifesto to the front page of a French newspaper, Le Figaro *(1909), or when they dropped political pamphlets from the bell tower of Saint Mark's cathedral onto the crowd of tourists and Venetians. In both examples, and in others, they target a very specific "you." This is exemplified in my manifesto as well; it is made for you, my teacher, to read, and therefore it targets you by name. This does not exclude groups from being viewers though, as groups can be specifically targeted and sought after.*

Raffaele Bedarida is an art historian and curator specializing in art, politics, and cultural diplomacy between Europe and America in the twentieth century. Assistant professor of art history at Cooper Union, he regularly lectures on modern and contemporary art topics at the Solomon R. Guggenheim Museum and MoMA.

LEARNING HISTORY AS DESIGN PROBLEM SOLVING

Michael Dooley

General problem: Students, particularly those on a design track, hate humanities studies in general.

With any luck, they mildly tolerate these courses. The most obvious reason is that they're often forced to take them as a graduation prerequisite. For this, they just have to accept what Santayana might have told them: "Those who cannot remember the past are condemned to repeat it next semester."

Particular problem: They don't care about graphic design history.

For them, even the words "graphic design" are quickly becoming dusty relics. So we enthrall them with the variety of ways in which this topic is vitally relevant. Such generalizations are somewhat helpful but only go so far. The deeper problem is why they don't care.

Specific problem #1: They're expected to read.

The cliché that designers hate reading is really about the fact that they hate required reading. But with recommended readings, their options are becoming practically unlimited. And design history texts are continually expanding, even faster than Steve Heller can write them.

Specific problem #2: They're expected to write!

Here, teachers can cut themselves some slack. Typically, schools with design courses either don't set or don't strictly enforce the most basic academic requirements such as minimum word count. Administrations are either aware or just don't care that only a handful of academically-minded students will actually put any genuine, worthwhile effort into their writing assignments.

Specific problem #3, the big one: They consider humanities/history classes as stealing precious time away from their "real" education.

Students can't just be told why graphic design history is important in the broad sense. As they see it, they're shelling out tuition money and taking out loans so they can produce portfolio projects that'll lead to big-bucks salaries. And any pursuit of knowledge that doesn't directly contribute to that objective is just old and in the way.

Solution, part 1: Have each student figure out why design histories are important to them.

My syllabus gives the students their goals and expectations:

- to practice methodologies of informed critical inquiry that produce relevant new perspectives and relationships both within and beyond the design field,
- to practice methodologies of perception and critical analysis that challenge design conventions and stimulate relevant thought and discussion,
- and so on.

They're heavy-duty requirements, so it's reasonable that they should reciprocate with their goals and expectations. So as I take attendance during my very first session, I begin to explore with each of them various ways in which the course could potentially benefit them. I work to provide options to connect their studies and interests to design history. Essentially, I become the class's Creative Director and they become the Designers, partnering to solve education problems. And in the process, which continues throughout the semester, I get to manage their expectations, to make sure their objectives are realistic, and that they stay on track. I also get to consider ways in which I can customize my lesson plans more effectively and efficiently. And, given enough care, a rich repertoire of resources, and a flair for flexibility, each term expands opportunities for them as well as for me. It also helps keep everything spiced up.

Solution, part 2: Have each student develop their own learning agenda. Every design historian, and every design history text, has at least one agenda. So again, it only seems fair that students start to develop theirs.

Therefore, their first assignment is to individually investigate which persons, groups, movements, issues, theories, philosophies, and so on will benefit them the most:

- best enrich their awareness of design history's value,
- best challenge their preconceptions, and
- best develop their analytical skills.

Any good design historian is also a good gumshoe, so this process itself becomes valuable design training. And my feedback helps shape and refine their direction.

Solution, part 3a: No in-class exams, no "just the facts, ma'am." No multiple choice, no fill in the blanks, no true/false or any other such nonsense. Such tests are ideal for lazy teachers: they're simple to create and easy to grade. Bam, done. But for teaching histories, I've found them to be essentially worthless. Here's how such tests work or rather, don't work:

- Throughout the semester, students dutifully transcribe their professor's lectures.
- Then they review these notes and readings.
- Then they go to class, get these stupid exams handed to them, and answer what they remember and take their best shots at what they don't.
- Finally, they pass in their paper, they exit the door, and poof! Most everything they've crammed into their heads gently rises and floats away.

And if they're good at retaining short-term details, they've successfully passed "Figuring out what'll be on their exams." But that's about it. If all they're doing is memorizing historical details and dates, they're just wasting their time, now more than ever, what with the world of facts at all our fingertips, just a quick Google search away.

Solution, part 3b: Give the students all their grade test questions at the beginning of the semester.

I let my students know at the outset that they'll be graded by how they perform on four types of projects:

- in-class participation, which includes reading/image reports,
- guest speaker analysis reports,
- mid- and end-term exam essays, and
- a final presentation to the class.

Oh, and I also include the following on my syllabus: all the prompts they must address on their reports, on their essay exams, and in their presentation, as well as the primary questions I'll be asking in class. This gives them an entire semester to work out their answers. And here's why I do that: each of these projects is an "examination" in the truest sense of the word: "The process of closely and carefully investigating and analyzing persons and things in order to make discoveries and determinations about relevant aspects of these persons and things." Their answers are not simply about retaining facts in their memories for just one semester. They're about exploring, and then comprehending, absorbing, connecting, comparing, analyzing, and critiquing. And ultimately, they're about clearly and concisely communicating how all this information is meaningful to them. Again, that's asking a lot, so it's only fair that they're given plenty of time to do due diligence in their detective work.

I'll get to that in a second, but first a word or three about overall instructional structure.

Solution, part 4: Teach the students the three "C"s.

To help students achieve their goals, I have a three-tier hierarchy of central components, "contents," "concepts," and "contexts," which I use to structure my rubric and assignments, and which I demonstrate—i.e., model—throughout my presentations, and which I apply in my feedback critiques.

- **Contents**. These are just the facts, mere starting points, the "whos, whats, whens, and wheres." They're elements of the questions rather than answers. Students get no grade credit for such information, which, again, is easily accessed with an instant Wiki-search by anyone who knows the difference between Bauhaus the school and Bauhaus the band. What contents alone fail to address is what's most relevant, the "whys" and the "hows." For that, we bring in the other two "C"s.
- **Concepts**: Creative methods, the workings of the mind, "interior" processes. They're the ways in which ideas become reality, when bicycle handlebars becoming Breuer chairs. This is news they can use.
- **Contexts**: This is the most important component, because history without context becomes irrelevant. They're the "exterior" circumstances such as culture, politics, technology, and the other factors that have led, say, from Behrens to Bauhaus to Berlin and beyond.

And now the projects.

Project #1: In-class participation, reading reports.

Beyond the students' own self-motivated questions and comments, I give "Readings / Images Analysis Assignments." Each assignment has topic groupings, based on upcoming classroom discussions. For example:

A. Ukiyo-e: Japan (1650s–1850)
B. Art Nouveau: England/America/France (late 1880s–1910)
C. Glasgow School: Scotland / Vienna Secession: Austria (late 1880s–1910)
D. Jugendstil: Germany (late 1880s–1910)

Students choose to research whichever one of these topics they consider most important and submit one or more images based on their readings. For example, if they select ukiyo-e, they can submit anything from the Great Wave to a Japanese caricature of Commodore Perry to a photo of a nineteenth-century geisha side-by-side with an Utamaro illustration. I'll then incorporate these images into my slide presentation, and then the student will "Analyze the significance of their images to their topic."

Project #2: Guest speaker analysis reports.

1. **Impressions:** Discuss all new ideas, insights, and connections generated by the lecture and analyze why they are important.
2. **Inquiries:** Discuss questions you asked the speaker(s) during the lecture and analyze what you learned from the answers.
3. **Improvements:** Discuss any changes in the lecture you would like to have seen.

Project #3: Exam essays.

This takes various forms, set within an overall structure of three sections: Profile (within the time period of the designer, movement, philosophy, etc.), Preface (prior to that time period), and Progress (from that time period to the present and future). The students are presented with contents (facts) and are required to "examine" the concepts and contexts. For example:

1. Profile.
    - **Facts:** Such as the achievements and development of the designer or movement, one representative design artifact, a relevant quote, etc., Each of these components can be presented as separate components.
    - **Examination:** Analyze and explain, with specific examples, why and how the concepts and contexts of each of the above facts are historically significant.
2. Comparisons: Preface.
    - **Facts:** Names of designers, movements, etc., both locally and internationally, at any point prior to and during that era, that share similarities and differences.
    - **Examination:** Analyze and explain, with specific examples, why and how the similarities and differences are significant.

3A. Reprising #2 in a different context: Progress.

- **Facts:** Names of designers, movements, etc., locally and internationally, at any point after that era, that share similarities and differences.

- **Examination:** Analyze and explain, with specific examples, why and how the similarities and differences are significant.

3B. Evaluation: Progress.

- **Facts:** Various ways in which your designer, movement, etc., has been criticized, during that time and up to the present.
- **Examination:** Analyze and explain.
- **Critique:** The contents, concepts, and contexts of these negative evaluations, using specific examples.
- **Commentary:** Your personal POV, explaining and justifying why and how aspects of your topic may be worthy of criticism and re-evaluation, using specific examples.

Project #4: Final presentation.

Students choose any topic based on what's become most relevant and valuable to them in the course of the semester. The only qualification is that it's different from everything else covered in class. In sharing their research and analysis with their classmates, they're expanding the scope of class content in a very personal way. And, they've taken their first step in creating their own, personal design history.

Creative director, professor, author, and photographer Michael Dooley teaches Histories of Design, Comics, and Animation at Art Center and Loyola Marymount University. He's lectured at schools and cultural institutions such as CalArts, the Hammer Museum, Museum of Contemporary Art, and San Diego Comic-Con. He's been a Print *contributing editor since 1990.*

READ

FURTHER READING

This is a selected listing of books on the history of graphic design and designers. It is not a complete list by any means. There are monographs and collections of many designers and design styles and movements. Please also refer to the reference notations and bibliographies accompanying many of the essays and syllabi in this book.

Bass, Jennifer and Pat Kirkham. *Saul Bass: A Life in Film & Design.* Laurence King Publishers, 2011.

Blackwell, Lewis, and David Carson. *The End of Print: The Grafik Design of David Carson* (2nd ed). Laurence King Publishing, 2000.

Brandle, Christian, Karin Gimmi, Barbara Junod, Bettina Richter, Museum of Design Zurich (Eds.). *100 Years of Swiss Graphic Design.* Lars Muller Publishers, 2014.

Cifuentes-Caballero, Beatriz. *Design: Vignelli: Graphics, Packaging, Architecture, Interiors, Furniture, Products.* Rizzoli International Publications, 2018.

De Jong, Cees W., Alston W. Purvis, and Jan Tholenaar (Eds.). *Type: A Visual History of Typefaces and Graphic Styles, 1628–1938.* Taschen, 2017.

Drucker, Johanna and Emily McVarish. *Graphic Design History* (2nd ed). Pearson, 2012.

Eisele, Petra, Annette Ludwig, and Isabel Naegele. *Futura: The Typeface.* Laurence King Publishing, 2017.

Eskilson, Stephen J. *Graphic Design: A New History* (2nd ed). Yale University Press, 2012.

Friedman, Mildred (Ed.). *Graphic Design in America: A Visual Language History.* Abrams, 1989.

Glaser, Milton. *Milton Glaser Posters: 427 Examples from 1965 to 2017.* Abrams, 2018.

Heller, Steven. *Merz to Emigre and Beyond: Avant-Garde Magazine Design of the Twentieth Century.* Phaidon Press, 2003.

Heller, Steven. *Paul Rand.* Phaidon Press, 2000.

Heller, Steven and Georgette Balance (Eds.). *Graphic Design History.* Allworth Press, 2001.

Heller, Steven and Greg D'Onofrio. *The Moderns: Midcentury American Graphic Design*. Abrams, 2017.

Heller, Steven and Louise Fili. *Typology: Type Design from the Victorian Era to the Digital Age*. Chronicle Books, 1999.

Heller, Steven and Seymour Chwast. *Graphic Style: From Victorian to Hipster* (4th ed). Abrams, 2018.

Heller, Steven and Véronique Vienne. *100 Ideas that Changed Graphic Design*. Laurence King Publishing, 2012.

Hollis, Richard. *Graphic Design: A Concise History* (2nd ed). Thames & Hudson, 2002.

Lewis, John. *The Twentieth Century Book*. Studio Vista, 1967.

Livingston, Alan and Isabella Livingston. *The Thames & Hudson Dictionary of Graphic Design and Designers* (3rd ed). Thames & Hudson, 2012.

McNeil, Paul. *The Visual History of Type*. Laurence King Publishing, 2017.

Meggs, Philip B. and Alston W. Purvis. *Meggs' History of Graphic Design* (6th ed). Wiley, 2016.

Müller, Jens and Julius Wiedemann (Eds.). *History of Graphic Design: Vol. 1, 1890–1959*. Taschen, 2018.

Müller, Jens and Julius Wiedemann (Eds.). *History of Graphic Design: Vol. 2, 1960–Today*; Taschen, 2018.

Müller, Jens and Julius Wiedemann (Eds.). *Logo Modernism*. Taschen, 2015.

Müller-Brockmann, Josef. *A History of Visual Communication*. Niggli 1999.

Poynor, Rick. *Typographica*. Princeton Architectural Press, 2001.

Poynor, Rick. *Uncanny Surrealism and Graphic Design*. Moravian Gallery, Brno (2010).

Purcell, Kerry William. *Alexey Brodovitch*. Phaidon Press, 2011.

Rand, Paul. *Paul Rand: A Designer's Art*. Princeton Architectural Press, 2016.

Reagan, Kevin and Steven Heller. *Alex Steinweiss: The Inventor of the Modern Album Cover*. Taschen, 2011.

Remington, R. Roger. *American Modernism: Graphic Design 1920 to 1960*. Yale University Press, 2003.

Remington, R. Roger. *Lester Beall: Trailblazer of American Graphic Design*. W. W. Norton, 1996.

Thomson, Ellen Mazur. *The Origins of Graphic Design in America, 1870–1920*. Yale University Press, 1997.

Weill, Alain. *Graphic Design: A History*. Abrams, 2004.

Wolff, Laetitia. *Massin*. Phaidon Press, 2007.

Websites

https://designarchives.aiga.org/#/home

http://www.designishistory.com/

http://designishistory.com/1850/posters/

http://www.designhistory.org/

http://www.glaserarchives.org/

https://letterformarchive.org/

https://library.rit.edu/gda/

http://lubalincenter.cooper.edu/

https://miscmagazine.com/a-brief-history-of-graphic-design/

https://woodtype.org/

ACKNOWLEDGMENTS

I am eternally grateful to Tad Crawford, publisher of Allworth/Skyhorse Press, for publishing this and over thirty other books I've edited, authored, and coauthored. His enthusiasm and encouragement are invaluable. To Chamois Holschuh, editor at Allworth, sincere thanks for the time and effort she has devoted to this project. And to Rick Landers, a frequent collaborator, thank you for your wonderful design of these disparate elements.

Much appreciation to all the contributors who have not only shared their ideas and words in this volume, but who also are responsible for making huge contributions to design history pedagogy.

Of course, those who make history cannot be ignored. Without the efforts of visionary designers, there would be no history to teach.

Finally, thanks to David Rhodes, president of the School of Visual Arts, New York, who has long supported me and Allworth Press in our design education projects.

—STEVEN HELLER, SEPTEMBER 2019

INDEX

INDEX

BOOKS FROM ALLWORTH PRESS

Advertising Design and Typography
by Alex W. White (8½ × 11, 224 pages, paperback, $29.99)

Becoming a Design Entrepreneur
by Steven Heller and Lita Talarico (6 × 9, 208 pages, paperback, $19.99)

Brand Thinking and Other Noble Pursuits
by Debbie Millman with Rob Walker (6 × 9, 336 pages, paperback, $19.95)

Citizen Designer (Second Edition)
by Steven Heller and Véronique Vienne (6 × 9, 312 pages, paperback, $22.99)

Design Literacy
by Steven Heller with Rick Poynor (6 × 9, 304 pages, paperback, $22.50)

Design Thinking
by Thomas Lockwood (6 × 9, 304 pages, paperback, $24.95)

Designers Don't Read
by Austin Howe with Fredrik Averin (5½ × 8½, 224 pages, paperback, $19.95)

The Education of a Graphic Designer
by Steven Heller (6 × 9, 380 pages, paperback, $19.99)

The Elements of Graphic Design
by Alex W. White (8 × 10, 224 pages, paperback, $29.95)

How to Think Like a Great Graphic Designer
by Debbie Millman (6 × 9, 248 pages, paperback, $24.95)

Listening to Type
by Alex W. White (8 × 10, 272 pages, paperback, $29.99)

POP
by Steven Heller (6 × 9, 288 pages, paperback, $24.95)

Starting Your Career as a Graphic Designer
by Michael Fleishman (6 × 9, 384 pages, paperback, $19.95)

Teaching Design
by Meredith Davis (6 × 9, 216 pages, paperback, $24.99)

Teaching Graphic Design (Second Edition)
by Steven Heller (6 × 9, 312 pages, paperback, $24.99)

To see our complete catalog or to order online, please visit www.allworth.com.